PERSPECTIVES ON THE ENLARGEMENT OF THE EUROPEAN UNION

EDITED BY

CAMERON ROSS

BRILL

LEIDEN · BOSTON · KÖLN

2002

This book is printed on acid-free paper.

Deutsche Bibliothek – CIP-Einheitsaufnahme

Perspectives on the enlargement of the European Union/
Cameron Ross (ed.). – Leiden ; Boston ; Köln : Brill, 2002
ISBN 90-04-12471-3

Library of Congress Cataloging-in Publication data

Library of Congress Cataloging-in-Publication Data is also available

ISBN   90 04 12471 3

PRINTED IN THE NETHERLANDS

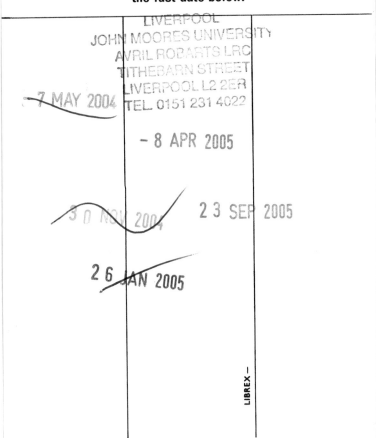

CONTENTS

INTRODUCTION

This edited volume, on the theme of European Union enlargement, brings together eleven articles, which were first published in the journal, *Perspectives on European Politics and Society* (Leiden, Netherlands: Brill Academic Publishers). Seven of the articles come from a special issue of the journal devoted to this theme (Vol. 1, No. 1, December 2000). In addition, I have included four articles on this topic, from the second issue (Vol. 2, No. 1, May 2001). One of the primary aims of the journal is to provide a forum for academics, throughout all parts of Europe, to engage in scholarly debate, and, in particular, to give scholars in Eastern Europe new opportunities to exchange ideas with their counterparts in the West. In this volume we have included contributions from academics in Bulgaria, the Czech Republic, Italy, Britain and Australia.

By 1965 the number of members of the EU had risen to fifteen, a significant increase from the six original members of the EEC in 1957. Following the collapse of communism in Eastern Europe in 1989, and the disintegration of the Soviet Union in 1991, new opportunities arose for the eastward enlargement of the EU, and for the inclusion of countries from the former Soviet Bloc. In a historic decision at its Copenhagen Conference in June 1993, the EU gave the green light to such an eastward expansion. Initially, invitations to join the EU went out to just six countries of the former Soviet bloc: Poland, Hungary, the Czech and Slovak republics, Romania, and Bulgaria. However, it was not long before there was a queue of other applicants from Eastern Europe pressing at the EU's gates. But, as William Wallace note in Chapter 1, according to agreements made in Copenhagen, before candidates could be considered for admission, they would have to meet the following economic and political entry criteria: 1) the creation of stable institutions, guaranteeing democracy, the rule of law, human rights and respect for and protection of minorities; 2) the development of a functioning market economy with the capacity to cope with competitive pressure and market forces within the Union; 3) the ability to take on the obligations of membership, including adherence to the aims of political, economic and monetary union. This would be no easy task for countries which had just been liberated from forty years of communism and Soviet domination.

For many East European leaders, there was a perception that the tough entry requirements laid down at Copenhagen were deliberately designed to be impossible to meet, and to halt the expansion of the EU before it had even begun. The Western leaders, it appeared, had little understanding of the momentous problems which the countries of Eastern European faced in their 'triple transitions' from totalitarianism. For not only did they have to simultaneously reform their economies and polities, they also had to re-orientate their foreign policies. And in moving closer to the EU, they had to be careful not to alienate Russia.

There were real fears in some quarters that the economic reforms demanded for entry into the EU would bring about more 'shock' than 'therapy' in Eastern Europe, and that a rapid move to the market (with the inevitable consequences of high inflation, high unemployment, and greater poverty) would undermine support for democracy. Moreover, as our case studies of the enlargement process clearly demonstrate, (see chapters 7-11) there was also a growing perception in Eastern Europe, that the preconditions for application, set down at Copenhagen, were far in excess of any previous demands made by the EU in earlier rounds of enlargement. It looked as if it would take decades, rather than years, before any of the applicants would be in a position to meet the stringent conditions of the EU's *acquis* (see chapter 1).

However, after a series of delays, protracted negotiations, and numerous setbacks, the most serious of which was created by the civil war in Yugoslavia, a positive decision to press ahead with enlargement was finally decided at Helsinki in 1999, and more flesh was put on the bones of these agreements at the EU's Intergovernmental Conference, which was held in Nice in December 2000. At this Conference it was agreed that the EU should be expanded to twenty five members, with the inclusion of ten new states from Eastern Europe. However, no set timetable for membership was laid down, and further questions about the status and representation of the new members within EU institutions will now have to wait until after the completion of yet another Inter-Governmental Conference, which is due to take place in 2004.

As William Wallace notes, the most likely future scenario is that Hungary, Poland, Estonia, the Czech Republic, and Slovenia will gain entry to the EU in 2003. These will, in all likelihood, be followed soon after by Slovakia, Latvia, and Lithuania, and some time later still, by Bulgaria and Romania.[1] And the process is unlikely to stop there. In the more distant future we may also expect to see EU membership being widened even further, to include,

Croatia, Macedonia, and Albania, not to mention the Ukraine, and perhaps, even Bosnia.

This volume of essays, by a group of internationally recognised experts, focuses on the eastward expansion of the European Union and the EU's relations with the applicant states. The primary aim of the volume is to provide a historical and analytical account of the enlargement process and to provide readers with a scholarly road map to guide them through the intricacies of the rapidly changing enlargement terrain. Scholars from both the East and West provide new insights and perspectives, not only on the accession process itself, but also on the EU's wider relations with Eastern Europe and post-communist Russia, at a time of unprecedented change and uncertainty over the future contours of Europe.

In the first five chapters of the book we provide region-wide studies of the enlargement process, and these are followed in Chapter 6 by a study of EU-Russian relations. Chapters 7-11 then move on to provide in-depth case studies of eight countries: Bulgaria, Romania, the Czech Republic, Slovakia, Croatia, Serbia, Poland, and Estonia.

In Chapter 1 William Wallace provides us with a historical overview of the EU's relations with Eastern Europe, from its foundation in 1957 to the Nice Conference in December 2000. Here, the author carefully maps out the ups and downs of the enlargement process and the fears and frustrations felt by the applicant countries in the wake of the stringent preconditions set out for EU membership in Copenhagen in 1993. In a carefully argued exposition the author guides us through the myriad of protracted negotiations and the endless series of setbacks and delays. In the end, as Wallace demonstrates, it was the nightmare of ethnic cleansing in Yugoslavia, and the EU's debacle in Kosovo, which finally goaded the EU into overhauling its policies, 'to the point of considering eventual enlargement to the whole of Eastern Europe'.

In Chapter 2 Neill Winn, in a multidisciplinary study combining contributions from political science, sociology and international relations, examines 'the place of the EU in the new Europe in an era of unprecedented change and contested versions of Europe'. To this end Winn sets himself three major tasks: '1) to capture the characteristics of the EU as an economic and political order, given its growing salience in the European and global environment; 2) to delve into the distinctiveness of the Union and its mode of governance in search of ways of analysing it; and 3) to explore the re-configuration of territory, identity, and function in Europe'. Locked as it is, 'between the territorial national-state, regionalism, localism, multi-level governance, globalisation and the politics of identity', it is 'the experimental and the innovative nature of the EU', Winn concludes, 'that enables it to respond to multiple agendas and Europe's diversity in a flexible manner'.

Geoffrey Pridham in Chapter 3 argues that the study of EU enlargement has paid insufficient attention to domestic impacts in accession countries. Pridham develops a novel four part analytical framework to examine the relations between domestic politics and the enlargement process. His study examines, 'a) historical, motivational and cultural factors; b) governance, c) the political arena and d) the socio-economic arena'. And he concludes, 'that while Europeanisation pressures on domestic politics have been significant and fairly extensive, interactions between these four different levels within domestic politics have so far been restrained'.

In chapter 4 Jackie Gower turns to an examination of EU-Russia relations'. In particular, she focuses on three key questions: 'how Russia has reacted to the prospects of the EU's eastern enlargement, the specific issues arising from enlargement, and the kind of long term relationship that might develop between Russia and an enlarged EU'. EU enlargement if not handled properly poses the risk of isolating Russia from the rest of Europe. It is therefore essential, notes Gower, 'to find ways of ensuring that Russia can be fully integrated with Europe while almost certainly remaining outside the EU itself'. Gower also notes that new opportunities for a more stable and productive relationship have arisen under President Putin. And she concludes, 'If EU enlargement is going to have a positive impact on the long-term stability and security of Europe, it will therefore be important to seize the opportunity to ensure that relations with Russia are substantially strengthened before it takes place.'

This is followed in chapter five by Martin Dangerfield's study of multilateral sub-regional cooperation initiatives in Central and Eastern Europe, and the potential for such bodies (the Barents Euro-Artic Council, Council of Baltic Seat States, Baltic Free Trade Area, Central European Initiative, Central European Free Trade Area, Visegrad Group, South European Cooperation Initiative) to act as a 'supplement' or even a 'substitute' for EU membership. Dangerfield provides a detailed study of each of these groups, and he concludes, that with the partial exception of the Central European Free Trade

Area, none of the others 'qualify as even hypothetical alternatives to the EU'.

In Chapter 6 Aleissa Vatta provides a careful study of a much neglected area - social dialogue and European Union enlargement. Vatta focuses on the development of corporatist tripartite bodies (trades unions, employers' organisations and government) in ten countries: Estonia, Latvia, Lithuania, Bulgaria, The Czech Republic, Hungary, Poland, Romania, Slovakia, and Slovenia. And she studies the impact of the enlargement process on the development of corporatist organisations. In conclusion, the author argues that the role of representative groups will have to be strengthened before we can hope to see an effective implementation of the EU's reform agenda.

In Chapter 7 we turn to our first case study. Here, Antoaneta Dimitrova and Rilka Draagneva evaluate Bulgaria's progress in preparing for accession. The authors provide a positive assessment of Bulgaria's readiness for EU membership. In particular they argue that, 'perceptions of the country in the West have not caught up with the most recent considerable achievements in the areas of law reform, economic transformation and democratisation'. Furthermore, they argue that the EU, 'has failed to take into consideration Bulgaria's positive developments in establishing democratic and constitutional stability, the lack of ethnic conflict in the country, and the adoption of a comprehensive legal framework for administrative reform and enhanced border controls'.

In Chapter 8 David Phinnemore examines the fears and frustrations in Romania's quest for EU membership and he assesses claims that the EU and NATO have thwarted Romania's entry into Europe. Phinnemore critically examines Romania's progress in meeting EU entry requirements, and he discusses the prospects of the country remaining stuck in, 'a grey zone of economic, political and social instability in south-eastern Europe'.

In Chapter 9 Lenka Anna Rovna turns to an examination of the Czech Republic and its prospects for a speedy entry to the EU. Rovna argues that although the, 'Czech Republic is now closer to becoming a functioning and stable democracy with a prosperous market economy and a modern effective state', there are still a number of drawbacks which will have to be overcome. 'Problematic voucher privatisation, the as yet unfinished transformation of big companies, the absence of a clear legal framework, and the lack of the reform of the civil service', she notes, 'are the most pressing problems still to be solved'.

In Chapter 10 Heather Field provides us with case studies of Slovakia, Croatia and Serbia, which she calls 'awkward states' because of their slow progress in meeting EU entry criteria. After a close examination of the background and progress of membership negotiations in general and a study of membership criteria, including an assessment of the attitudes of citizens in these countries towards the EU, Field moves on to discuss the vexed question of EU decision-making issues. Field also argues that, 'political change has been and remains the key factor in turning awkward states into suitable and enthusiastic would be members'. And she concludes, 'that in this context Slovakia is already there, Croatia is on its way, but in Serbia such change is only just now in prospect'.

Finally, in Chapter 11, David Brown discusses the problems encountered by Poland and Estonia in implementing the internal security *acquis* ('the Tampere agenda') - which was agreed at the Tampere European Council in October 1999. In his detailed empirical study of, 'the administrative and logistic capacities required for full implementation', Brown argues that, 'neither country is within reach of successfully completing the Justice and Home Affairs *acquis*', within the current deadline.

All of the chapters provide a critical assessment of the EU's work in the enlargement process and they shed new light on the complex interrelations between the domestic politics operating within the applicant states and the external demands and pressures made by the EU relating to the enlargement process. Whilst, on the one hand, the EU's preconditions for membership have undoubtedly helped to promote free markets and democratisation, there is the real possibility, that if these countries are not rewarded soon, then the whole process could backfire, and we may see a slowing down or, even in some cases, a reversal of the democratic process in Eastern Europe.

Note

1   Bill Wallace, 'The coming enlargement of the European Union: the prospect for business', Scottish Council for Development and Industry, *Occasional Paper*, 2001, p. 1.

William V. Wallace

Enlarging The European Union - An Overview

ABSTRACT

Enlargement has been fundamental to the idea of European unification from the start, and between 1957 and 1965 the EU grew from six to fifteen members. But it was not necessarily ready to welcome others when communism collapsed in Eastern Europe in 1989. For their part, the newly liberated countries were too pleased to have regained their independence to be prepared to surrender it to what they saw as another possible overlord. The dissolution of the Soviet Union in 1991 and the realisation of the mutual advantages that might flow from the enlarged EU changed attitudes on both sides and terms were set out at Copenhagen in 1993. Since then, this meeting of minds has been strained by problems and suspicions in both East and West and by the disintegration of Yugoslavia. However, the recurring crises over Yugoslavia have brought the EU to the point of considering eventual enlargement to the whole of Eastern Europe, and extensive negotiations are in train with a view to the first new members joining in 2003. But a real meeting of minds depends on the outcome of the inter-Governmental Conference already meeting. It needs to ensure that the terms of entry for the new East European members do not involve any greater loss of precious sovereignty than for the present fifteen.

West Europeans and Enlargement

The idea of creating a union of identifiably European entities goes back a long way. But the present

European Union (EU), emerging from the waste of the post-First World War depression and the need for post-Second World War reconstruction, had a specific economic objective - to create a large single market that would promote internal prosperity and maintain international competitiveness. But this could not be maintained without a serious degree of country-to-country cooperation; and there was the further crying need to put an end to the destructive cycle of intra-European wars. So there was a second aim of fostering political harmony. And in due course there was added a third, that of reinforcing Europe's security in face of a perceived Soviet threat. In this way Europe advanced from the Coal and Steel Community to the Economic Community (EEC) and ultimately to the Union. It also grew in numbers. Provision for enlargement was included in the Treaty of Rome that was agreed by the six founder members in 1957. Three new members were admitted in 1973, another in 1981, two more in 1986 and a further three in 1995. The process provoked much debate, not to say anguish. But based on the original objectives there was a certain inevitability about it. It even proved possible to sign Association Agreements, implying eventual membership, with three less obviously European candidates, Turkey in 1963, Malta in 1970 and Cyprus in 1972.

Turkey actually applied to get in before communism collapsed in Eastern Europe. Yet in spite of being a member of the Council of Europe since 1950 and of the North Atlantic Treaty Organisation (NATO) since 1952, it was turned down. The reasons were complex. Openly it was considered too poor to contribute positively to the overall economy and, in a world paying more attention to human rights, it was thought to be politically unacceptable. Less openly it was regarded as alien in language and culture, though this argument was couched in terms of geography. In the course of 1989, too, there was a desire to do nothing that would upset the delicate political balance within President Gorbachev's changing version of the erstwhile Soviet bloc. Late in 1989 as communism crumbled in Eastern Europe West European leaders had no thought of enlarging their bailiwick. There was a wide array of feelings from, at one extreme, thankfulness that its peoples had been freed, to at the other, *schadenfreude* at the Soviet Union's discomfiture. Chancellor Helmut Kohl was more agile than most but even he did not initially believe that Germany could be united, let alone Europe. If a serious question had been raised, it would have received very much the Turkish answer -

Eastern Europe was underdeveloped, undemocratic and, in parts, rather alien.

East European and Enlargement

In fairness, snuggling up to Western Europe was not the first thought in the minds of most East Europeans either. Their communist leaders would have regarded it as apostasy but were gone or going. Their new leaders were still emerging, certainly experienced in opposing old policies, but not in proposing radical alternatives. And for the vast majority of ordinary people disposing of communism was essentially a matter of getting rid of foreign domination and finally securing the national independence they had struggled for so long to gain and to retain. It might be all right for West Europeans to contemplate surrendering some or all of their sovereignty to a developing Union, but in 1989-90 East Europeans were at the much earlier stage of celebrating the recovery of theirs. Appreciating this is essential to an understanding of their attitude to possible membership of the EU both then and since.

All the countries re-emerging in 1989-90 had rich traditions reaching back to the first millennium. But none of them had a continuous history of political independence. The Bulgarians succumbed to the Turks in the fifteenth century, the Romanians and the Hungarians a century later. The Czechs and the Slovaks fell to the Habsburg empire in the seventeenth century, while in the following century the Poles were partitioned among the Habsburg, Russian and Prussian empires. As the Ottoman empire steadily declined in the late eighteenth and nineteenth centuries and other powers argued over its Balkan legacy the Hungarians were able to win near equality with the Austrians inside the Habsburg empire, while piece by piece into the early twentieth century the Romanians and Bulgarians managed to build independent states. And last but not least, cultural revivals and revolutionary ideas of the kind that inspired Italian and German nationalism had the same effect on the Czechs, the Slovaks and the Poles, preparing them to make use of the opportunity to bid for freedom that, as chance would have it, came with the outbreak of war in 1914.

Yet the national states that were recognised at the end of the First World War were in large part shaped to meet the selfish interests of Britain and France.

Germany and Austria-Hungary were defeated. Bolshevik Russia stood in self-imposed exile. Turkey barely remained within Europe. The United States of America had advocated self-determination but abandoned the Versailles peace conference in a not altogether unjustifiable huff. So, while they paid some attention to East European views, Britain and France were free to give greater weight to what they saw as the need above all else to prevent a recurrence of German and Austro-Hungarian aggression and the westward spread of bolshevism.

With this in mind they advantaged Poland over Germany in the west and allowed it to seize what it could from Russia in the east. They encouraged the Czechs and the Slovaks to join together in a single state and assigned them a strategically defensible rather than an ethnically justifiable frontier which meant that a third of the population was neither Czech nor Slovak. Fearing a Habsburg revival, they created a separate Hungary but reduced it in size so that a quarter of its population was located outside in Czechoslovakia and Romania. For its part, Romania was allowed to seize Bessarabia from Russia, but Bulgaria was deprived of territory as a pre-war rival of Romania and a war-time ally of Germany. In an ethnically confused situation, gravely overlaid with historical claims and counter-claims, a perfect East European settlement was impossible. But the one that was reached left Eastern Europe once more dependent on outside powers. The winners needed the continued support of the 1918 victors and the losers wanted the eventual return of the 1918 outcasts.

In the event, both lost. The Czechoslovaks made a reasonable job of developing their economy and creating a democratic multi-ethnic society. But at the infamous Munich Conference in 1938 the British and French abandoned them to Hitler. Though less successful economically and less liberal politically, the Poles secured a British-French guarantee of support in the spring of 1939 but in the autumn could not be rescued from a Hitler-Stalin carve-up of their country. During the Second World War the Romanians, the Hungarians and the Bulgarians, impoverished and embittered, found themselves clinging to Hitler in the vain hope that they could salvage something of their national independence. Of all the East Europeans the Poles suffered most at the hands of the Nazis but none escaped and few forget.

As a result of their previous behaviour Britain and France had forfeited much of their right to shape the new peace settlement. The United States was better placed morally but accepted that the Soviet Union's part in liberating most of Eastern Europe gave it a *de facto* authority. The Soviet Union could also argue that like Eastern Europe it had been a victim of the Versailles settlement and therefore had an entitlement to play a determining role. Currently, too, it enjoyed a political edge. There were many well-meaning communists in the East European resistance movements and there was some popular sympathy for Soviet achievements. After all, Stalin had forged an industrial society out of a predominantly peasant land and had gone on to defeat the Nazis. Life might be hard in the Soviet Union, but the burdens and rewards appeared to be shared. Much of Eastern Europe, too, still awaited an economic and social revolution, and a little help from the east might not go amiss.

This tolerance was not meant to involve giving up territory, still less surrendering independence. It was aimed at defending Eastern Europe against a possible Nazi revival and at promoting the economic and social development so lacking in the inter-war period. Sadly, however, the East Europeans ended up with less freedom of national action than before the war, and they also had imposed on them a completely alien and unsuccessful economic and social system. Stalin secured frontier changes that strengthened his hold over Eastern Europe as a whole. He then proceeded to terrorise the population at large and to purge the politicians to ensure that Soviet-style communism would prevail. By the time of his death in 1953 Russian domination was total.

Politically speaking, Stalin's dictatorship was counter-productive. The elite might be happy with their privileges and conform to Russia's will. But while ordinary citizens followed orders, they did so unwillingly and inefficiently. Yet as huge industrial plants were built and most of the land collectivised, great areas of Eastern Europe were translated from the nineteenth into the twentieth century. If only a few people were rich, not many were poor. But Stalin's successors could not make their rule widely acceptable. In 1956 Nikita Khrushchev permitted Poland to decollectivise agriculture. But in the same year he brutally suppressed the Hungarian Uprising. Leonid Brezhnev fared no better. Initially in 1968 he tolerated the Prague Spring with its slogan of 'communism with a human face'. There were no ugly crowds or wild demands. But during the summer he interpreted Czechoslovak plans to allow more than one party to function as a serious threat to the communists' tenure of power everywhere in Eastern Europe. And in August he ordered an invasion that destroyed the only chance Soviet communism encountered of achieving reasonable popularity. The so-called Brezhnev Doctrine declared East European national independence dead.

Yet Soviet hegemony might still have been tolerated if its economic conse-quences had not been so abysmal. But central planners were no more able to anticipate demand and facilitate supply in Eastern Europe than in the Soviet Union, while those who managed or laboured in the industrial plants and collective fields lacked the authority or the incentive to make improvements of their own. With better communications, too, Eastern consumers became increasingly aware of the higher standard of living enjoyed by their Western counterparts.

Serious discontent surfaced first in the Gdansk shipyards in Poland where in 1980 Lech Walesa, backed by the Catholic Church, brought the trade union Solidarity out on strike. This won such extensive support that Brezhnev inter-preted it as a threat. Retaliating in 1981 with martial law simply spread oppo-sition within Poland and elsewhere in Eastern Europe and prepared the ground for a widespread re-assertion of political and economic independence. All that was needed was Gorbachev's initiation of reform in the Soviet Union itself. Through the autumn and winter of 1989 the once solid communist gov-ernments collapsed. As a result of Walesa's skilful manoeuvring the Polish regime was the first to fall. In face of Nicolae Ceascescu's security apparatus the Romanian was the last. Dissidents, trade unionists and intellectuals led the way, but it was ordinary people who poured on to the squares and streets and showed in no uncertain manner that they had had enough of rule from outside and wanted to be masters in their own countries, free to reshape their own future.

From One Meeting of Minds to Another

In a strange way, therefore, there was a meeting of minds. The EEC did not want to take on any further burdens, while the newly liberated East European countries had no wish to exchange one subordination for another. The two sides could be very good friends but should mind their own business. Yet there was soon a rather different meeting of minds. It was part of the EEC's writ to foster foreign trade. It was also vital for Eastern Europe to be able to switch as much as possible of its trade away from the east in order to escape continued economic dependence upon the Soviet Union and at the same time acquire Western know-how. Discussions started in 1990 and led a year later to the first of the Europe Agreements, as they were called, with Czechoslovakia, Hungary and Poland. These were important though they still contemplated little more than tariff reductions and technical co-operation.

Gradually, however, a few other issues were raised. In the course of 1990 there was a good deal of western political rhetoric about promoting democracy. This was partly honest sympathy for inexperienced peoples struggling to create unaccustomed representative systems. But it was also propaganda intended to reinforce Gorbachev's attempts to liberalise Soviet politics. This then produced an ill-defined discussion of East European security; and the question was even raised as to whether enlargement would be of any assistance. Nevertheless not much more resulted than an inconclusive, mainly internal debate on who in the EEC would benefit most and least from an increase in numbers. The walls were not to be stormed.

Yet on into 1991 and 1992 the mood in Eastern Europe began to change. There was still a good deal of political satisfaction. On the other hand, among the problems that arose were those of selecting a model to emulate in a world in which democracy took many forms and of finding enough fresh talent able and willing to operate the chosen system. Many communist politicians refused to fade away; and many communist civil servants could not be ousted because they were still essential for the day-to-day running of the country. Dissidents were accustomed to protesting against governments, not to participating in them; and talented non-communists were frequently too disillusioned with the old style of politics to want to get involved in the new. In spite of this, however, parliamentary republics began functioning reasonably well in Czechoslovakia, Hungary and Poland though less freely in Romania and Bulgaria. But economically there was increasing dissatisfaction. The legacies of communism were forbidding. There was obsolescent industry and agriculture, inefficiently run by bureaucrats lacking in understanding of market practices and without the backing of such modern financial and other services as would make an alternative economy work. And specifically there were unnecessary and expensive military and manufacturing enterprises to be got rid of, pollution on a grand scale to be dealt with and scarce consumer goods to be found for the shops. People had hoped things would get better. In fact they got worse. As Table 1 illustrates, gross domestic product as a whole suddenly declined, with industrial output particularly hard hit. As goods became scarcer, prices rose; and for most consumers, record inflation on top of rising unemployment made for harsher conditions than in the Soviet period. During the winter of 1990-91 the cry went up for something drastic to be done; and the new politicians translated this into a demand for a second Marshall Plan, this time for Eastern Europe.

Table 1 - Eastern Europe Economic Indicators 1990-92

	Czech Republic	Hungary	Poland	Romania	Bulgaria
% Gross Domestic Product Growth					
1990	-1.2	-3.5	-11.6	-5.6	9.1
1991	-11.5	-11.9	-7.0	-12.9	-11.7
1992	-3.3	-3.1	+2.6	-8.7	-7.3
% Industrial Production Growth					
1990	-3.5	-9.3	-24.2	-23.7	-16.0
1991	-22.3	-18.4	-8.0	-22.8	-27.8
1992	-7.9	-9.7	+2.8	-21.9	-15.0
% Rate of Inflation					
1990	10.8	28.9	585.8	5.1	26.3
1991	56.7	35.0	70.3	161.0	333.5
1992	11.1	23.0	43.0	210.9	82.0
% Rate of Unemployment					
1990	0.8	1.9	6.1	NA	1.5
1991	4.1	7.5	11.8	3.0	11.5
1992	2.6	12.3	13.6	8.1	15.6

Sources: *European Bank for Reconstruction and Development, Transition Reports, Transition Report Updates* and *Annual Reports*.

There was, of course, no chance of such a plan being realised. It would have required initial sums that not even the United States could afford; and Americans were in any case determined to pass most of the responsibility on to West Europeans. Nor was much hope entertained at a serious level in Eastern Europe. Yet there were important responses. The area might still be comparatively poor but, if developed, it could be a useful market of around a hundred million. So the European Investment Bank was strongly encouraged to include East European countries in its proposed Trans-European Network and various technical assistance projects. The European Bank for Reconstruction and Development was established to help facilitate a speedy transition from command to market economies. The European Commission provided funds for a series of programmes such as PHARE designed to improve performance in public and private services. And discussions around the Europe Agreements began to hint at possible enlargement.

What probably clinched the argument was the final collapse of the Soviet Union at the end of 1991. In so far as its patent hostility had provided one argument for coming together in the first place its disappearance might have been expected to undermine the case for enlargement. It has been suggested that the event was taken as an opportunity to lay the political foundation for a European superpower. And the fact is that NATO has since moved eastwards. But at the time the proposal was seen within Eastern as well as Western Europe as a possible means of preventing the Soviet rot spreading. The ethnic divisions that rapidly sharpened in Ukraine and Moldova, for example, could easily have affected Poland, Hungary and Romania. And it has to be remembered that in July 1991 Slovenia and Croatia had just declared their independence of Yugoslavia and begun to demonstrate what might happen in societies that were internally divided and externally unprotected.

But some of the enlargement reasoning was more positive. Romania and Bulgaria might perhaps present a dismal picture but, by 1992, Poland was already recording growth. For its part, Hungary had pulled in some $5 billion in foreign investment, nothing to do with official EEC schemes, and it was reckoned to be one of the safer bets in the developing world. Nor was Eastern Europe any more quite such a lonely place. The International Monetary Fund (IMF) and the World Bank were also active, lending dollars for economic restructuring.

The Decision for Enlargement

So by 1993 there was a new and firmer meeting of minds. Yes, there was a case for enlarging the Union. The EU set out its entry conditions at its Copenhagen Council in June 1993. It would be open to six countries to apply: to Poland and Hungary; since Czechoslovakia had divided by agreement, to the Czech and Slovak Republics; and to Romania and Bulgaria. But approval of the applications would depend both upon the applicants' readiness and upon the absorptive capacity of the existing Union. It was set out in this way:

> The associated countries in Eastern Europe that so desire shall become members of the Union. Accession will take place as soon as a country is able to assume the obligations of membership by satisfying the economic and political conditions. Membership requires: that the candidate country has achieved stability of institutions guaranteeing democracy, the rule of law, human rights and respect for and protection of minorities; the existence of a functioning market economy, as well as the capacity to cope with competitive pressure and market forces within the Union; and the ability to take on the obligations of membership, including adherence to the aims of political, economic and monetary union

and

> The Union's capacity to absorb new members, while maintaining the momentum of European integration, is also an important consideration in the general interest of both the Union and the candidate countries.

In short, there was to be no messing about. The East Europeans knew what they had to do; but the last word would be with the West Europeans. Informal talks with the applicants got under way in 1994. But no official negotiations were scheduled to take place until after an Inter-Governmental Conference (IGC) convened in 1996-97 to consider inter alia the likely impact of enlargement upon the Union's existing policies and future financing and on the possible strengthening of transitional arrangements.

Interim Developments

The best guess at the time was that definitive negotiations would get under way early in 1998. How long they would last was not clear. The previous set (with the Austrians, Swedes and Finns) had taken just thirteen months; but the set before that (with the Spaniards and Portuguese) had gone on for seven years. To some in Eastern Europe it looked a daunting prospect. But short or long, the obvious course seemed to be to get on with improving the applicants' political and economic performance.

In the years since 1993 the East Europeans have made quite a lot of political ground. Proportional representation has thrown up a multiplicity of parties and a series of coalitions that have leaned sometimes to the left and some-times to the right but that have jolted basic reforms forward. The one clear exception until November 1998 was Slovakia where the prime minister twice attempted to circumvent a democratic constitution that stood in the way of his personal ambition; and recent party manoeuvres in Romania and Bulgaria have provoked awkward questions. The Czech Republic, too, has had a brief brush with corruption. But in the same period several EU members have had not altogether dissimilar problems.

On the economic front the record has been uneven, with some of it very good. As Table 2 shows, Romania and Bulgaria ran into difficulties in the late nineties while the Czech Republic suffered a sharp setback.

Table 2 - Eastern Europe Economic Indicators 1993-99

	Czech Republic	Hungary	Poland	Slovakia	Romania	Bulgaria
Population in Millions						
	10.4	10.3	38.4	5.3	22.7	8.4
% Gross Domestic Product Growth						
1993	+0.6	-0.6	+3.8	-3.7	+1.5	-2.4
1994	+2.7	+2.9	+5.2	+4.9	+3.9	+1.8
1995	+5.9	+1.5	+7.0	+6.8	+7.1	+2.1
1996	+4.1	+1.0	+6.0	+6.9	+4.1	-10.9
1997	+1.0	+3.0	+6.0	+4.5	-6.6	-7.0
1998	-2.3	+5.1	+4.8	+4.4	-5.4	+3.5
1999?	-0.2	+4.5	+4.1	+1.8	-3.2	+2.5
% Industrial Production Growth						
1993	-5.3	+4.0	+6.3	-10.2	+1.2	-11.8
1994	+2.1	+9.6	+12.1	+6.4	+3.1	+7.8

Table 2 (*cont.*)

	Czech Republic	Hungary	Poland	Slovakia	Romania	Bulgaria
1995	+8.7	+4.6	+9.7	+8.3	+10.0	-6.3
1996	+6.4	+3.0	+8.5	+2.5	+8.2	-7.9
1997	+2.0	+7.5	+8.0	+3.5	-5.5	-9.0
1998	+1.6	+12.6	+5.0	+4.6	-17.3	-12.7
1999?	-3.1	+10.5	+4.4	-3.4	-8.0	-12.5
% Rate of Inflation						
1993	20.8	22.5	35.3	23.2	256.1	73.0
1994	10.0	18.8	33.2	13.4	137.0	96.3
1995	9.1	28.2	27.8	9.9	32.2	62.0
1996	8.8	23.6	19.9	5.8	39.0	123.0
1997	9.5	18.0	16.0	6.5	145.0	1049.0
1998	10.7	14.3	11.8	6.7	59.2	22.3
1999?	2.5	9.0	7.0	10.6	45.0	2.0
% Rate of Unemployment						
1993	3.5	12.1	15.7	14.4	10.2	16.4
1994	3.2	10.4	16.0	14.8	11.0	12.8
1995	2.9	10.4	14.9	13.1	9.9	10.5
1996	3.5	10.5	13.6	11.1	7.8	12.5
1997	4.5	10.0	12.5	13.0	8.0	15.0
1998	7.5	9.1	10.4	15.6	10.3	12.2
1999?	9.4	9.1	13.0	19.2	11.5	16.0
1990s Foreign Investment $BN						
	14.9	17.8	20.0	2.1	5.3	2.3
% Economy Privatised						
	80	80	65	75	60	60

Sources: as Table 1.

But the first two are now recovering with the assistance of the IMF and the third continues to enjoy the confidence of foreign investors. Poland and

Hungary performed exceptionally well. It is a clear measure of their progress that by the end of the year 2000 Poland's gross domestic product should reach 128 per cent of what it was in 1990 while Hungary's should reach 104 per cent. The corresponding figures for Romania and Bulgaria are seventy six per cent and seventy per cent.

Since 1993 the number of applicants has also grown. Following its breakaway from Yugoslavia, Slovenia adjusted its politics and developed its economy to the point where it could sign an Association Agreement with the EU in 1996. Its gross domestic product is now confidently heading for the 112 per cent mark. Estonia, Latvia and Lithuania, emphasising their separation from Russia and supported by their Baltic neighbours, concluded Association Agreements in 1995. But they have had more difficulty recovering from the effects of fifty years of direct rule by the Soviet Union, and their gross domestic product predictions for the end of 2000 are not as impressive as Slovenia's - eighty nine per cent, sixty one per cent and sixty three per cent respectively.

In general the fifteen EU members have expressed their satisfaction with signs of progress as they have appeared. From the start things seemed to be proceeding in the right direction. But from the start, too, members' expectation of informal and then formal negotiations was that they would secure conformity with the EU's so-called *acquis* - that is, the totality of previous treaties, legal decisions and agreements. The thirty-one headings under which the *acquis* appear are worth listing as an indication of the complexities that lay ahead: Free movement of goods, free movement of people, free movement of services, free movement of capital, company law, competition policy, agriculture, fisheries, transport, taxation, economic and monetary union, statistics, social policy and employment, energy, industrial policy, small and medium enterprises, science and research, education and training, telecommunications and information technology, culture and audio-visual policy, regional policy, environment, consumer and health protection, justice and home affairs, customs union, external relations, common foreign and security policy, financial control, financial and budgetary provisions, institutions and other.

In 1993 the Copenhagen timetable seemed to some in Eastern Europe just a little dilatory; and as the years have passed it has appeared that way to rather more. The EU has been criticised for inaction. But there was a great deal to be done that not everyone appreciated. And other problems arose.

The Yugoslav Complication

From the EU angle Slovenia introduced a special complication. During the Cold War Yugoslavia had been an ally in all but name and, at least until recently, it had been a relatively stable and prosperous society. It had, as it were, no right now to complicate the post-Soviet world. However, what this view overlooked was that, irrespective of the ambitions of some politicians and the irreconcilability of conflicting claims, the several peoples who made up Yugoslavia believed that at various times in the past their legitimate aspirations had been frustrated. At the end of the First World War the Yugoslav state that was put together by Britain and France was mostly in their own interest. The small Serbia that had previously fought for and won its independence from the Turks was not allowed to create a greater Serbia; the Croats and Slovenes who had effectively been imprisoned within the Habsburg empire were not permitted to celebrate their liberation in separate national states; and there were others, such as some Macedonians, with somewhat similar complaints. After the Second World War the external Soviet threat and the semi-egalitarianism of Marshal Tito's communism might have made life in the republic broadly bearable. But after the events of 1989 there appeared to be no reason why the disgruntled in Yugoslavia should not use the same opportunities as their brethren elsewhere in Eastern Europe and break free of their bonds.

The EU was split on the issue. It was one thing to recognise the independence of the former Soviet republics when the USSR actually collapsed at the end of 1991 or the division of Czechoslovakia when it was accomplished by agreement at the start of 1993. But to appear to encourage the break-up of a sovereign state could have all sorts of disruptive consequences, not least for Hungary, Romania and Bulgaria. On the other hand, both justice and expediency could be argued in favour of amending two faulty peace settlements. And it was somewhat illogical to exclude Yugoslavia from the business of completing the unification of Europe. There was one consolation in the case of Slovenia. It won a quick victory in a territory with no other major ethnic group and then settled down politically and prospered economically. Croatia presented an entirely different case. Its war started at the same time but dragged on and merged into a struggle with the Moslems and the Serbs for control of what was left of Bosnia. This not only broke the ethnic, democratic and economic principles at the heart of the EU's enlargement policy. It threatened to extend civil war throughout the rest of Yugoslavia and provoke intervention from outside, not least from President Yeltsin's reassertive Russia.

The situation was further complicated by pressure from the United States which was anxious that, by enlargement or otherwise, the EU should maintain the peace in Europe and therefore in Bosnia. Independently for the sake of its own survival in a new role - and under similar American pressure - NATO pushed for an end to the Bosnian war. The UN joined in as well. So from 1992 to 1995 the EU tried to broker when it did not dither. In the end it was NATO aircraft and tough talking at an American air base that produced the Dayton Accord, a settlement of sorts. But for several years the whole Croatian-Bosnian business distracted the EU from what it might have done by way of a speedier follow-up on the Copenhagen resolutions. Yet in 1996-97, as promised, it did convene an IGC designed to spell out the major implications of enlargement for its own working as well as the detailed procedure of enlargement for those who wanted to join. But on the first item it failed, and on the second it disappointed a number of aspirants.

Other Complications

It is sometimes argued that the EU could have reformed itself quickly if it had not had to bother about Eastern Europe. Certainly the prospect of enlargement has emphasised the problems and made settling them more difficult. Given that some members are bigger than others, and that some favour more integration than others, then divisions have always been inevitable. But enlargement on the scale proposed has raised the financial stakes and implied a considerable redistribution of power, so that in particular the question of who decides what has become much more serious.

Currently there are twenty Commissioners, with the five biggest countries having two each. Ought there to be just fifteen as a fair and sensible working number and, following enlargement, should it be kept at fifteen or be allowed to rise at the rate of one for each new member? Voting in the Council is weighted specifically according to population, and qualified majority voting is used on less touchy matters. Should it be employed more widely to stop small groups holding up business, and not least when the number of members is increased? These were some of the issues that the IGC discussed but failed to resolve by the middle of 1997.

This might have been disastrous for enlargement. But taking cognisance of East European progress - and perhaps shamed by the IGC fiasco - the EU decided to start official negotiations with six applicants. Poland, Hungary, the Czech Republic and Slovenia were accepted as front-runners. Estonia was squeezed in while Cyprus was viewed as a special case. So far, so good. But the remainder, including those previously encouraged to apply, were given no more by way of consolation than that their cases would be reconsidered year by year. Things could have been worse. Negotiations might have been put on hold for everyone. Certainly there was ill-feeling. Even the chosen had their doubts. Talks were not to start till the spring of 1998. The *acquis* had begun to look like, of all things, old-fashioned foreign domination. And the pre-accession funds intended to assist applicants to adapt to the acquis requirements would not be available until 2000 and looked wholly inadequate. For their part, EU members were disinclined to lower their entry standards, while some of them thought that East European politicians were good on promises but poor in delivery - and not a little greedy. There might be a meeting of minds on the broad issue of the desirability of enlargement; but the practical details revived mutual suspicions.

Since 1997 several differences have assumed a special importance. The Common Agricultural Policy (CAP) has been bitterly contentious within the EU, with France as champion and Britain as critic. It absorbs almost half the Union budget to help six per cent of the working population turn out three per cent of gross domestic product. At first the East Europeans disclaimed any interest in gaining CAP support. But the corresponding statistics of twenty seven per cent of their labour-force producing eight per cent of their output made them think again; and their protestations led in 1999 to a doubling of the pre-accession funds made available for restructuring agriculture through the so-called SAPARD programme. They are now campaigning openly for full CAP support on entry, a demand that will not be conceded willingly, if at all. On another tack, EU businessmen fear competition based on cheap labour. But East European politicians resent excessive buying-up of their best enterprises and development sites. Some EU countries object to migrant labour from the east. But much of Eastern Europe resents the brain drain to the west. In addition it takes a lot of imagination on both sides to envisage a time when per capita national incomes will even remotely approximate since the lowest in the west is twice the highest in the east - and the highest in the west is thirty times the lowest in the east! And more than most factors, money matters are likely to intensify existing suspicions.

The European Union Solution

However, if the 1997 deal was disappointing to the second-rankers among the East European countries, help was at hand as a result of the EU's response to the Kosovo tragedy. It remains to be seen what will really emerge from of its 'stabilisation and association process' for those Balkan nations not otherwise covered by its enlargement thinking. It has promised funds and is looking world-wide for more. But the declared objective in the middle of 1999 was to open negotiations with a view to the full integration of both Croatia and Bosnia into EU structures as well as the two states, Macedonia and Albania, that were finally emerging from their isolation and poverty. As a result of this there was little alternative but for the Helsinki Council that met in December 1999 to put an end to the EU's two-stage timetable by sanctioning official talks with all existing applicants, that is, including Slovakia, Romania, Bulgaria, Latvia and Lithuania - as well as Malta, now recovered from its self-imposed exclusion.

The terms for entry remain the same (except for an understandable demand that all frontier disputes should be settled). But it is up to each country to make the best speed it can. In a sense, ill-feeling between the two East European batches is being replaced by a competitive free-for-all. Whether this will create new east-east tensions, never mind remove east-west tensions, is another question. Other issues remain open. Is this the moment for Turkey to re-activate its application? Should Ukraine and Moldova be considered for entry? But with a new President and a fresh Commission, with greater participation by Parliament in decision-making, and with the euro trying to work, much of the talk within the EU at the moment is about expediting membership for those that are adapting most rapidly. It is therefore hoped that by December 2000 the new IGC will have resolved the outstanding differences over internal governance and thus have prepared the way for the first of the new entrants to be admitted in January 2003.

Clearly who is to decide what in the enlarged EU is a serious matter; and with the proposal to establish a military force the stakes have become much higher. Yet there are strong incentives for agreement. An enlarged Europe appears likely to be richer economically and stronger internationally, able to stand up to the other big players and perhaps help some of the smaller ones. But reforming the EU's internal governance is as important to East European applicants as to present members. They are no longer prepared to be dictated to by outside powers; but they are willing to limit their freedom of action so long as they have a fair share in central decision-making and all members accept the same limits on their freedom of action. This is what is supposed to happen. Both sides making it happen should see the final meeting of minds.

University of Glasgow
bwallace@ifb.co.uk

Neil Winn

In Search of Europe's Internal and External Borders: Politics, Security, Identity and the European Union*

ABSTRACT

This article argues that it is the experimental and the innovative nature of the European Union (EU) that enables it to respond to multiple agendas and Europe's diversity in a flexible manner. In this view, the EU is a harbinger of trends in political and economic order, locked as it is between modernity and post-modernity - between the territorial national-state, regionalism, localism, multi-level governance, globalisation and the politics of identity. In the final analysis, the Union represents a form of deep regionalism in contrast to other regionalisms in the world. From eastern Europe to Latin America and North America the EU model is copied and diffused into world politics. It might be concluded that imitation is the finest form of flattery.

The following analysis considers the place of the European Union in the new Europe in an era of unprecedented change and contested versions of 'Europe'. It argues that the new Europe is characterised by multiple agendas on a number of layers of organisation. The new politics of the new Europe is organised around universalist western principles of human rights, individual autonomy and representative democracy. The European Union is the key political and economic actor in the new Europe, but still has not captured the hearts and minds of the region's citizens. Identity formation mechanisms remain largely local, regional and national in scope. This is a huge paradox, given the ever greater inter-penetration of national-states in Europe by the economic and political forces associated with globalisation. Contemporary Europe is characterised by a post-sovereign regional political system based on a nexus of complex interdependencies.[1]

The present article aims to raise pertinent questions related to the development of the new Europe rather than provide definitive answers. It sets out to explore three main objectives considered by Laffan, O'Donnell and Smith in their recent critique of European integration:

* To capture the characteristics of the European Union (EU) as an economic and political order, given its growing salience in the European and global environment.
* To delve into the distinctiveness of the Union and its mode of governance in search of ways of analysing it.
* To explore the *re-configuration of territory, identity and function* in Europe.[2]

The approach of this article is multidisciplinary, highlighting the distinctive contributions of political science, sociology, international relations and European studies approaches to the analysis of modern Europe.

Europe has changed dramatically in the past decade. With the end of the cold war, the east-west divide has been dissolved, and new structures of economic, political and military interaction between the various European states are being developed. The European Community, an integral part of the cold war security architecture in Europe, has been superseded by a new European Union, for which the incorporation of central and eastern European states has become a major strategic goal.

Within the next five years the complex European polity (the political system comprising the European Union, its member states, and all actors orientated towards them) is therefore likely to become even more complicated. Three events will be the sources of such a development towards complexity: first, the introduction and working of the single currency (the euro); second, the eastward enlargement of the European Union; third, the endeavour to promote wider political integration by means of building new institutions and giving them policy capacity. These future events are likely to complicate the working of the European polity in three crucial ways.[3]

First, the launching of EMU will both reinforce and threaten the level of integration within the European polity. On the one hand, anticipating the advent of EMU, member states have reached a higher degree of policy co-ordination in some policy areas; on the other hand, they have made an attempt to find new policy instruments in order to keep some possibilities to affect independently their competitive position in other policy areas. The trade-off between benefits and losses involved in the choice between policy co-ordination and policy autonomy is likely to continue after the start of EMU.

Second, the widening of the European Union involves a serious complication of decision-making.[4] It will be even more difficult to agree on common policies if the number of member states increases beyond fifteen. The extension of qualified majority voting (QMV) will not ease things. It will just render more important the game of building or preventing blocking minorities in the Council of Ministers. In addition, an eastward enlargement may create a new division of 'first class' member states, running ahead with a whole series of policy areas, and a second division of states lagging behind. This is likely to complicate policy-making even further.[5]

Third, deepening and widening of the European polity will not only accentuate the increasing interdependence of economic, geopolitical and social dimensions of politics, but it will in particular prioritise the issue of security on multiple European policy agendas.[6] Including central and eastern European states into the European polity implies the inheritance of their geopolitical security problems. Their acceptance of the *acquis communautaire* will make them part of 'western' concerns relating to security, society, economics and politics. In addition it will create pressure on the working and performance of these 'new' democracies and the transition towards 'Europeanised' political and economic systems. The new members of the European Union will also have to bring their human rights regimes - as expressed through foreign and security policies - into line with the western European members of the Union. More importantly, however, the new member states will need to align their foreign and security policies towards the premises of the Common Foreign and Security Policy (CFSP): protection of individual and human

rights; promotion of democratic principles; acceptance of the market economy for economic transactions and providing services; and acceptance of the
rules and procedures of CFSP.[7] The process of 'widening' the European Union
moreover not only affects the existing member states and (prospective)
new members, but also the larger European region: the New Europe from
the Atlantic to the Urals, and from the Arctic to the southern rim of the
Mediterranean.

All three consequences share three common features that are relevant for any
study of the European polity. First, the *institutional framework* will be complicated. Not only will the European Union develop more institutional room
for manoeuvre *independently* of its member states in various policy domains
(the right to *decide* as well as the right to *act*) but the incorporation of the
national institutions of (prospective) *new* member states will also add to the
level of complexity. Second, the number of transnational actors whose interests are no longer confined by national borders and laws is likely to increase
rapidly.[8] Third, and most significantly, changing *normative preference structures*
and *concomitant identities* will greatly impact on the policy-making structures
and practices of the new Europe. These features deserve to become focal
points of new research on European politics.

Framework for Analysis

A threefold analytical framework is proposed, based on the recognition of
the EU's inter-connectedness and contingency: the relationship between *territory, identity and function.* The article will then go on to consider the European
Union as an actor in Europe and the wider world. This framework draws on
the interdisciplinary work of Brigid Laffan, Rory O'Donnell and Michael
Smith.[9]

To turn briefly to *territory*: The territorial nation-state is under stress from
above and below. Some authors like the Danish political scientist Ole Waever
and the French analyst Pierre Hassner maintain that the territorial nation-
state is dying or even already dead.[10] Indeed, the very notion of territory
somehow seems anachronistic in the early twenty-first century in western
Europe. Territory is a porous concept given the inter-connectedness of international interdependence: a nexus of networks operate across states ignor-

ing sovereignty and national borders. Since the mid-1960s there has occurred a blurring of responsibilities and identities between state, nation, international organisation whether intergovernmental (IGO) or non-governmental (NGO) and multinational company (MNC). The 'new diplomacy' - as we might term it - involves all of the above actors vying for policy space in a series of relational interactions encouraged by complex interdependencies: state-to-state; state-to-MNC; state-to-IGO; state-to-market; state-to NGO; NGO-to-MNC; IGO-to-market; MNC-to-market, etc. State-to-state interactions are only one of many possibilities in the modern international environment.

We focus now on the concept of *identity*. Here we refer to *identities* in the plural. As a concept identity is highly contested. Multiple and contested identities have emerged since 1989 to complicate an already complex situation in Europe. Identities can be local-particularistic, regional, national, what we might term 'idealised European' (which is itself highly contested), and even 'idealised international' (which is also contested). We must also add 'creolised-cosmopolitan' to this list, that is, the internationalisation of societies identity formation structures through the homogenisation of cultures into one global culture.[11]

As a reaction against 'creolisation' individuals have reacted in varying degrees against what they perceive as homogenisation.[12] Nevertheless, in the conscious pursuit of being 'different' they themselves often become 'creolised'. This is the dilemma of modern identity: the need to be different, but also to be similar in a social-cultural sense. Indeed, there are non-western societies which actively want to become modernised, creolised, homogenised, Americanised, re-fashioned and re-constituted. They chase the dream of becoming 'westernised' as they perceive massive benefits compared to their normal situation.

What actually matters, however, is the *perception* of those holding a particular identity. For example, a citizen of the United Kingdom from Edinburgh might choose to define his identity in terms of being Scottish. He could also choose to identify with Edinburgh as a city. He might also choose to identify with the UK. Alternatively, he could, for example, say that he is Scottish and European thereby choosing to adopt multiple identities.

But why has the contestation of identities become more common in the past thirty years? This process is encouraged by a number of inter-related factors: First, the fall-out and reaction to the end of the cold war in central and eastern Europe. New and older identities have emerged and re-emerged to redefine civil societies in these states. Second, the regional policies of the European Union encouraged regional particularisms to seek a greater say in their own political fate. Examples of this would be devolution in the UK (in Scotland, Wales, Northern Ireland); regional autonomy in Spain (in the Basque region and Catalonia); and federalism in Belgium. This has served to reinforce regional identity through the principle of subsidiarity. Subsidiarity is a contested concept and can mean a number of things in this context: subsidiarity as proscribing or prescribing central intervention; subsidiarity as the allocation of political powers; subsidiarity as the exercise of political powers; and subsidiarity as adding or removing issues from political decision-making.[13] In the present analysis we are mainly concerned with subsidiarity as a procedural device in decision-making. Hence we might define subsidiarity as doing things at the lowest possible level of appropriate decision-making. This form of subsidiarity has served to reinforce regional identity where already strong regional identities existed. This in turn was administratively reinforced by the creation of the Committee of the Regions in 1992 at Maastricht. 'Regionalisms' have learned from the success of, for example, Ireland in the political, economic and cultural fields over the past 20 years in Europe. This has encouraged new self-confidence in others.

Third, the EU itself represents a form of 'thin identity'. It still substantially lacks basic legitimation structures associated with the nation-state. Individuals' *perceptions* of legitimacy in Europe are still based largely on national foundations underpinned by *national* civic, ethno-cultural and legal reference points.[14] Fourth, individuals' loyalties cling to local, regional and national myths in the face of globalisation and creolisation. Individuals are essentially conservative and either dislike or fear change. They cling to what they know.[15] Local, regional and national identities are like an old pair of slippers - a dependable, worn but still comforting thing that is familiar to its owner. Fifth, 'ethnic identities', old hatreds and new prejudices have arisen in the east of Europe and the former Soviet Union to challenge 'civic identities' from below. The result has been catastrophic in some cases: Bosnia, Kosovo and Chechnya come to mind. Mature and democratic political institutions - and concomitant political cultures - are conspicuously lacking in these recently liberated totalitarian and authoritarian regimes. Democracy and capitalism will take time to implant their presence on political, cultural and social thought processes: the problems associated with the transitions in the east are as much socio-psychological as they are political or economic in nature.

We now turn to the concept of *function*. We live in a world of multi-level and multi-tiered governance structures.[16] Traditional hierarchies of authority and sovereignty in government have been actively challenged by *horizontally-formed* governance structures: Epistemic communities, policy networks, policy regimes and transnational networks cut across national state structures.[17] National state political and economic systems have become increasingly Europeanised and (paradoxically) decentralised. At the same time, sovereignty is being transferred at a pace to Brussels in a whole range of policy areas. Monetary union is just one example along with environmental protection, and even possibly foreign policy in the future.

Indeed, the EU is a complex system with formal as well as more fluid layers of competencies and the subsidiarity principle does not fix competencies as in a static federal constitution. In addition, the Union is a political system in which public and private actors vie for policy space on a number of levels. The actual distribution of power in any given policy area is the product of formal and informal networks, hierarchies and nodes of authority reflecting the participation of public and private interests. Actual EU policy may thus reflect the interests of a combination of public, private, informal, subnational, national, transnational and supranational actors. This has further encouraged the 'Europeanisation' of national political and economic systems. 'Europeanisation' is here defined as: the emergence and development at the European level of distinct structures of governance, that is, of political, legal and social institutions that formalise and routinise interactions among the actors, and of policy networks specialising in the creation of authoritative European rules. Europeanisation involves the evolution of a new layer of politics . . .[18]

The table below outlines the relationship between political institutions, identity, and security in the Europeanised new Europe. It does this by comparing the conditions of the new Europe with the classical European state system and the cold war state system.

Table 1: Political Institutions, Identity and Security

Eras	Political institutions	Identity	Mode of security
Classical states system	Nation-states	Patriotism	External defence and internal pacification
Cold war	Nation-states Blocs Transnational institutions	Ideology - freedom or socialism	Deterrence Bloc cohesion
The new Europe at the Millennium	European Union Nation-states Regionalism	Human rights Multiculturalism Tolerance and diversity	Extension of rule of law and civil society Elimination of inter-state war Humanitarian intervention

Source: M. Kaldor 'Europe at the Millennium', *Politics*, 20(2) 2000, p. 60 (with author's amendments).

In summary, there is no unified global society but there are exceptional levels of global interdependence. Secondly, unpredictable shock waves spill out 'chaotically' from one part of the system as a whole to affect other parts. Thirdly, there are not just 'societies' but massively powerful 'regimes' - which some would term 'hegemonies' - roaming the globe which are arguably altering and reconfiguring collective and self-perceptions and identities of host populations of which the EU, McDonalds, AT&T, Siemens and the USA are all prime examples. Lastly, there is mass mobility of peoples, objects, goods, and services all of which encourages the interpenetration of societies and identities.[19]

Where does the European Union fit in?

Within our framework we can identify five key ties and tensions. The first is between states and markets, the second between the EU as a polity and a problem-solving arena, and the third between different levels of policy-making. There is a fourth tension between the EU universe and its wider global environment and lastly, and most importantly, there is a tension between the EU as a practical political project and a normative project.[20] Due to its experimental nature the EU is able to respond to multiple agendas and Europe's diversity in a flexible way. The EU can be characterised as a harbinger of trends in political and economic order, locked as it is between modernity and postmodernity. ('Postmodern' here means 'after the modern, or territorially based Westphalian state', and does not refer to the cultural theory of post-modernism.) This analysis is therefore somewhat unconventional and designed to challenge the conservative 'either/or' debates on the nature of integration in traditional analyses.[21]

By 'either/or' is meant debates focusing on issues such as the fruitfulness or otherwise of studying the EU through intergovernmental, neo-functionalist, federal and neo-federal frameworks. These debates tend to restrict the analysis of the governance structures of the EU as do narrow debates on forms and types of governance. In this type of analysis the EU itself and its complexity becomes squeezed by the positivist demands of the models under scrutiny. That form of analysis also ignores the normative underpinnings of policy preferences. Here we are concerned to situate the analysis firmly away from the study of integration *per se*, and, instead, attempt to ground it in political *practice* with reference to state/EU/international level interactions through an interdisciplinary dialogue. In doing so we challenge the relatively recent trend of analysing the EU according to elegant but parsimonious models of governance and policy-making. Here, following Laffan and her colleagues, we seek to present how it might be possible to write a comprehensive account of the *unsettled* nature of political and economic interactions in the new Europe and further afield.

In this new Europe the nation-state has been undermined by not only international economic pressures, but also by the pace and rate of change at the national level itself. Europe, in the terminology employed here, is therefore 'unsettled'. Globalisation, regionalism and localism have all served to undermine the nation-state. Bottom-up impulses from the level of the individual upwards are the new arena of identity politics in the new Europe. Nevertheless, as Lyotard has commented: 'A *self* does not amount to much, but no self is an island; each exists in a fabric of relations that is now more complex and mobile than ever before'.[22] Indeed, there are those who argue that notions of territory, identity and function are self-constructed, oblivious to exogenous preferences.[23] We must never forget, however, that international and structural factors still impinge greatly on the self, the state, the EU and the wider

Europe. We must also be aware that domestic pressures from host populations - so-called 'people power' - directly influence what we term international relations.

Where do eastern and central Europe fit in?

'People power' was a major stimulus behind the revolutions in eastern and
central Europe in 1989-90. The contemporary western European-east central
European relationship is asymmetrical, heavily favouring the west. Indeed,
as one commentator has suggested: 'one paradox evident in central and eastern Europe after 1989 has been the reassertion of national sovereignty and
independence within a political and economic framework which depended
on access to sovereignty-constraining western institutions'.[24] East looks west
whilst the west determines who is eligible to join international institutions
according to western criteria and standards. In order to meet these standards
the states of eastern and central Europe have reorientated their political and
economic systems to meet EU standards.[25] However, commitments to western integration were made well before the implications for national autonomy and identities were understood.[26] National identities have been torn
between the demands of Europeanisation, globalisation, the market economy,
liberal democracy and a revival of old traditions.

The main questions concern boundaries (both intellectual and geographical),
identities and institutionalisation in east central Europe. The question of
boundaries is extremely important, including boundaries which impinge on
identities. However, the main questions currently revolve around dividing
the 'ins' from the 'out' states in terms of joining international institutions.
The core - Poland, the Czech Republic and Hungary - will shortly be joining
the EU and have already joined NATO. The Baltic states are in a more pre-
carious position given the nature of Russian hegemony in the region. Indeed,
the Baltic states have sizeable Russian minorities looking towards Moscow
for protection against the nationalism of the dominant populations. The likes
of Bulgaria and Romania have been largely overlooked by the EU given their
relatively low levels of democracy, high levels of patronage, and poor democratic and capitalist reform programmes over the past decade. The Balkan
states and other parts of south-eastern Europe - save Turkey - have no prospects
of joining the EU given that the region is dominated by dictatorship, law-
lessness and (potential) ethnic wars. Russia is a former world power reeling

from a loss of status and prestige in world and European politics.[27] Moscow is unhappy with the decision by NATO to welcome Poland as a member state for security reasons. It is also unhappy with the prospect of Poland joining the EU and the Baltic states joining the EU and NATO. The latter prospect would cause ructions in pan-European and transatlantic politics at a time when 'Eurasianist', nationalist and anti-reformist camps are influencing Russian foreign policy alongside reformist westernisers.

All of this will mean that policy-makers will need to reform their mental maps of Europe. Enlargement of the EU and NATO will create 'ins' and 'outs' in the new Europe. Those belonging to the 'in' group will have freedom of movement in the EU, the freedom to work in the Union, extensive legal protection from the European Court of Justice (ECJ) and the expectation that national political systems will deepen processes of European institutionalisation.[28] The exclusion of 'out' groups - including Russia - will lead to new divisions in the new Europe. In the final analysis, progress in the centre and east of Europe is inextricably linked to developments in western Europe and in international institutions located in the west: the EU-east central European relationship is based on asymmetrical dependence in terms of political and economic and distributions of rewards.

Europe in the International Political Economy

In any analysis of the new Europe, therefore, we must at least partially focus on the structure of Europe's relationship with the international political economy (IPE). The contested relationship between territory, identity and function casts light on the EU's 'incompleteness' as an economic actor. The EU combines 'regulatory statehood' (*via* the regulatory diplomacy of the European Commission) and 'multilevel policy-making' (a product of the Europeanisation of national political systems) in a world demanding just these new qualities.[29]

Traditionally, analyses of EU economic policy have focused on their subject in terms of the old argument that the Union is *sui generis*, that policy is the product of intergovernmental agreements regulated by the member states, that the EU after the Single Market and the Single European Act (SEA) is a neo-liberal economic order, and that the EU is not merely a scaled-up version of the nation-state.[30] An alternative approach might instead characterise the Union's economic policy as a new model of internationalisation: analyses might therefore focus on the *amount* of policy competence at the EU level (for example through the Rome Treaties as amended), and also on the *pattern* of policy-making and implementation (who was involved and who did what to whom and when) The idea of the *EU as a new model of internationalisation* expresses both its systemic and novel nature. This is prescient when considering the role of economic and monetary union (EMU) in the international political economy. While open economy macroeconomics tells us a certain amount about international economic interactions, this approach retains the traditional macroeconomic notion of the national economy. EMU is more akin to the political economy of the international monetary *system*.[31] In terms of its trade politics EU policy derives from intra-Union decision-making structures on the one hand, and on the other, from the nature of the international political economy. This also emphasises a new model of internationalisation. Meunier suggests that this relationship might be more precisely articulated as follows: '. . . I argue that the EU's effectiveness as an international trade negotiator is determined partly by two distinct, but correlated, institutional mechanisms: the *de facto* voting rules used by the EU Council of Ministers and the negotiating competence delegated to Commission representatives',[32] both of which are *sui generis* in the international political economy.

Normative Perspectives: Security, Democracy, Legitimacy, Citizenship and Identity

The EU is more than a regulatory project. It is also a reflection of 'bottom-up' impulses from national populations. It makes sense, therefore, for us to consider normative issues related to important identity politics issues. The most obvious areas are democracy and legitimacy. It is important to compare the EU not just to national democracy but also to traditional diplomacy. At present the Union policy style resembles something akin to Jean Monnet's pragmatic technical incrementalism. From the perspective of national democratic systems the Union can seem undemocratic. However, from the perspective of traditional diplomacy the EU is normatively attractive as an institutionalised regulatory system which protects welfare gains (*via* a succession of Directives since the 1960s in the social field), human rights (by way of the ECJ and Commission regulations) and fundamental equality through the rule of law (also *via* the ECJ). The EU has also been a major sponsor of the International War Crimes Tribunals on Former Yugoslavia and Rwanda.[33]

The European Union co-exists within a European superstructure of nation-states each possessing diverse national security interests, national identities and conceptions of European citizenship. The challenge for the post-Amsterdam Union as the new millennium dawns is to come to terms with non-state and non-traditional forms of identity, related forms of security, and citizenship.[34] This section of the article is concerned with assessing and analysing differing conceptions of European Union security, identity, and citizenship. It is argued that new forms of non-state identities have emerged as a condition and response to the European integration process. An interesting preliminary exercise therefore is to link the concepts of identity, security, and citizenship to the empirical outcomes of the European integration process. It is also instructive to focus on the methodological, ontological and philosophical underpinnings of the above concepts in comparative normative context.

In order to analyse the exigencies of European Union identity, security, and citizenship it is useful first to review literature in the fields of security and identity. The following contested definitions of security rely on Krause's recent excellent review of pertinent international relations and political science security literature.[35] New thinking on security can be classified along one of three axes. Traditionally, security has been defined in strictly classical 'foreign policy' and diplomatic-political terms. The first definition attempts to broaden the narrow orthodox conception of security away from 'the political' to include conceptions of security that are derived from economic, social and environmental threats to the state.[36] Such threats include immigration and human rights abuses in third party states. This school of thought has been accompanied by attempts to deepen the agenda beyond its state-centric focus by moving either up or down to the level of individual or human security, or up to the level of international or global security. This school of thought is associated with the so-called Copenhagen School of international relations.[37] A third school of thought has remained within a state-centric approach, but deployed diverse terms as modifiers to security in order to assess different forms of interstate security co-operation.

As Krause intimates, all three of these efforts are problematic.[38] Attempts to expand the security agenda or the levels on which security is discussed seldom explain clearly how the various issues or levels are to be brought together, and whether or not there remains an analytic core to the concept.[39] On the other hand, the expanded state-centric approach remains trapped by the logic of international co-operation and conflict. Then there is the charge of epistemological and ontological 'deficits' in the definitions used for security. Indeed, it can be argued that all three schools confuse 'problems' with 'threats'.[40] To the social scientist, therefore, the concept of 'security' is an essentially contested one with multiple meanings and methodological, ontological and epistemological underpinnings.

The concept of security is inextricably linked to the contested concept of identity. To Ernest Gellner identity is a multifaceted phenomenon derived essentially from a western conception of 'civilisation'.[41] The concept of identity is a more or less fluid, more or less constraining, resource through which actors identify themselves, with its fluidity or constraints depending on the facts of history and societal opinions. Identity, therefore, is an essentially empirical issue at its heart.[42] The analysis of collective identity must begin with the process of its construction. The problem is to interpret what an apparent national or societal identity means, to test the extent and depth of subscription to it, and draw germane conclusions. New identities emerge as potential rivals to the state, generated outside its control, thus changing the nature of security in a wholly new context of political behaviour.

To what extent then is the European Union a challenge to state identity and independence in the field of European security? Are new concomitant security identities being forged outside of state structures? What implications do these changes have for political organisation in contemporary Europe? What implications does this have for conceptions of European citizenship and rights? In order to consider these questions it is necessary to define differing forms of identity in the contemporary EU. To the eminent Czech statesman and author, Vaclav Havel, the Union is based on a long European tradition of Christian values, the rule of law, and a clearly defined sense of civil society.[43] This set of western values has its own clear moral foundations, anthropomorphic morphology, and distinct identities. The EU lacks its own identifiable spirit and concrete loyalties from largely 'national' populations. One of the most important tasks facing the Union today is coming up with a new and genuinely clear reflection on what might be called European identity. This will involve a new and clear articulation of European responsibility, an intensified interest in the very meaning of European integration in all its wider implications for the contemporary world, and the creation of a 'Union ethos'. If the citizens of Europe perceive the Union as an autonomy-enhancing organisation, with well-defined ideas on the nature of human community and freedom, the EU might then begin to co-exist alongside the nation-state in people's hearts and minds.

A Few Definitions of European Identity [44]

Havel suggests that a common European identity exists that is derived from Graeco-Roman traditions and Christianity. To be a European, according to this view, is to live in a society that has developed through a distinctive series of historical stages. The cumulative legacy of classical thought, Christianity, the Renaissance, the Enlightenment, industrialisation, and modernisation has, it is suggested, endowed those who live in the EU with broadly compatible views on the appropriate ends and methods of legitimate government.[45] Indeed, particularisms have long been repressed by nation-state monopolies on mass identity formulation thus developing mutual commonalities. The optimists, in post-Hobbesian vein, argue that the Union possesses a *telos* myth: the post-1945 goal of avoiding war. 'Ever closer union', tempered nationalism and so forth provide compelling visions of a post-national European order based on transnational indeterminate forward looking identities.[46] The parallel argument is that Europeans face a common future in the face of globalisation and the diffusion of multi-tiered power centres in the wider international system. This, it is claimed, will contribute to forging some form of European identity.[47] Nevertheless, not all analysts are so optimistic on the prospects for a European identity. Some argue that the historical experiences of those who live in the Union are as likely to divide as unite Europeans. Indeed, the EU is not yet a full economic and political union with institutional stability. It is objected that the Union has no prospect of rivalling the nation as the dominant site for individual and collective loyalties. The nation, in this view, has been the carrier of a special authority to contain and arbitrate more diffuse identities. For, as Havel has presciently observed, the EU lacks mythical foundations, an ethnic affiliation, and a sense of shared cultural community.[48]

An alternative view is that national identity is 'constructed', rather than ethnically determined. The EU, in this view, was put together at the end of an
evolutionary time-scale and is thus immature in terms of identity formation.
Because nation-states relatively successfully captured a whole series of factors and functions in the 19th and 20th centuries in a single body politic, they
assumed an organic character.[49] This was accepted by generation after generation with a few blips such as localised national revolutions of various
kinds. This presents two major problems for the Union. First, the conditions
that produced national identities are non-repeatable at the EU-level: the Union
has somewhat of a 'man-made' veneer. Second, it is suggested, that the
national-state is a frozen political identity with mass support. Politics, economics, education, socialisation and culture are all perceived to be 'national'
in orientation by the masses.[50]

The Union is therefore captured within its pre-existing national identities.
Its prospects for identity loyalties will also be shaped by the kind of political system it purports to be. If the Union were to act like a polity - which
it cannot at present - this would lessen the exigencies of identity formation
at the European level. Additionally, the existence of the EU system has not
yet succeeded in changing perceptions at the level of collective identification in mass publics, and it still seems incapable of convincing academics
to revise their traditional concepts and categories of analysis.[51] The Union
makes far lighter demands on the loyalties of European citizenry compared
to the nation-state. It still cannot, for example, order armies to fight in the
name of Europe; it cannot set common rules for immigration; and it cannot
directly administer criminal justice systems. Hence the Union is less a constitutional charter governed by constitutional law than a treaty governed by
international law.[52] Indeed, at present it is all too easy for national polities to
disguise EU policies as a mere extension of domestic politics which in fact
underpin national identities. In order to stand any chance of forging a form
of 'EU identity' the Union must reach in a more direct fashion to the citizenry of Europe.[53] One prerequisite is to persuade citizens that direct elections to the European Parliament (EP) are worthwhile. Another is to encourage
people to vote along European and not national lines in these elections. At
present about sixty per cent of the EU electorate vote in EP elections every
five years.[54]

The Union has created a number of 'EU' level symbols to help boost its image. Some of these have the classic characteristics of purposeful identity formation. These include the EU flag, the European passport, direct elections to the EP, the right to vote in local elections for third country nationals, and the use of the European Court of Justice to override national courts when administratively appropriate. Scharpf goes further and argues that an EU identity can only be created through common participation in common political processes and structures. Only in this way can an EU identity be formed beyond the nation-state. Therefore the institutional structure of the Union is a key component in forging a European identity.[55]

The nation-state is under pressure from a number of sources which offer possibilities from the development of the EU. First, there is globalisation. One perspective on this argues that the territorial state is dying and the loyalties and identities of individuals are increasingly mediated by international and not national concerns. As Waever has stated, 'Europe is experiencing not just confusion, but a logical confusion. The key variable, the organising abstraction - territorial sovereignty - has lost its grip, and all the concepts hanging on it - in particular national conceptions of identity - are sliding too.'[56] Second, the state is under pressure from multi-level governance in the EU. Governments are increasingly constrained to formally admit sub-national actors to the European arena, thus undermining the natural authority of the national capital. In the longer term mass publics may be beginning to shift identity loyalties to different and multi-tiered power centres. In short, multiple forms of identity formation and multiple power centres have emerged in response to wider sociological factors in national societies, and to the end of the cold war in Europe.[57]

A further classification of European identity is one formed around a shared commitment to civic values. Gellner points out that as identities become more complex, alternative forms of western civil societies will emerge.[58] The EU is increasingly taking on tasks previously reserved for nation-states. Joseph Weiler points to a series of boundary abuses between territorial nation-states, the state and the nation, and the nation and the individual. Weiler suggests that the nations of Europe are increasingly drawing their identities from EU stimuli, from ethno-cultural sources, and from an increasing EU civic culture.[59] Indeed, it is argued that the EU is developing constitutionalist principles that are based on the institutional and procedural learned civic values contained in the Treaty of Paris, the Treaties of Rome, the Single European Act, the Maastricht Treaty on European Union, and the Amsterdam Treaty. A certain degree of constitutional patriotism exists without one constitution for Europe.[60] However, the absence of one European constitution will prove problematic in terms of defining and fashioning a European Union identity. Shared civic values are not present in a deeply structured fashion towards the EU; the union must overcome centuries of historical national memories and political cultures. This will undoubtedly prove to be very difficult when the EU itself possesses a considerable democratic deficit in decision-making. The Union can therefore to be elitist, out of touch with mass publics, and alien.[61] One possibility, as Havel has suggested, might be a Charter for European Identity and Citizenship based on legally enforceable EU laws. The ECJ might thus be a natural motor for European cultural and social integration.

What are characterised as 'thin identity' values can be endogenously formed and reinforced *within* political systems.[62] Gellner assumes that citizens form relationships and identities across all cultural categories based on shared idioms.[63] These shared idioms are often based around one single act. Identity formation in the EU, in this view, is directly proportional to individuals internalising and articulating commitments. Such thin identities are formed through the creation of commitment-making obligations, and standardised confidence-building measures. Additionally, the participants in the European integration process have little choice but to work together for as long as they can foresee. This may add to opening windows of opportunity for creating relatively defined EU identities over a number of issues that are changeable and yet determinate. A number of factors that may explain support for the EU are significant in this context. The work of Beetham and Lord on democracy and legitimacy in the EU is particularly useful here as it makes extensive use of exhaustive primary source opinion poll data.[64] First, the growth of support and identification with the Union would seem to be linked to the passage of time rather than to economic benefits of integration. This implies that identities are formed in a long-term sweep rather than in response to short-term policy stimuli. Second, there would seem to be an important role for political leadership. Mass publics filter their views on European integration through national politics. Third, the Union is based on learning over time as well as institutions. The Union is made up of social and economic cleavages - social class, economic status, party political identification - to the same degree as national polities. This may prove problematic. Fourth, there has been a growth in trust in terms of the formation of supranational identity both within and between member states especially since the single market programme was launched in the mid-1980s. Evidence points to a cognitive mobilisation in support for European integration amongst mass publics. Fifth, mutual trust is at a relatively high level historically between the nation-states of the EU - the UK being the most prominent exception. This bodes well for the future prospects for European identity formation.

In the foreseeable future the EU system of governance will be dependent on the politics of identity. Majone has recently argued that the EU is a fourth arm of governance in Europe based on regulation as opposed to the more demanding spheres of social redistribution and economic stabilisation.[65] The theory is that mass publics are more amenable to regulatory forms of governance in that they can see the tangible benefits most clearly. A European identity formed around the fulcrum of regulation might in turn contribute to an EU identity in the socio-economic field. Majone has suggested, for example, that building mutual trust based upon economic transactions in the context of the Single European Market has formulated new forms of European regulatory identities in an era of reinvigorated integration.[66] Scharpf warns, however, that the burden of the welfare state and economic and monetary union (EMU) may undermine Majone's hypothesis that regulation will replace redistribution and regulation. In these circumstances mass publics will be more likely to back national solutions over supranational regulatory solutions.[67] However, EU influence 'over who gets what, when and how' in western Europe is considerable. First, a large part of the administrative charge of European governance is an EU responsibility. Second, sub-national implementation of European level legislation is governed by EU norms and rules. These rules form a distinct type of European political identity formed around ideas of shared governance. Nevertheless, these new forms of political intercourse are only stop-gaps in the development of a European identity or demos. Deeper inroads into the psychological make-up of national citizenships will have to be achieved through other forms of non-institutional identity formation.

In the above section we have underlined the varieties of European identities in terms of an ethno-political dimension, a civic cultural dimension, and an administrative cultural dimension. We must now seek to link notions of European identity to European citizenship. Identity and citizenship interact guaranteeing individuals' autonomy and self-determination as human beings. Both of the above concepts are central to the EU's democratic process and provide the core of the EU's rationale for existence.

Some Definitions of EU Citizenship

Three developments in the fields of EU identity and citizenship stand out as being significant for analysis. These are firstly, the severing of the link between rights and nationality within the EU; secondly, the concomitant development of certain EU social rights, and thirdly, the recreation of citizenship at the Union level. There have been calls for the creation of a 'European Social Contract' for the EU as a whole along the lines of Havel's Charter for European Identity. However, such a concept of social contract is necessarily imprecise and lacks conceptual clarity.[68] EU citizenship reflects an indirect link between an individual and the Union, mediated by nationality of a member state. EU citizenship is a legal status consisting of a set of positive rights. The idea of citizenship is directly linked conceptually and practically to the idea of identity. If the EU wishes to go beyond what exists it will need to develop a sense of civil society. In a civil society diverse, incompatible and perhaps incommensurable conceptions of good and the wider world can coexist in a peaceful sense. A second feature of civil society is that, in it, both government and its citizens are constrained by the rule of law. In any civil society, most social and political activities will take place in autonomous institutions that are protected by the rule of law. A third feature of civil society is the institution of private or joint property. Property is the enabling device for modern societies.[69]

The EU clearly possesses all of the above attributes to varying degrees perhaps excluding the most important one: a conception of common European identity that is based on shared values, culture, language, and common galvanising institutions. The institutions of the Union, as Havel reminds us in his proposals for a Charter on European Identity, are perceived as being remote, technocratic, undemocratic, and out of touch with modern national societies in the cultural sense. The Union has begun to tackle the problem of its own civil society deficit through a number of active regulatory programmes in the Majone regulatory sense. One of these was the creation of the SEM in the mid-1980s was a means to enshrine liberal democratic and liberal economic visions of European societies at the EU level thus engendering a broad consciousness as to the benefits of the internal market in mass publics. The there is the forthcoming Single Currency and European Central Bank will have a direct impact on identity formation in a regulatory sense in the post-Amsterdam period.

Returning to our initial definition of citizenship, it is a truism that the EU will have to forge a sense of civil society if it is to capture the hearts and minds of mass publics. At present citizenship possesses a formal legal definition. The EU must move beyond this. At present EU citizenship has a liberal economic-legalistic profile that is bereft of sociological and communitarian underpinnings. To Garcia the only meaningful cleavage that justifies the existence of EU citizenship is nationality based on the idea of equality of nationalities and non-discrimination against nationalities *via* rulings of the ECJ. However, the ECJ will increasingly come up against a constitutional limit to its powers in this controversial field. Nationalists will accuse EU of social engineering. Additionally, EU citizenship relies on member states nationality, but the gatekeepers of this citizenship are national not supranational actors. This poses a logistical problem for those seeking to deepen notions of EU citizenship. If the gatekeepers are national it seems likely that they - individuals, groups and institutions - will wish to attain some control over conceptions of citizenship. EU citizens, therefore, may be in a situation of inequality *vis-à-vis* third country nationals. Further, in the sense of regulationist orthodoxy there exist explicit derogations in the Treaties of Maastricht and Amsterdam from the application of EU 'economic' citizenship in national contexts: the core communitarian principle is explicitly excluded from the logic of the single market in Articles 48(4) and 55 of the EC Treaty as amended at Amsterdam in 1997.[70]

In both normative and conceptual terms European citizenship is typically defined against the classical political and civil rights dimension. This fails to capture the more subtle questions of importance to identity and citizenship. As Ferrajol points out, an alternative classification might be ordered around notions of *personal autonomy*. Social rights include, for instance, the right for families to be together thus establishing familial autonomy. Social rights also include the right to education, life and democracy in the strict sense of the French revolution and Enlightenment project. Ferrajol also identifies the status of the recipient of rights, distinguishing fundamental and citizenship rights.[71] The importance of Ferrajol's work derives from the fact that it produces a new conception of rights in practice where social rights are not linked to the status of citizenship. However, there are a number of problems in the EU context. First, there exists a heterogeneous mixture of national conceptions of rights in the Union. Second, this lack of commonality is obstructed by the lack of channels for formulation of new values. Indeed, the EU champions national forms of rights and citizenship in its own official documentation.[72] To Majone EU rights can be achieved in one of two main ways: either by social regulation *or* by the development of a social and political identity based on moral and political reasoning. In this way the holy trinity of citizenship, rights and identity are fused.[73]

There are those who argue that the EU citizenship needs to be more than the sum of its official and legal pronouncements. This implies a commitment to the duties and rights of a civil society - and a related civic culture - covering discrete areas of public life. On the other hand, critical commentaries of EU citizenship warn against the exclusivist character which is intrinsic in the notion of citizenship and identity itself.[74] Indeed, the EU directly challenges values incorporated in national concepts of citizenship, contract and identity, as well as solidarity, cohesion and redistribution in a social sense. Nevertheless, there is nothing to prevent EU member states from extending Union rights and citizenship into national legal and political systems. Much is dependent on how the national 'gatekeepers' of identity and citizenship choose to implement such legalistic EU concepts.

Other options include enshrining fundamental human rights and freedoms directly into the EU Treaties. This argument runs into two main problems. First, such fundamental freedoms are often already enshrined in national constitutions and human rights appendices. The two levels of responsibility - the EU and the national - might conflict and even cover the same ground. Second, human rights is the current 'responsibility' of well-established non-EU institutions such as the Council of Europe, and the more recent International

War Crimes Tribunal on former Yugoslavia. Since the Nuremberg and Tokyo trials of 1945-47 human rights have been a central element in the collective European psyche and identity. It might seem appropriate, therefore, that the EU take on board fundamental human rights considerations in its deliberations on citizenship and identity.

This EU and its member states have more recently taken a stand on the issue of human rights and representative democracy in Austria (itself a member state of the Union). The inclusion of the nationalist *Freilheitlichte Partei Öster-reichs* in the federal government of Austria caused uproar in Brussels and the other member state capitals. The other EU member states suspended bilateral relations with Austria in protest against the FPÖ's nationalist style of politics.[75] This is a contested example of the Union and its member states seeking to expand the EU's policy competencies to include fundamental human rights and freedoms. This argument might be taken further to include so-called 'cosmopolitan democracy' implying all the world's citizens enjoy fundamental human rights and obligations. This doctrine argues that fundamental human rights exist alongside political, economic and social-cultural rights. The EU has been a particular champion of this concept. Where fundamental human rights are breached, according to this doctrine, the international community (legitimised by the UN, NATO and the EU) has the right - indeed the obligation - to intervene in a third parties state boundaries. This occurred, for instance, recently in Kosovo to prevent greater harm. This 'just cause', to paraphrase Walzer, derives from the liberal international values that have grown up since 1945. This process started in 1945-47 with the Nuremberg and Tokyo war crimes trials.[76] This does not necessarily imply a concept of world citizenship, but does imply that universalist values - derived from the Enlightenment project - apply to everyone.

Critics of 'cosmopolitan democracy' criticise political leaders for applying the doctrine selectively. Indeed, there exists a degree of moral inequivalence in the application of the doctrine across cases. For instance, why does NATO/UN not intervene in African conflicts more given the severity of such conflicts? Why does NATO/UN not pressurise Turkey to desist from human rights abuses towards ethnic Kurds? Why did the UN not intervene in East Timor until 1999? Critics have gone even further and argued that 'cosmopolitan democracy' is essentially a western construct that is indiscriminately applied to the developing world. In this view the west will use the doctrine to shape political behaviour in developing countries.[77] Nevertheless, the question must be asked: who would protect human rights in the absence of the west? A reformed UN with greater third world participation? Regional rapid reaction corps modelled on NATO's and legitimised by the UN? The EU as an international actor working alongside NATO, the US and developing countries? Indeed, to what extent is the EU able to take on greater international responsibilities in an increasingly conflict-riven world?

The EU as an International Actor

Security arrangements in Europe have undergone a period of rapid transition since 1989. The demise of the Soviet Union, the Warsaw Treaty Organisation (WTO), the unification of Germany, the movement towards a common foreign policy in the Europe Union, and the triumph of western liberal democratic capitalist values have been much commented upon on both sides of the Atlantic. Much is made of the new uncertainties of the post cold war world both in the popular media and in academic debates. On the eve of the twenty-first century Europe was said to be returning 'back to the future', reverting to the dark days of old style balance of power politics.[78] However, as the foregoing discussion suggsts, the new Europe is characterised essentially not by cold dark classical realism but instead by transnationalism, democratisation, interdependence, and multilateral co-operation. Human rights is the organising principle of the new world order just as anti-communism was for the cold war.[79] The contemporary international system is based on liberal internationalism with numerous multilateral interventions under United Nations mandates.

Many of the certainties that had characterised the cold war in Europe were actually based on very fragile underpinnings: the past was never as stable it was presented in the academic literature. It is worth noting that on both sides of the east-west divide there were problems. On the Soviet side this took the form of fragile regimes in east Europe which both economically and politically presented a continual management problem for the Kremlin (as was ilustrated in 1956 and 1968 with Soviet intervention to subdue the Hungarian and Czech uprisings). On the western side there were tensions, though of a different kind, which resulted from the tension between Atlanticism and Europeanism - how the United States related to the west Europeans and *vice versa.* So the notion that the division of Europe represented a neat solution is one that needs to be treated with caution.

Although the past was more complex than perhaps we thought, it is the case that the new Europe is characterised by a host of novel problems. Bipolarity has given way to mutipolarity and the fragmentation of the eastern bloc has presented a new series of challenges at both state and regional levels.[80] This has in turn presented new problems for the EU. Traditionally the Union has been a 'civilian power' concerned with welfare generation and economic regulation).[81] As an international actor the EU is ambiguous. The EU has always, and inescapably, been a foreign policy project, but that does not mean that it is cast in the constraining mould of the statist version of foreign policy.[82] The Union's status as a kind of 'great experiment' has clearly had an impact on the wider Europe, and on the international arena through processes of emulation and diffusion. One only has to think of the copies of the EU's common market: NAFTA, ASEAN and MERCOSUR bear witness to the broader influence of the EU in world politics. Indeed, as one author has recently maintained: '(i)ncreasingly, the EU seems to be influencing the behavior of other actors in the international political economy. Above all, the EU is a model for other regional integration efforts. Countries in Asia, North America, and Latin America are trying to imitate the apparent successes of the EU in the commercial sphere'.[83]

Nevertheless, the same author acknowledges that others contend that the EU's international capacity is greatly attenuated by a number of crucial factors:

First, the lowest common denominator position prevents the EU from making innovative proposals and therefore from having a lot to offer its negotiating opponent in order to extract concessions of a similar nature. Second, the institutional design of the EU deprived negotiators of one crucial element: uncertainty. Because member states reveal their position during the Council meetings . . . the EU cannot hide its bottom line. Finally, as a result of the shared power between the Commission and the member states, the EU is ill-equipped to act swiftly in the final hours of a negotiation, when agreements are always hammered out.[84]

The EU foreign policy project is unsettled, both in the sense that it has dynamism and fluidity and in the sense that it lacks a definitive outcome. It is still evolving, but seemingly gathering momentum. It is a journey in search of a destination. As such, it is a metaphor for much international action in the global arena of the early twenty-first century.[85] Indeed, the EU is significantly extending its roles into the military and civilian areas of responsibility.

Conclusion

This article has argued that it is the experimental and the innovative nature of the EU that enables it to respond to multiple agendas and Europe's diversity in a flexible manner. In this view, the EU is a harbinger of trends in political and economic order, locked as it is between modernity and post-modernity - between the territorial national-state, regionalism, localism, multi-level governance, globalisation and the politics of identity. In the final analysis, the Union represents a form of deep regionalism in contrast to other regionalisms in the world. From eastern Europe to Latin America and North America the EU model is copied and diffused into world politics. It might be concluded that imitation is the finest form of flattery.

University of Leeds

n.winneleeds.ac.uk

Notes

[*] This article is a revised version of a paper presented to the conference 'In Search of Europe's Internal and External Borders' at the Catholic University of Leuven in April 2000 when the author was Visiting Professor of European Studies there. The author would like to thank Professor Emiel Lamberts and Alona Lyubayeva for their invitation to present a paper in the 'Idea of Europe' seminar series.

[1] W. Wallace, 'Europe after the cold war: interstate order or post-sovereign regional system?', *Review of International Studies*, 25 (Special Issue) 1999, pp. 201-223.

[2] B. Laffan, R. O'Donnell and M. Smith, *Europe's Experimental Union: Rethinking Integration* (London: Routledge, 2000).

[3] See R.O. Keohane and S. Hoffmann, *The New European Community: Decision-Making and Institutional Change* (Boulder CO: Westview Press, 1991); G. Marks, *et al.*, *Governance in the European Union* (Oxford: Oxford University Press, 1996).

[4] Laffan, O'Donnell and Smith, *Europe's Experimental Union*, p. 49.

[5] See 'Adapter les institutions pour réussir l'élargissement', *Bulletin of the European Union*, Supplement Number 2, 2000.

[6] N. Winn, 'The future development of external europe: From Maastricht I to Maastricht II', *National Security Studies Quarterly*, 2(3) 1996, pp. 67-88.

7   N. Winn, 'The proof of the pudding is in the eating: The EU joint action as an effective foreign policy instrument?', *International Relations*, 13(6) 1997, pp. 19-32.

8   B. van Appeldoorn, 'Transnationalization and the restructuring of Europe's socio-economic order: social forces in the construction of 'embedded liberalism'', *International Journal of Political Economy*, 28(1) 1998, pp. 12-53; M. Green Cowles, 'Setting the agenda for a new Europe: The ERT and the EC 1992', *Journal of Common Market Studies*, 33(4) 1995, pp. 501-26.

9   Laffan, O'Donnell and Smith, *Europe's Experimental Union*, pp. 3-10.

10 See B. Buzan, *et al., The European Security Order Recast* (London: Pinter, 1990); O. Waever *et al., Identity, Migration and the New Security Agenda in Europe* (London: Pinter, 1993); B. Buzan *et al., Security: A Framework for Analysis* (Boulder CO: Lynne Rienner, 1998); P. Hassner, 'Mensonage et illusion: les pathologies de l'échec', *Esprit*, January, 1995, pp. 177-180.

11 G. Therborn, 'At the birth of second century sociology: times of reflexivity, spaces of identity and no theory', *British Journal of Sociology*, 51(1) 2000, pp. 37-58.

12 See M. Castells, *The Power of Identity* (Oxford: Blackwell, 1997).

13 A. Follesdal, 'Subsidiarity and Democratic Deliberation' in E.O. Eriksen and J.E. Fossum, *Democracy in the European Union* (London: Routledge, 2000), p. 85.

14 N. Winn, 'Europe, une question d'identité', *Projet*, 255, 1998, pp. 23-30.

15 U. Beck, *What is Globalization?* (Cambridge: Polity Press, 1999), p. 2.

16 G. Marks, *et al., Governance*, p. 1.

17 N. Winn, 'Who gets what when and how? The contested disciplinary and political nature of governance and policy-making in the European Union', *Politics*, 18(2), 1998, pp. 119-32.

18 S. Bartolini, *et al., Between Europe and the Nation-State: The Reshaping of Interests, Identities and Political Representation* (Florence: European University Institute, 1999), p. 16.

19 J. Urry, 'Mobile sociology', pp. 185-203.

20 Following Laffan, O'Donnell and Smith, *Europe's Experimental Union*, pp. 3-10.

21 Laffan, O'Donnell and Smith, *Europe's Experimental Union*, pp. 8-10.

22 J.-F. Lyotard, *The Postmodern Condition*, (Manchester: Manchester University Press), 1984, p. 15.

23 See, for example, N. Onuf, *World of Our Making* (Columbia SC: University of South Carolina Press, 1989); K.E. Jorgensen (ed), *Reflectivist Approaches to European Governance*, (London: Macmillan, 1998); K.E. Jorgensen; *et al.*, 'Reflectivist appraoches to European integration', *Journal of European Public Policy*, 2000, (Special Issue); J. Berejikian and J.S. Dryzek, 'Reflexive action in international politics', *British Journal of Political Science*, 30(2) 2000, pp. 193-216; A. Wendt, *Social Theory of International Politics* (Cambridge: Cambridge University Press, 1999).

24 W. Wallace, 'Europe after the cold war', p. 210.

25 S. Bartolini *et al.*, *Between Europe*, p. 2.

26 W. Wallace, 'Europe after the cold war', p. 210.

27 H. Adomeit, 'Russia as a great power in world affairs', *International Affairs*, 1995, pp. 1-25.

28 'Adapter les institutions', p. 3.

29 G. Majone, 'Towards a Fourth Arm of Government? Regulatory Statehood in the European Union', Working Paper SPS, European University Institute, 1995, p. 1.

30 Laffan, O'Donnell and Smith, *Europe's Experimental Union*, pp. 101-35.

31 B. Eichengreen, *European Monetary Unification* (Cambridge, MA: MIT Press, 1998), p. 6.

32 S. Meunier, 'What single voice? European institutions and EU-US trade negotiations', *International Organization*, 54(1) 2000, pp. 103-35.

33 Laffan, O'Donnell and Smith, *Europe's Experimental Union*, p. 46.

34 N. Winn, 'Western Europe's international identity after Amsterdam: An evolutionary perspective', *International Journal of Political Studies*, 1(2) 1999, pp. 361-79.

35 K. Krause, 'Theorizing security, state formation and the "Third World" in the post-cold war world', *Review of International Studies*, 24, 1998, pp. 126-30.

36 This school of thought is formed around the work of: T. Moran, 'International Economics and National Security', *Foreign Affairs*, 69(5), 1990-91, pp. 74-90; J. Tuchman Mathews, 'Redefining Security', *Foreign Affairs*, 68(2), 1989, pp. 162-177; M. Weiner, 'Security, Stability, and International Migration', *International Security*, 17(3), 1992-93, pp. 91-126.

37 This perspective includes works by B. Buzan, *People, States and Freedom* (Hemel Hempstead: Harvester Wheatsheaf, 2nd edition, 1991); O.Waever *et al.*, *Identity, Migration and the New Security Agenda in Europe* (London: Macmillan, 1993). B. Buzan, *et al.*, *Security: A Framework for Analysis* (Boulder CO: Lynne Rienner 1998).

38 K. Krause (ed), *Culture and Security* (London: Frank Cass, 1999).

39 K. Krause (ed), *Culture and Security*, p. 127.

40 For these debates see D. Baldwin, 'Security studies and the end of the cold war', *World Politics*, 48, 1997, pp. 117-141.

41 E. Gellner, *Conditions of Liberty* (London: Hamish Hamilton, 1994), p. 1.

42 B. McSweeny, 'Durkheim and the Copenhagen school: A response to Buzan and Waever', *Review of International Studies* 24, 1998, pp. 137-140.

43 V. Havel, 'A Charter of European Identity', Speech Made to the European Parliament, Strasbourg, 8 March 1994., http://www.eurplace.org/diba/citta/havel.html.

44 This section of the analysis relies heavily on D. Beetham and C. Lord, *Legitimacy in the European Union* (London: Longman, 1998).

45 N. Davies, *Europe: A History* (Oxford: Oxford University Press, 1996), p. 1278.

46 J. Weiler, 'The transformation of Europe', *Yale Law Journal*, 100(8) 1991.

47 C. Closa, 'Citizenship of the Union and nationality of member states', *Common Market Law Review*, 32, 1996.

48 On the possible component parts of a common culture in Europe see, J. Gray, *Enlightenment's Wake: Politics and Culture at the Close of the Modern Age* (London: Routledge, 1995), pp. 112-17.

49 Beetham and Lord, *Legitimacy*, Chapters 3 and 4.

50 Beetham and Lord, *Legitimacy*, p. 62.

51 P. Schmitter, 'The European Community as emergent and dominant form of political organization', Working Paper No. 26, (Juan March Institute: Madrid, 1991).

52 J. Weiler *et al.*, 'European democracy and its critics', *West European Politics* 18(3) 1995, pp. 4-39.

53 Beetham and Lord, *Legitimacy*, p. 64.

54 See, S. Hix and C. Lord, *Political Parties in the European Union* (London: Macmillan, 1997). See also; S. Hix, *The Political System of the European Union* (London: Macmillan, 1999).

55 See, F. Scharpf, 'Community and Autonomy: Multilevel Policy-Making in the European Union', Robert Schuman Centre Working Paper 94/1, (Florence: European University Institute, 1994).

56 O. Waever, 'Identity, integration and security: solving the sovereignty puzzle in EU studies', *Journal of International Affairs*, 48(2), 1995.

57 O. Waever, 'Territory, Authority and Identity: The Late Twentieth Century Emergence of Neo-Medieval Political Structures in Europe', Working Paper (Centre for Peace and Conflict Research: Copenhagen, 1992).

58 E. Gellner, *Conditions of Liberty*, page 1.

59 J. Weiler, *et al.*, 'European democracy', pp. 4-39.

60 Beetham and Lord, *Legitimacy*, Chapters 3 and 4.

61 A. Follesdal, 'Subsidiarity and Democratic Deliberation', pp. 85-110.

62 N. Winn, 1998, 'Europe une question . . .', p. 24.

63 E. Gellner, *Conditions of Liberty*, p. 4.

64 Beetham and Lord, *Legitimacy*, pp. 4 and 5. See also Lord, *Democracy*.

65 G. Majone, 'The European Community as a Regulatory State', *Proceedings of the European Academy of Law* (Dordrecht, Kluwer Law International, 1994).

66 G. Majone, 'Mutual Trust, Credible Commitments and the Evolution of Rules for a Single European Market', Robert Schuman Centre, Working Paper 95/1 (Florence: European University Institute, 1995).

67 F. Scharpf, 'Community and Autonomy', p. 7.

68 C. Closa, 'EU Citizenship as the Institutional Basis of a New Social Contract: Some

Sceptical Remarks', Robert Schuman Centre, Working Paper 96/48 (Florence: European University Institute, 1996), p. 1.

69 J. Gray, 1995, *Enlightenment's Wake*, p. 135.

70 C. Closa, 'EU Citizenship', p. 7.

71 L. Ferrajol, 'Cittadinanzia e diritti fondamentali', *Teoria Politica*, 9(3), 1993, pp. 63-6.

72 See, for example, the preamble to the EEC Treaty of 1957 or the definition attached to citizenship in the Maastricht Treaty on European Union.

73 G. Majone, 'The European Community between social policy and social regulation', *Journal of Common Market Studies*, 31(2), 1995.

74 See for example J. d'Olivera, 'Union Citizenship: Pie in the Sky?', in A. Rosas and E. Antola, *A Citizens' Europe* (London: Sage, 1995).

75 I. Wallerstein, 'The Albatross of racism', *London Review of Books*, 18 May 2000, pp. 11-14.

76 See M. Walzer, *Just and Unjust Wars* (New York: Basic Books, 1977); M. Walzer, *Just and Unjust Wars* (New York: Basic Books, 2nd edition, 1992).

77 D. Chandler, *Bosnia: Faking Democracy After Dayton* (London: Verso, 1999), p. 4.

78 J. Mearsheimer, 'Back to the future: instability in Europe after the cold war', *International Security* 15(1) 1990, pp. 5-56.

79 Winn and Kennedy-Pipe, 'Europe: Old Institutions'.

80 Krause, 'Theorizing Security', pp. 126-130.

81 H. Bull 'Civilian power Europe: a contradiction in terms?', *Journal of Common Market Studies*, 21(2) 1982, pp. 149-164.

82 Laffan, O'Donnell and Smith, *Europe's Experimental Union*, pp. 167-186.

83 S. Meunier, 'What single voice?', p. 133.

84 S. Meunier, 'What single voice?', pp. 105-106.

85 P. Muller, 'Gouvernance européenne et globalization', *Revue Internationale de Politique Comparée*, 6(3) 1999, pp. 707-717.

Geoffrey Pridham

EU Accession and Domestic Politics: Policy Consensus and Interactive Dynamics in Central and Eastern Europe

ABSTRACT

The study of EU enlargement has not paid sufficient attention to domestic impacts in accession countries and how these might complicate the process. The arguments for looking at this problem are greater than ever before given the EU is more demanding of such countries over prior conditions and the scope and degree of European policy implementation before membership may take place, compared with previous enlargements. Furthermore, countries in central and eastern Europe (CEE) are undergoing multiple transformations with economic change, and in some cases, state- and nation-building alongside political democratisation. On the other hand, political consensus over EU membership is distinctly broader in CEE countries compared with previous cases of accession. The article therefore concentrates on the strength of this consensus and how far it should withstand the increased pressures that will come as accession negotiations advance. To this end, a four-part analytical framework is developed and then applied in more detail to CEE. It looks successively at: (a) historical, motivational and cultural factors; (b) governance; (c) the political arena; and, (d) the socio-economic arena. It concludes that while Europeanisation pressures on domestic politics have been significant and fairly extensive, interactions between different levels within domestic politics have so far been restrained. On the other hand, risks may come from a growing gap between political elites and mass opinion in what are still fragile new democracies and from any serious delay in accession dates.

> The [European] Community process is not confined to what takes place within the formal framework of the Community institutions. Rather it embraces a network of relationships and contacts among national policy-makers in the different member states, both directly through involvement in the Community arena and indirectly as that arena impinges on national policy processes. Consequently, ... the Community process ... can be analysed only as the tip of a much larger iceberg formed by the domestic contexts that set constraints on each member government. In addition national policy-makers are caught up in other kinds of transnational activities including other international agencies and a variety of informal links both multilateral and bilateral. These arenas of discussion sometimes complement or reinforce the Community process, but on occasion may complicate or undermine it'.[1]

This statement draws attention to two important, and still somewhat neglected, areas of European integration research: 'informal integration' parallel to official EU activity, including transnational networking of not only policy-makers but also non-governmental actors; and, the reality that much EU policy activity is directly or indirectly affected by developments at the national levels in what are now fifteen member states. This statement from 1977 is still broadly true even though the scope of integration has much increased since, so that national decision-making has to a large extent been permeated by the EU. This has set off a continuing dynamic process whereby growing 'European-isation' pressures harmonise or conflict with domestic ones along the lines indicated at the end of the statement.

It is reasonable to suppose that the balance between both sets of pressures is different in applicant states since they are not yet formally and fully integrated into the EU. Hence, it is likely that domestic pressures are uppermost or at least play a considerable part during entry negotiations because of the influence of domestic policy-making structures and attitudes. Governments in applicant states have to maintain political consensus behind their European policies, pass through parliamentary procedures and deal with different and sometimes conflicting interests as well as maintain public support. Some applicant countries have then completed the process with a referendum on accession; and, those from central and eastern Europe (CEE) plan to do the same in most cases. The essentially one-sided nature of accession negotiations means that governments in applicant states do not have much room for manoeuvre in playing off domestic pressures against EU demands and so have to confront these themselves.[2] Particularly applicable to them is Bulmer's argument that national governments hold a key position at the junction of national and of EU politics and that negotiations at the EU level are between so many dependent, not independent, variables.[3]

At the same time, and applying the notion of 'informal integration', it is clear that a basic distinction should be drawn between accession and integration as a whole given the extended pre-accession period of developing links with EU institutions. While accession eventually opens the way for full integration by virtue of becoming a member state, integration is a longer process that commences well before accession and indeed before negotiations start. During this period, for instance, transnational linkages develop among a variety of actors notably political parties and NGOs; and, integration already takes place to a large extent at the level of trade, as is now the case with most post-Communist states. For this reason, the 'battle of deadlines', whereby national leaders in CEE and also to some degree European Commission officials have engaged in competing versions of accession dates, distracts from the real process of integration. Accession dates are, of course, a matter of great historical symbolism; but they are also inclined to be subject to domestic calculations and expectations as well as a means for putting public pressure on Brussels.

There are parallel forms of weaker integration into Euro-Atlantic structures including the membership of post-Communist states in the Council of Europe (commonly seen in CEE as an intermediary stage towards EU membership), the Organisation for Security and Cooperation in Europe (OSCE) and, in a few cases, even NATO, not to mention institutional links with financial organisations like the World Bank, the International Monetary Fund and the European Bank for Reconstruction and Development (EBRD). These only contribute to the integrative effects, occurring through convergence with the EU, on domestic politics of applicant states, which may be summarised as follows:

* the prospect of eventual EU entry, with its energizing effects on prospective member states and impacts on their policy direction;
* the gradual involvement and socialisation of national political elites in the EU institutional framework, such as through membership negotiations and

preparations for entry but also mechanisms linked to intermediary stages such as Association (Europe Agreements);

* pressure exerted from the application of democratic conditionality by the EU on political conditions in applicant states, including through economic aid programmes;

* the binding policy commitments that come from adoption of the *acquis communautaire* and that increasingly impinge with a variety of effects - direct and indirect - on domestic politics and different economic interests;

* the growing involvement of political and economic elites and groups in transnational networks linked to the EU and other European organisations.

While the growing literature on eastern enlargement has concentrated on official links between Brussels and respective national capitals, and on the economics and costs and benefits of eventual accession, little attention has been given to the domestic politics of accession.[4] It is important, therefore, to develop a framework for analysing the interactive dynamics may develop between Europeanisation and domestic pressures in applicant states. This will be done in the next section and then applied to central and eastern Europe in the following one.

Explaining European/Domestic Interactions in the Context of Enlargement

Various considerations may assist in approaching the fairly complex question of interactions between Europeanisation and domestic pressures during the accession period. Firstly, it is reasonable to suppose that Europeanisation impacts are much more easily identifiable in accession countries, and perhaps also new member states, than in established or long-standing member states.[5] This is because integration effects are recent, deriving from a European strategy adopted only some years before, as well as rather extensive and fairly abrupt. This is because applicant countries have to adopt and implement the whole of EU legislation in an almost comprehensive range of policy sectors (which comprise some thirty 'chapters' in the negotiations) - commonly known as the *acquis communautaire*. This has to be done under considerable pressure of time. It is thus possible to measure Europeanisation impacts at the policy level, sector by sector as previous national legislation has to be modified or, if non-existent, the *acquis* fills the legislative void. With new democracies the situation is special because their policy directions, as indeed their political systems, are still in a formative phase so that, notionally, the scope for Europeanisation impacts is especially large.

Secondly, one should differentiate domestic pressures in terms of levels of political involvement and interest within accession countries. This may be done by focusing on government and institutions as well as the wider political arena and also the socio-economic arena. The emphasis should be on those actors and influences that are relevant to both consensus building and mobilisation potential over EU accession. This will provide a measure of how far an applicant country's European strategy is elite-driven or whether it has wider motivation or deeper forms of support that will probably reflect on its subsequent behaviour as a member state. It will, furthermore, make it easier to identify from which quarters domestic problems derive during the course of what are usually lengthy and complicated negotiations for accession.

Thirdly, some lessons may be drawn from previous cases of EU enlargement. These can highlight the usual pressure points from European and domestic directions, and how interactions between them develop. At the same time, they may reveal differences between these and the CEE accession processes which may qualify any such lessons.

These three considerations will now be discussed comparatively. In looking first at Europeanisation pressures, it may be supposed that at the public and societal level Europeanisation pressures are minimal and possibly more difficult to identify than at the institutional level because more diffuse. This is likely given the low level of information about the EU among accession publics in past and present cases. But what exactly is 'Europeanisation'?

So far, the term has been used in reference to the EU becoming part of the logic of policy and legislation but this needs some brief explanation as does the fact the term has various (loosely linked) meanings. A post-authoritarian European strategy involves a major external policy redirection. It amounts to a momentous departure in a country's politics so that motivation must include the *historical imperative*. This is evident in the stress on grand issues during accession and in the rhetoric of political leaders, especially those committed to EU entry. But there are various related imperatives, including the *security imperative*, the *democratic imperative* (the EU and other Euro-Atlantic organisations together provide a structure for guaranteeing the chances for new democracies) and also the *modernising imperative* (especially economic but with implications for cultural modernisation).

Since joining Euro-Atlantic organisations has effectively been 'the only external game in town' for post-authoritarian countries, this may mean that real political debate is not great. When, however, attention moves to specific issues, then the scope for mobilisation may however increase since different economic or social interests can become affected by the prospect of accession. Much then depends on their own lobbying capacity and public links, but clearly too the handling of issues by the media is also important. One key feature to watch is elite linkages with the wider political and socio-economic arenas and whether accession pressures help to widen the gap in such linkages, endangering consensus building and maintenance which is essential during negotiations with the EU.[6] The sheer policy overload deriving from these - all in addition to normal government business - as well as the enormous time pressure involved tend to encourage a decidedly elitist approach in practice. It follows that interactions between EU accession and domestic politics have a potential for creating tensions, prompting governmental errors and public misunderstandings given the general difficulties in projecting the EU onto national publics (a problem also encountered by member states). Thus, a crucial variable is whether a wide political consensus exists from the start of accession negotiations, and how firm that is since it will be subject to some erosion as negotiations proceed.

This leads us straight into looking more closely at domestic pressures. Accession usually produces changes in institutions and procedures both for carrying through negotiations (invariably involving cross-ministerial coordination) but also for implementing the *acquis*. The latter, being a monumental task, places a considerable onus on effective administration. Furthermore, as studies of practical as distinct from formal policy implementation in member states show, this is not a purely administrative problem. It is one that may also involve the functioning of the state structure (including centre-periphery relations), political factors like national policy styles as well as economic factors (notably, where applicable, the costs of applying EU legislation but also the pressure of economic interests) and even cultural and attitudinal matters. The last refers to policy understanding but also views towards, and knowledge of, the EU and its legislative role on the part of national but also sub-national policy-makers.[7] But applicant countries are procedurally less prepared than member states and almost certainly have a much less developed awareness and knowledge of EU affairs. This points to a major role played by political parties as intermediary actors between the institutions and society. Parties are vital to building and maintaining political consensus, and they have an obvious mobilisational capacity, although in new democracies they may be less developed organisationally and less rooted in society than their equivalents in established democracies and member states of the EU.

Regime change is normally still in progress during membership negotiations with new democracies. It is a clear prerequisite that an applicant state should be on course for an unambiguous liberal democracy. Any developments that contradict this are almost certain to stall negotiations if not prevent them being opened.[8] But CEE countries are undergoing other transformations than political and economic ones. In several cases these involve state- and nation-building). Developments here may have various effects on EU membership prospects. On the economic front, severe or persistent difficulties in any key aspect - whether macro-economic stabilisation, price liberalisation or structural reforms - may call into question future EU membership.

Given the economic dislocation that still exists in CEE, with public concern about differential effects (gainers and losers), any trend of discontent displacement against the EU becomes significant, that is to say, it begins to be blamed for economic ills whether directly responsible for these or not. The potential for this is enhanced by Brussels pressure for satisfying the conditions of a functioning market economy. This phenomenon may be called *exaggerated policy interlinkage* where there is some linkage which, however, becomes overstated either through the way economic policy concerns overspill into EU affairs or because of its exploitation by oppositional forces.

As to the third transformation, state- and nation-building, the risk is that this remains predominant for a time and perhaps occasions problems of national identity or nationalist tendencies which might conflict with the ethos of European integration. While the EU has much less of a direct role to play here compared with its role in economic change, its sensitivity to issues of minority rights does provide an area where pressure can at times be quite intense and domestic responses accordingly swift or reactive, depending on the outlook of the government in power.

A brief survey of past EU enlargements underlines some relevant patterns but also one important difference compared with the post-Communist accession process. The historical imperative was decidedly strong following the precedent of post-war Federal Germany's escape from its recent traumatic past. New democracies like Greece and Spain put aside international isolation and at the same time aimed to buttress their still fragile regimes through joining an integrative organisation. Small states like Ireland and the Scandinavian countries have sought to both gain enhanced international status but also some protection and hence security. In all cases, a basic policy redirection occurred which could also be called historical. With the 1995 enlargement, Austria, Sweden and Finland were free to join once their neutrality was no longer relevant after the end of the cold war.

While historical and political motivation was invariably strong in earlier enlargements, economic and in some cases political commitment on the part of all the main forces was often lacking during negotiations and did not develop until after membership. In Portugal, the Communists opposed EC as well as NATO membership for some time but were relatively isolated domestically, while in Greece the then main opposition PASOK took a deviant line on EC entry but abandoned this once in office from 1981 because of the advantages for Greek society it found in EU resources. Accession in Ireland and Spain was relatively consensual (in Spain's case all three imperatives - historical, democratic and modernizing - were present), but not in Denmark where cross-party support was long checked by a vibrant anti-EC movement. In Britain, despite a quarter century of membership, still no real political consensus has emerged. Over time, therefore, domestic support has gradually but sometimes with difficulty spread across the political spectrum, though excluding the political extremes.

It is in this respect that central and eastern Europe is remarkably different. While historical and political motivation is certainly strong, it has been accompanied from early on by broad consensus in applicant countries. This should bode well for the current accession process, but the question still remains: how firm is this consensus or is it more formal than substantial? This will only eventually be answered by the test of long negotiations; but, meanwhile, it should not be forgotten that CEE applicants are undergoing a more arduous change process than in previous enlargements, so that the pressures on their broad consensus are likely to be heavy. The Mediterranean accessions involved new democracies that were primarily concentrating on political change, although they had also to undergo some economic restructuring and modernisation but at a pace much less intensive than that recently witnessed in post-Communist countries. Furthermore, CEE countries have to accept far more European legislation than in the southern enlargements.

Two other differences are already apparent in comparison with previous enlargements. The EU is now more demanding and interventionist towards accession countries than ever before. This is evident from the political conditions set out in the Copenhagen criteria of 1993 and monitored in the European Commission *avis* of 1997, the Accession Partnerships of 1998 and, in some detail in the annual Progress Reports of 1998, 1999 and 2000. Brussels made various bland political demands of Spain, Greece and Portugal, invariably along the lines of formal democracy (concerning democratic institutions and political pluralism). But not only has the EU extended these demands more precisely and into areas of substantive democracy (including, for instance, civil and political as well as socio-economic and cultural rights and the protection of minorities). This reflects the fact that there is now hardly an area of domestic policy that is not in some way affected by policy plans and action in Brussels. Altogether, therefore, the scope for domestic political impacts through accession is much greater than was the case in southern Europe.

On the EU side, the whole business of enlargement is on a scale which is unprecedented. Whereas previous enlargements have entailed usually three countries (1973 and 1995) or three in two stages (Mediterranean enlargement in 1981 and 1986), eastern enlargement potentially involves a dozen or maybe more new member states over the next decade or longer. This has enormous implications for an EU which has not as yet prepared itself convincingly in terms of either institutional or policy reform. Any consequent delay in accession in an attempt to resolve this problem may of course have repercussion effects on CEE applicants, hence their ability to hold the momentum and consensus behind the drive for accession.

EU Accession and Post-Communist Politics

From the above discussion, a framework for analysis may be constructed, based on unscrambling the domestic politics of applicant states and looking at motivation as well as key actors within different interlocking arenas. It is structured as follows: (a) historical, motivational and cultural factors; (b) governance, comprising policy approaches and institutional aspects; (c) the political arena, including parties, the media and public opinion; and, (d) The socio-economic arena, including different interests and the possibilities for civil mobilisation.

It postulates interactions not only within domestic politics but also especially between that and the EU in a two-directional sense: inner-directed, with Europeanisation pressures impacted on the domestic front; and, outer-directed, with domestic pressures responding to inner-directed ones as well as those originating internally. Conceivably, inner-directed pressures may stimulate intensified interactions among different domestic actors and influences. In order to take some qualitative measure of such pressures, one may distinguish between those which are policy-substantial, instrumental or opportunistic and polemical or populist, - which distinction does not of course exclude some combination of these. It goes without saying that democratic transition and movement towards liberal democracy is a virtual precondition of this framework. If, however, this persists as a problem, then we can expect some disruption of domestic politics with outer-directed impacts on Brussels, which in turn might make special demands on any such difficult applicant state. This framework will be applied to the CEE accession countries comparatively under each heading.

(a) Historical, Motivational and Cultural Factors

The historical imperative behind the basic policy redirection from east to west has been present from the start and it still generates grand political rhetoric, sometimes being linked to geo-strategic and security concerns as well as the need to reinforce democratisation. There are, however, some variants of this policy shift such as the escape-from-the-past imperative. In the Baltic states, for instance, this takes the form of retraction from the Russian embrace having been formerly part of the USSR, and inevitably it has contained a strong security motive driving their European policies.[9] No doubt, too, small country status enhances this imperative, perhaps all the more, as Moscow has threatened serious consequences for European security if the Baltic republics join NATO. But consensus is not undermined by the existence of strong

Russian minorities in two of these states, for the EU favours these by providing pressure for more liberal language laws and its membership offers far
better economic prospects than could ever be achieved in Russia.[10] A similar
imperative has been evident in some Balkan countries, which saw the EU as
offering a political if not economic and geo-strategic escape mechanism from
that region's troubled past and present. While Slovenia successfully extri-
cated itself from its Yugoslav entanglements in the early 1990s, 'escaping'
from the Balkans is now an unmistakable element in the thinking of political
elites in Bulgaria and Romania, which have now opened negotiations for EU
membership. In Bulgaria, the consensus among political actors has remained
overwhelming, and such historical imperatives help to reinforce this.

Historical factors and memories have also complicated European policy in
some cases. The vestiges of anti-German feeling in the Czech Republic would
be one example. However, this historical legacy has not seriously affected
broad support among the parties for Czech integration in Europe; indeed,
the EU is widely perceived as the optimal framework for coming to terms
with past issues and for bilateral international reconciliation.[11] Relations
between Poland and Germany have been rather less fraught because of past
hostility, once outstanding issues like confirming the border were resolved
in the early 1990s.

The security motivation needs some explanation. A distinction should be
drawn between direct or military security as provided for by NATO membership and the broader sense of security, including 'soft' security matters,
that comes from joining the EU. This distinction has a bearing on political
consensus as NATO has been more contentious than the EU in several countries (such as the Czech Republic, Slovakia and Bulgaria), all the more after
NATO action over Kosovo, but not in those where security motivation is high
such as the Baltic republics and Poland. But how much linkage is made
between NATO and the EU, and does controversy over the first affect the
second in domestic politics? Some linkage is made in opinion trends over
the one membership reinforcing chances for the other.[12] But political actors
have not greatly exploited this because of their strong consensus over the
EU, except for some extremist parties. Given public opinion is in many cases
more antipathetic to NATO, there would be a risk of parties losing control

over opinion in the event of too much instrumental linkage between these parallel issues.

Issues of national identity have arisen in some cases but, as a whole, they have not been presented in conflict with the values of European integration. Occasionally, the view is voiced that national sovereignty, recently acquired, will soon be ceded to Brussels, but this is most common in those states that were previously part of a larger political system, such as Slovenia and Estonia. In Estonia's case, cautiousness about compromising national independence comes from its experience under the USSR as is illustrated by suspicion toward the term 'union' in reference to the EU.[13] Such concerns about national sovereignty have usually remained unfocused and are rarely politically driven in an anti-EU direction. Political consensus in Estonia is strongly pro-accession; and only in Lithuania among the Baltic states is there a small Eurosceptic movement which argues that EU membership would be detrimental to national identity and independence.[14] Poland is by far the largest of the CEE applicants but there consensus among political elites accepts that the country's interests and identity will be enhanced through membership. Only in fundamentalist Catholic circles are reservations expressed in terms of western liberal and secular threats to traditional Catholic values, but such sentiments are not always channelled politically.[15]

In general, historical and political motivation as well as definitions of national interest and identity tend to reinforce the European strategies of post-Communist countries. Elements of Euroscepticism do exist, as in more recent statements of Czech opposition leader Vaclav Klaus, but there an impression of the instrumental or polemical about these. Difficulties in enlargement negotiations may encourage such behaviour, but what mainly counts is whether political consensus on these grounds is firm enough to withstand such pressures. Since the shift in external strategy from east to west involves an unambiguous rejection of the past, conclusions about the effects of different imperatives point to a fairly strong convictional drive behind accession policies.[16] So far at least, reaction to Europeanisation pressures has not been particularly value-ridden or ideological. Rather, it has taken the form of some impatience with Brussels' fairly stringent and numerous demands but also of some sectoral concerns over the policy implications of EU membership. Whether opposition from such sources mounts and then utilises grand arguments of an historical or cultural nature remains to be seen.

(b) Governance

This is variously defined as both policy-oriented and institutional. It is to be expected that Europeanisation will be considerable on the policy level through the adoption of the whole *acquis*. For, Brussels expects not merely legislative incorporation of this but also its practical implementation.[17] As to institutional procedures and structures, change is likely to be less radical but pressures are very real already, as applicant states have to manage their negotiations competently at the domestic level. Moreover, Brussels pays serious attention to the administrative capacity of accession countries as central to their ability to assume the obligations of membership, and requires administrative reform to be carried out prior to membership.

At this stage of the process, the European policies of post-Communist countries are essentially responsive. Their predominant concern is to negotiate entry to the EU and in the course of this accept more or less uncritically the legislative output over time of the EU. It is in the traditionally domestic policy sectors that most attention is focused - as nearly all of the 'chapter' headings indicate - with the most difficult likely to include agriculture (because of structural change required) and the environment (due to economic costs and the vastly complicated task of implementing highly technical legislation). Since the easier 'chapters' tend to be placed first in the order of negotiations it is only really those applicants that commenced negotiations in 1998 that are feeling the pressure at a wider political level.[18] Special issues have come to the forefront with some potential for creating anxiety, like migration and land purchase in the Czech Republic and notably agriculture in Poland because of the size of the farming business in that country.

In the Czech Republic, reform of the judiciary has been slow as highlighted in the 1999 Progress Report. Now, a whole range of further measures are planned under different headings: short-term priorities (for example, improving the qualifications of judges and training them in the application of European law, improving the accessibility of information for decisions by judges); medium-term priorities (e.g. modernising public administration in the field of justice, using information technology to improve management and measures to promote judicial self-administration); institution building needs (for example, rationalising the court workload and simplifying proceedings in court); and, financial needs, including EU assistance.[19] According to officials in the Finance Ministry, drafts of new laws are invariably sent to Brussels for consultation with relevant directorates-general and also where applicable with member states.[20] Slovakia has only recently started negotiations but already in the environmental field the government has made various institutional changes in different ministries and has adopted or is planning a raft of measures on air protection, waste management, water protection, nature and landscape protection, industrial pollution, noise pollution and nuclear safety.[21] A particular feature of policy harmonisation with the EU is the new practice of institution building twinning arrangements involving the secondment of officials from selected member states. In 1998, for instance, Slovenia had in the agricultural field such arrangements for veterinary and phytosanitary control, farm registry, rural structural development, market intervention and strengthening quality control.[22]

Despite general strategic agreement over EU entry, it is not impossible that the deadline pressures of negotiations and differences over specific policy sectors might place an added onus on national governments already facing policy difficulties on other grounds. This may cause difficulties in the area of European policy especially when there is a policy linkage problem. In Slovakia, the new Dzurinda Government was under sustained pressure to prove the country's democratic credentials after the Meciar period and demonstrated this with a series of decisions satisfying the EU's political conditions. One final measure required was a more liberal language law concerning the use of Hungarian, as a virtual *sine qua non* for opening negotiations with Brussels. This was duly passed in summer 1999, but only after serious differences between the Hungarian Coalition Party (SMK) and some other parties in the Government, but which did not in the end threaten government stability.[23] Of course, where there exist some basic differences over European integration between or within coalition partners then the impact of pressures from negotiations may be more damaging, as eventually occurred in the case of the Solidarity Electoral Action-Freedom Union (AWS-UW) government in Poland (1997-2000).[24]

As to institutions, coordinative structures are a familiar part of the government machine in applicant states. But, in general, the record so far is mixed with some cross-national variation but there are also predictable efficiency problems in countries that abandoned Communist rule only a decade ago.

The Visegrad countries are better prepared than most having introduced some bureaucratic streamlining at the top level to cope with the intense policy implementation pressures, such as Poland's civil service reform and establishment in 1996 of an effective Committee on European Integration to facilitate inter-ministerial co-ordination.[25] However, the Czech Republic has at times been criticised for poor organisation, lack of reform and modernization and a shortage of trained staff despite a structural overhaul in the mid-1990s.[26] Quite common to all countries is a shortage of suitable and sufficient expertise of EU affairs among their public administrations, but this will probably in the course of time be resolved. More serious perhaps is the absence of an enforcement culture, due to bureaucratic inheritances from the Communist period, such as in countries like Romania, so that monitoring implementation of the *acquis* becomes difficult.[27]

(c) The Political Arena

While areas of governance in accession countries are very largely engaged in the official business of convergence with the EU, thereby conforming with demands from Brussels, the wider political arena is not so subject to this basic constraint, so that criticisms and dissent are more likely to surface at this level as well as in the socio-economic arena.[28] Much depends on how political parties and the media handle issues and whether this promotes some debate that is informative or rather polemical. Since publics in accession countries are not as a rule well-informed about EU affairs, there is a tendency for them to be influenced by opinion-makers. Elite consensus is itself somewhat inhibiting to wider debate. This has been particularly true in cases like Hungary, unlike in some other countries where criticism of the EU has stimulated responses. This occurred in the Czech Republic with Klaus's condemnation of European monetary union and the EU approach to social policy.[29] In Poland, too, the advance of negotiations has profiled some issues that have begun to arouse concern despite cross-party support for accession. Such a development has however remained so far restricted, but the 'bite' of negotiations may well provoke new or predictable tension points in political exchange. It is much less in evidence in those countries which have only recently opened negotiations, although Slovakia has a background of polarisation between government and opposition parties, especially during the Meciar period. Such polemical handling of European policy had some impact on the public.

Accordingly, party supporters tend there to follow party lines over this question with significant divergence of opinion between supporters of each sides.[30]

Parties have a central role in maintaining political consensus. Since they both reflect ideological standpoints but also harness popular concerns while seeking to maximise their electoral prospects, under Europeanization pressures they may voice public concerns in a way that either does not challenge consensus or in populist fashion departs from this for partisan advantage. The general picture until now is one that broadly confirms a view of overwhelming political consensus. Governing parties support official policy except where (as in Poland) there has been some dissension within the government camp. While opposition parties also adhere to their countries' European strategies, differences emerge on specific issues and sometimes tactics in negotiations with Brussels. To some degree, such positions may be opposition politics. Beyond that, however, interest lies in how far policy-substantive differences have any wider meaning. In the Czech Republic, the Civic Democratic Party (ODS) emphasises a looser political construction for the EU and opposition to further supranational plans. The KDU-CSL, on the other hand, has supported the strong pro-integration position of fraternal Christian Democrats in western Europe. The Social Democrats meanwhile, more pro-integration than the ODS, have stressed the value of the Social Charter.[31] Such differences do indeed reflect party ideologies, although it does not follow this will lead to a significant divide over accession. Such party-political differentiation is much less in evidence in countries like Bulgaria where political consensus among the parties is very high but negotiation issues have not yet had much wider impact.

The ability of parties to hold with the political consensus on accession will depend also on the role of the media and the tendencies of public opinion. In other words, they may not be able to control what limited debate there has been up to now if pressures from both these directions start mounting. Debate in Poland has intensified not least because parties and the media have pursued lively arguments, albeit polemically. But this is also because the country's position in talks with Brussels has become more complicated and government impatience has increased, while there has been a decline in public support for accession (from admittedly a very high level).[32]

Again, the difference between countries that commenced negotiations in 1998 and 2000 is apparent. In Romania, for example, the quality of media coverage has been largely factual with generally positive views about integration, but the connection with economic reform is rarely made and the possible impact of EU membership on the economy little discussed.[33] In Estonia, on the other hand, more than two years of negotiations have produced more media debate but then there was little of that before they started. Media attention has focused on the practical implications of accession, with a tendency to treat some issues of concern in a populist way.[34] Similarly, in the Czech Republic, media coverage has grown with negotiations, the Amsterdam Treaty of 1997 being a turning-point. Since then, coverage of issues has become more concrete and there is now more technical understanding of EU affairs compared with the somewhat amateurish approach of the Czech media in the earlier 1990s.[35] Given the political pressures that surface with negotiation problems, predictably the media selectively popularise some issues over others such as the criticisms from Brussels in the annual Progress Reports. All this does not have to represent serious Euroscepticism but rather normal political life where Europeanization pressures are transmitted through the usual mechanisms of political pluralism on the domestic level.

Public opinion may be described as broad but shallow in accession countries. Popular support combines with a low level of information about the EU; and this does not seem to have so far changed significantly with the onset of negotiations. In Poland, for example, the high level of support has been accompanied by widespread ignorance about the specific costs and benefits of joining.[36] However, a decrease in support in the past two years has coincided with occasional confrontation between the government and Brussels, as over new visa rules that aroused protests from some areas of local opinion.[37] The same pattern has been present in the Czech Republic, where stable support for entry is linked to low issue awareness, but there debate has been less emotional than in Poland. Yet there appears to be a limit as to how far national publics may be mobilised on concrete issues and their ignorance of fairly complex EU affairs overcome. Some survey evidence suggests it is still broader questions, like support for democracy and a free market economy, that affect backing for EU entry rather than utilitarian factors like individual financial well-being.[38]

The issue of NATO is usually more divisive in EU accession countries, for, whereas the EU image is generally rather positive, that of NATO is still affected by past memories from the Communist period and therefore arouses feelings. Somewhat by contrast, government leaders have tended to prefer more rational arguments in favour of EU entry. This perhaps gives a clue about difficulties in projecting the EU onto domestic politics. Any disillusionment of expectations about EU accession is not likely to be exploited by influential political forces.

(d) The Socio-Economic Arena

Limited public engagement with the politics of accession casts some light on European/domestic interactions in the socio-economic arena. This explains why there has been little exaggerated policy interlinkage involving spill-over effects onto this question from other policy areas, especially economic.

The EU does provide a fairly consistent pressure for economic reform. It could be argued that this contributes, perhaps indirectly, to social and economic hardship that ensues. Decision-makers are certainly aware of this connection, but there is so far little evidence of such awareness among the wider arenas, whether political or socio-economic. It is indicative that parties which depart from the European consensus do not as a rule exploit economic issues, or if they do, this is not the dominant issue but rather matters relating to national identity and culture. In the Czech Republic, for example, there is no convincing evidence of increased economic dissatisfaction having affected views on the EU.[39] In Bulgaria, there was a severe economic crisis some years ago, but this has not affected the strong political consensus there on the EU; and, indeed, the timing of this was such that it occurred well before EU negotiations were opened. In this context, it is interesting that the wider arena is, if anything, more aware of the accession process as such rather than the broader integration process - a distinction made at the start of this article. This is not surprising since the rhetoric of politicians is very largely focused on the former - and on entry dates. Only when negotiations have begun does the media pay serious attention to EU matters, and opinion research concentrates on support for EU membership. Other European organizational links (apart from NATO membership) make much less impact, and this includes the Europe Agreements with the EU itself which have been in force in many cases since the mid-1990s.[40]

It might be supposed that economic interests would be more informed about the broader integration process, because of the EU's early attention to commercial and economic links. But the signs are of not strong involvement by them as yet on EU matters although there is some national variation. In the Czech Republic, no major interest groups have opposed EU entry, but some like state-owned enterprises and agricultural workers might prove sensitive to negotiations and there are already indications that difficulties in economic transition are adversely affecting the ability of economic actors to adapt to the EU's *acquis*.[41] In Estonia, some sectors have voiced concerns including parts of industry as well as farmers (who have objected to the mound of hygiene and veterinary regulations from Brussels), but support remains high among the influential business community.[42]

It is, however, in Poland - another 'first wave' applicant country - where the one major exception so far is to be found. It is therefore relevant to ask why this is so. The reasons are partly linked to the advance of negotiations but not exclusively. Indeed, the fact this has happened in Poland more than in other 'first wave' countries suggests there might be some national-specific explanation. EU issues are now well-covered in the media and a connection has been made here with sectoral interests. In summer 2000, for instance, the situation deteriorated with trade unions angry about redundancies and the rise in inflation, farmers anxious about their livelihood being possibly destroyed through the imposition of EU policies and standards. There were also stories about companies losing business because of their inability to conform to new environmental laws.[43] However, this situation arose at a time when negotiations had become more difficult and rumours were circulating that Polish entry might well be delayed, thus adding to the political impatience already present in Warsaw. National pride was evident too but there were also cultural factors at work. Poland has a particularly large agricultural sector, but it is not simply this factor which matters in terms of the magnitude of the problem of change posed by accession. The land and countryside has a special significance to Polish culture, so that it is not too difficult a step for the EU to be presented as a threat to Polish culture in some farming circles.[44]

The socio-economic arena is in any case a complex area entailing a mixture of factors including influences from past experience. In Slovakia, it has been found there is a link between anti-western attitudes and reservations towards the EU while younger Slovaks are more open than the older generation in trusting people from western Europe - implying the former were less conditioned by life under the Communist regime. This past influence also coloured the view taken by some people that Slovakia was a small and newly sovereign country that was vulnerable to exploitation by the capitalist western world. At the same time, there was an overwhelming preference among the public for EU states over Russia as partner countries. Furthermore, the picture was complicated in that party preferences cut across these patterns quite strongly, with supporters of Meciar's party finding western European countries less friendly than supporters of the Slovak Democratic Coalition (SDK) did. Politics therefore confused the influence of sociological factors. To illustrate this further, the Hungarian minority took a more favourable view of western Europe than Slovaks on average despite their being more rurally based and having a weaker educational background (both factors which normally indicate lower sympathy in that country towards the west). For Hungarian Slovaks, there was a political motive in seeing the EU as offering protection from discriminatory pressure at home - not surprising since the EU gave visibility to issues of minority rights.[45]

In conclusion, there are various issues and mentalities that could, with effective political mobilization, be brought to bear as a domestic pressure against EU accession, but the commitment of political elites and political parties to this European strategy has prevented this from happening so far. This commitment is likely to come under greater strain during the course of entry negotiations in the next years, but it does not follow this will open up to a wave of Euroscepticism. Summarising evidence quoted above, the picture is one of fragmented disaffection with - or concern over - European integration, and this presents some obstacle to full-scale campaigns against that.

Conclusion

The balance of pressures is decidedly in favour of the EU over those from domestic sources but this is not without the consent of policy-makers in applicant countries. That in turn reinforces the positive outlook in Brussels where EU officials place a strong emphasis on continuing political stability in these countries given the investment of effort, time and prospective resources involved in the enlargement process.

It is clear, too, that the relationship between EU accession and multiple trans-formation has not so far created a dangerous threat to this consensus despite the overall pressures and demands from these. The EU has acted as a regular outside stimulant and support agent in encouraging the completion of democratisation. This has by and large reinforced the positive image of the EU in these countries despite occasional polemics over lack of progress in meeting Brussels' rather stringent demands of democratic conditionality. Economic transformation has not had a profound effect on attitudes towards EU entry, notwithstanding pressure from Brussels on this front, but in many cases the worst of this transformation is over, especially in those states from east-central Europe which are ahead in negotiations. Issues relating to national identity have arisen but in a diffuse way, and except on the sensitive issue of minorities the EU has not impacted greatly on the problem of nation-build-ing. The pressures on new states and their institutional structures are cer-tainly intense - through the time pressure of negotiations - but this problem has not greatly affected the wider political arena.

Thus, Europeanization pressures on domestic politics have been significant and quite extensive. It is reasonable to suppose these will increase during the course of negotiations. So far, interactions between different levels within domestic politics have been fairly restrained given the magnitude of the task in joining the EU. This may well change once Platonic attitudes to EU mem-bership are replaced or challenged by new realities, although the Polish expe-rience may not be exactly repeated since national-specific factors do count. In the end, what is significant is how the complexities of enlargement are handled politically, and whether political actors find short-term advantage in exploiting disaffection with what is a long-term departure in their coun-tries' histories.

If, overall, this analysis comes to a somewhat more optimistic conclusion than expected, there are also some reasons for caution. There is a potential for the gap to widen between elites and mass opinion, all the more as the accession process is one-sidedly driven from Brussels. Enlargement negotiations, as do also negotiations among EU member states, tend to strengthen an elitist bias since they are traditionally dominated by government executives. There are public signs of this, as when decision-makers in CEE countries use EU demands to justify the passage and implementation of unpopular measures. This is a practice also adopted by EU member states when convenient. But the difference is that new democracies in post-Communist countries are more vulnerable to growing mistrust towards political elites on the part of national publics and perhaps also special interests. If that became a serious problem, then the political consensus behind their European strategies would indeed be at risk. And, this is all the more likely if the EU, unprepared as it is, seeks to delay accession. In those CEE countries affected, this could seriously affect the domestic dynamics behind their drive to join the EU.

University of Bristol
g.pridham@bristol.ac.uk

Notes

[1] H. Wallace, 'National bulls in the Community china shop: the role of national governments in Community policy-making', H. Wallace, C. Webb and W. Wallace (eds), *Policy Making in the European Community* (London: John Wiley, 1977), pp. 33-34.

[2] As the deputy head of the European Committee in Lithuania remarked, accession negotiations are 'not real negotiations in the classical sense' (interview with Darius Zervolis, Vilnius, July 2000). The European Committee, under the Prime Minister's office, is responsible for the domestic side of accession negotiations.

[3] S. Bulmer, 'Domestic politics and European Community policy making', B. Nelsen and A. Stubb (eds), *The European Union: Readings on Theory and Practice of European Integration* (Boulder CO: Lynne Rienner, 1994), pp. 145; 148.

[4] This is not so unusual when comparing with the literature on previous enlargements. Studies of the domestic politics of accession are few and include, for instance, F. Roy Willis, *France, Germany and the New Europe, 1945-1967* (London: Oxford University Press, 1968); F. Roy Willis, *Italy chooses Europe* (New York: Oxford University Press, 1971); U. Kitzinger, *Diplomacy and Persuasion: How Britain joined the Common Market* (London: Thames & Hudson, 1973); and, L. Tsoukalis, *The European Community and its Mediterranean Enlargement* (London: George Allen & Unwin, 1981), chapter 2. However, some attention is given to domestic politics in the current accession process in H. Grabbe and K. Hughes, *Enlarging the EU Eastwards* (London: Royal Institute of International Affairs: 1998), chapter 6 and K. Henderson (ed.), *Back to Europe: Central and Eastern Europe and the European Union* (London: UCL Press, 1999), part III.

[5] This point is made and explored in the case of Austria by G. Falkner, 'How per-

vasive are Euro-politics? Effects of EU membership on a new member state' in *Journal of Common Market Studies*, June 2000, pp. 223-50.

[6] Cf. comment of chairman of the Foreign Affairs Committee in the Lithuanian Seimas (Parliament) that the necessary response to anti-EU propaganda was an information campaign but, in particular, using 'the language of the people and not Brussels jargon', implying the latter reinforced elitist images (interview with Audronius Azubalis, Vilnius, July 2000).

[7] This multi-dimensional approach to policy implementation is outlined in detail and applied to the environmental sector in G. Pridham, 'Environmental policies and problems of European legislation in Southern Europe', *South European Society and Politics*, summer 1996, pp. 47-73.

[8] The main example so far of political conditions complicating a CEE state's chances of EU membership has been Slovakia, whose exclusion from the then 'first wave' of applicants was precisely on these grounds because of the authoritarian leanings of the Meciar Government 1994-98. The 1998 parliamentary election, resulting in Meciar's defeat and leading to the formation of a government by the democratic opposition, was greeted in Brussels with an immediate change of attitude on which the new prime minister Dzurinda capitalised by making Brussels (the EU and NATO) his first official visit abroad within days of his inauguration.

[9] Interview with Povilas Gylys, former Foreign Minister of Lithuania, Vilnius, July 2000, in which he argued that the EU was an 'escape from the Russian past', it 'means security' and is connected with democratic Europe.

[10] In 2000 a new political party for Russian speakers was formed in Estonia, called the Russian Baltic Party of Estonia. Its board member Viktor Lanberg emphasised they were 'looking forward to joining EU' and that their party would 'take into account the experience of European countries, as we have solid contacts with European parties like the Christian Democratic Party of Germany' (*The Baltic Times*, 29 June-5 July 2000).

[11] V. Handl and M. Zaborowski, *Comparative Czech and Polish Perspectives and Policies on the Eastern Enlargement of the EU and the Prominence of the 'German Factor'* (Institute for German Studies, University of Birmingham, 1999), pp. 19-20; 31-32.

[12] For instance, in Slovakia, there has been a strong majority of opinion agreeing with the view that NATO acceptance would increase the chances of EU accession., e.g. see GFK Slovakia, Bratislava, *Public Awareness Campaign - Research on EU information sources and target audiences in the Slovak Republic and a proposal for communication strategy on the EU in the Slovak Republic*, 1998, pp. 51-52.

[13] K. Hughes, H. Grabbe and E. Smith, *Attitudes of the Central and East European Countries to Integration*, Discussion Paper No. IGS99/3, (Institute for German Studies, University of Birmingham, 1999), pp. 22-3; 65.

[14] G. Herd, 'The Baltic states and EU enlargement' in Henderson, *Back to Europe*, p. 265.

[15] Only Radio Maryja mobilises the religious Right on this issue and has provided some support for the post-Solidarity AWS in elections. In Slovakia, the former KDH chairman Jan Carnogursky, has on occasions expressed similar views critical of western or American liberalism, but his party has remained firmly pro-EU alongside its partners in Christian Democratic transnational party organizations.

[16] This may be illustrated by the Slovak case. The Meciar government of 1994-98 formally supported EU accession but there were increasing indications that this policy was not based on conviction, whether through Meciar's apparent sympathies for (mainly commercial) links with Russia, nationalist pressures from within the government or persistent flouting of political conditions demanded by Brussels. However, the Dzurinda Government, elected in 1998, has shown every sign of its overwhelming commitment to EU. Indeed, this European strategy has been its most unifying force in what is a complicated multi-party coalition.

[17] According to the deputy head of the European Committee in Lithuania, there is a fall-back position with a transition period but it has to be argued for in each case (interview with Darius Zervolis, Vilnius, July 2000). This represents a much tougher requirement than was the case with Southern enlargement.

[18] This does not mean that applicants which started negotiations in February 2000 are not already feeling the sheer pressure of policy change. In the case of Slovakia, there is additional pressure to catch up with those other east-central European countries that started in 1998, in particular the Czech Republic not least because of difficulties that would arise from the customs union between the two countries if Prague joined before Bratislava. Slovakia's motivation to do this is strong because of having been excluded from negotiations in 1998 because of the policies of the then Meciar Government.

[19] Czech Government, *National Programme for the Preparation of the Czech Republic for Membership of the European Union* (Prague, 1999), section 1.1.2, pp. 4-12.

[20] Interview with Jiri Vetrovsky, Milena Horcicova and Jan Gregor, Ministry of Finance, Prague, March 2000.

[21] Government Office, Slovak Republic, *National Programme for the Adoption of the Acquis Communautaire* (Bratislava, 2000), section 3.6.1, pp. 284-323.

[22] European Commission, *Composite Paper: Reports on Progress towards Accession by ceach of the candidate countries* (Brussels, 1999), annex 4.

[23] The inclusion of the SMK in the Dzurinda Government was, among other things, motivated by EU considerations, and these helped to overcome reservations expressed during the government formation in autumn 1998.

[24] See G. Blazyca and M. Kolkiewicz, 'Poland and the EU: internal disputes, domes-

tic politics and accession', in *Journal of Communist Studies and Transition Politics*, December 1999, pp. 131-43.

[25] M. Rupp, 'The pre-accession strategy and the governmental structures of the Visegrad countries' in Henderson, *Back to Europe*, pp. 99-100.

[26] Henderson, *Back to Europe*, pp. 96-7 and Hughes, Grabbe and Smith, *Attitudes . . .*, pp. 54-5.

[27] Henderson, *Back to Europe*, p. 100. See European Commission, *1999 Regular Report on Romania's Progress towards Accession* (Brussels, 1999), pp. 59-60 and section 4 for critical comments on Romania's failure to carry out public administration reform.

[28] Senior officials as well as government ministers and those in positions of parliamentary leadership are only too aware of the 'one-sided' nature of negotiations with the EU and are prepared to admit so in private to some impatience with this, but they quickly make it clear this is accepted for the sake of joining the most important international organization in Europe (a conclusion drawn from interviews conducted in the Czech Republic, Hungary, Slovakia and Lithuania between March and July 2000).

[29] Grabbe and Hughes, *Enlarging the EU Eastwards*, p. 73.

[30] See, for instance, the results of the survey on attitudes to EU and NATO of the Institute for Public Affairs (IVO), Bratislava, 'Aku zahranicnu politiku pre nasu verejnost?' in *Sme*, 29 April 2000.

[31] Handl and Zaborowski, *Comparative Czech*, pp. 20, 37.

[32] H. Grabbe and K. Hughes, 'Central and east European views on EU enlargement: political debates and public opinion' in Henderson, *Back to Europe*, p. 193.

[33] Hughes, Grabbe and Smith, *Attitudes*, pp. 96-97.

[34] Hughes, *Attitudes*, p. 64.

[35] Interview with Petr Zavadil, head of foreign department, *Lidove Noviny*, Prague, March 2000. But he pointed out that the technical content of EU policies was difficult to project to the public, as 'the people in general don't understand the complex nature of enlargement'.

[36] Hughes, Grabbe and Smith, *Attitudes*, p. 83.

[37] Blazyca and Kolkiewicz, 'Poland and the EU', pp. 137, 142.

[38] See for example R. Cichowski, *Choosing Democracy: Citizen Attitudes and the Eastern Enlargement of the European Union*, (Robert Schuman Centre, European University Institute, working paper no. 12, 2000), pp. 15-26. The survey also confirmed the strong independent effect that political partisanship has on popular attitudes towards EU membership.

[39] Hughes, Grabbe and Smith, *Attitudes*, pp. 50-51.

[40] For example, the Czech press did not give much coverage to the Council of Europe - as 'it is difficult to explain what it is' - or to the meetings of the Joint

Parliamentary Committee between the Czech Parliament and the European Parliament, an institutional provision of the Europe Agreement, only 'if there is some story' coming from the latter (interview with Petr Zavadil, *Lidove Noviny*, Prague, March 2000).

[41] Hughes, Grabbe and Smith, *Attitudes*, pp. 51, 55.

[42] Hughes, Grabbe and Smith, *Attitudes*, pp. 67-68.

[43] Report in *The Times*, 20 June 2000.

[44] Hughes, Grabbe and Smith, *Attitudes*, p. 86.

[45] This paragraph draws on GfK Slovakia, *Public Awareness Campaign*, report, 1998, passim; also, conversations with Kamil Sladek, Director, Centre for European Policy, Bratislava and Grigorij Meseznikov and Olga Gyarfasova, Institute for Public Affairs (IVO), Bratislava, May 2000. It may be noted that the Russian-speaking minority in Estonia similarly supports EU entry as a way of improving their political and economic status.

Jackie Gower

EU-Russian Relations and the Eastern Enlargement: Integration or Isolation?

ABSTRACT

The external relations dimension of the European Union's enlargement to central and eastern Europe has received surprisingly little attention despite the fact that in the long-term the issues that it raises may be far more important than those currently dominating the debate. Nowhere is this more likely to be true than in relation to Russia for which the EU's enlargement poses a risk of increasing isolation from the rest of Europe. The danger of creating a new dividing line across Europe is widely recognised and the challenge therefore is to find ways of ensuring that Russia can be fully integrated with Europe while almost certainly remaining outside the EU itself. This article focuses on relations between the EU and Russia and address three key questions: how Russia has reacted to the prospect of the EU's eastern enlargement; the specific issues arising from enlargement and the kind of long-term relationship that might develop between Russia and an enlarged EU.

The European Union's eastern enlargement is not expected to extend as Far east as Russia, but it will inevitably change the context in which relations with Moscow are developed. The accession of many of the former Council for Mutual Economic Assistance (CMEA) members will have a profound impact not only on the Union itself but also on Russia's perception of it. So far Russia has generally reacted positively to the prospect of her central and east European neighbours becoming members of the European Union, in marked contrast to her total opposition to them joining NATO. However, there is increasing concern in Moscow that their accession to the EU may have some negative consequences on Russia's economic and political interests in Europe. The greatest fear, and it is one shared by many in the west as well, is that the enlargement of the EU will create a new fault-line across Europe, leaving Russia as an 'outsider' state, marginalised politically and excluded from the benefits of the single market.[1]

If EU enlargement is to enhance European security and stability, the challenge therefore is to find ways of integrating Russia into the wider Europe on the basis of shared values and common interests while accepting that her accession to the EU is extremely improbable. The assumption that Russia is not envisaging applying for EU membership in the coming decade (2000-2010) was confirmed in the opening paragraph of the *Medium-Term Strategy* document presented by Vladimir Putin at the EU-Russia summit in October 1999:

> During the period under review, partnership between Russia and the European Union will be based on the treaty relations, i.e. without an officially stated objective of Russia's accession to or "association" with the EU. As a world power situated on two continents, Russia should retain its freedom to determine and implement its domestic and foreign policies, its status and advantages of an Euro-Asian state and the largest country of the CIS and independence of its position and activities at international organisations.[2]

This was undoubtedly extremely welcome news in Brussels where a previous Prime Minister, Victor Chernomyrdin, two years previously had unexpectedly declared at a press conference in Brussels that Russia's long-term goal was to become a member of the European Union.[3] Although no-one, at least officially, would question Russia's right to apply for EU membership if it could meet the Copenhagen criteria,[4] the institutional and financial implications of including a state as large and as poor as Russia would make the problems of the current enlargement agenda pale into insignificance. However, if it is agreed that Russia must be part of the European integration project but not as an EU member, it does raise major conceptual as well as practical issues as to how that is to be achieved.[5]

In 1999 both the EU and Russia independently adopted official strategies for the development of their relationship which reflected the recognition of the increasing urgency and importance of meeting this challenge.[6] Significantly, both documents hold out the vision of a 'strategic partnership' evolving between Russia and an enlarged EU with cooperation across a very broad range of policy areas in order to minimise the possible negative impact of enlargement and create new opportunities for positive interaction. The legal framework for the realisation of this objective is the Partnership and Cooperation Agreement (PCA)[7] that came into force in December 1997 and the main policy instrument is the Technical Assistance for the CIS (TACIS) programme to support Russia's political and economic reforms. The scope of the cooperation has recently been expanded by the EU's 'Northern Dimension' initiative which is intended to provide opportunities for Russia to participate in specific projects with her near neighbours. There remains, however, considerable uncertainty about how in fact this critical relationship between the two major powers on the European continent will evolve and whether enlargement will have a positive or negative impact on it.

Three main questions will therefore be addressed. Firstly, how has Russia reacted to the prospect of the EU's eastern enlargement? Secondly, what are the specific issues arising from the enlargement that could affect relations between the EU and Russia? And finally, what kind of longer-term relationship will develop between Russia and the enlarged EU?

Russia's attitude towards the EU's enlargement

There has so far been very little media coverage in Russia of the EU's enlargement process and certainly no public debate about its implications. Unlike NATO enlargement, it arouses no great passions and indeed little interest except among a very few academics and government officials. To the extent that it is known at all, the European Union is seen primarily as an economic organisation and it is among the business community that reservations about its enlargement have so far mainly been heard.

However, it is important to keep in perspective the relatively little negative reaction to the prospect of EU enlargement compared to the frequent public denunciations of NATO's similar plans. Unlike NATO, which has a high profile in the Russian media as the symbol of western antagonism not only during the Cold War but also today after Kosovo, the EU is almost unknown to the general public, and even apparently to some members of the foreign policy community.[8] Its enlargement, therefore, to include many states that were in the sphere of influence of the former USSR, and indeed three of its constituent republics (the Baltic states), is not perceived as either a threat or a national humiliation in the way NATO 'expansion' undoubtedly is. However, this is almost certainly only true of the current group of applicants: if Ukraine, Belarus, Georgia and other CIS states were to submit applications (and some of them have indicated that they intend to do so), Russia's reaction would be very different.

The lack of public awareness of the EU has enabled the government to adopt a largely pragmatic policy on the enlargement issue, raising no fundamental objections to it but indicating a determination to press for measures to protect Russia's own interests. The *Medium-Term Strategy* has a specific section entitled 'Securing Russian interests in an expanded European Union' in which it foresees that the impact of EU enlargement is likely to be 'ambivalent' and it will be necessary to strive to achieve 'the best advantages' as well as 'preventing, eliminating or setting off possible adverse consequences.'[9] The important point, however, is that the Russian authorities regard the issues arising from EU enlargement as negotiable and the overall impact on EU-Russian relations is likely to be a greater intensity of interaction and an increased sense of purpose in the large number of official meetings and working groups that now function within the PCA framework. Some of the most important issues on the EU-Russia agenda in the light of the planned enlargement will be considered in the next section.

Although there clearly are genuine and serious concerns about the impact of EU enlargement, particularly in the economic field, there are seen to be some advantages from the perspective of Russia's foreign policy goals. In geostrategic terms it is very much in line with Russia's key objective of developing a multi-polar world order with the assumption that enlargement will make the EU not only economically but also politically more important. The

EU is seen to have at least the potential to act as a counter-balance to US hegemony although in the view of one Russian academic 'Russians tend to overestimate its "counter-American" nature.'[10] There is considerable interest in Russia in the idea of a triangular power structure in Europe based on Washington, Brussels and Moscow.[11] Russia's Ambassador to the EU, Vasily Likhachev, commented that it was no coincidence that the EU-Russia summit at the end of May 2000 would be followed by the EU-US summit two days later and then President Clinton's visit to Moscow at the beginning of June. He explained that 'This is the logic of how Russia sees international relations. The world is multi-polar, with both the EU and Russia looking for a new image.'[12]

Russia's perception of the EU is clearly very different from the Soviet interpretation of it as the economic wing of NATO and explains the marked differentiation in the official response to the two enlargement projects. European integration is generally seen as a positive post-war development, contributing to European stability and security and encouraging reconciliation between past enemies. Youri Borko, one of the few Russian academic specialists on the EU, described it as 'one of the cornerstones of stability in Europe' and suggested that it would be in Russia's strategic interest for that stability to be extended to her western borders.[13] Candidate countries are required to settle any border disputes with their neighbours before accession and membership itself imposes considerable constraints on the internal and external policies of all its member states. Both in the pre-accession period and after enlargement, therefore, the EU is expected to exercise a moderating and restraining influence over the central and east European states in their relations with each other and other states in the region that is generally welcomed by Russia.

This would seem to be particularly true with respect to the Baltic states which are seen as 'openly unfriendly' towards Russia[14] and potentially rather volatile and nationalistic. Furthermore, Russia has recognised the potential to use the Baltic states' goal of EU accession as useful political leverage to secure an improvement in the position of the large Russian minorities living in Estonia and Latvia and acceptance of the post Second World War borders.[15] In the Medium Term Strategy one of the objectives is 'to secure that the EU fully follows the high standards established by it as to the admittance of new members' and it specifically calls for consultations before enlargement 'to safeguard, in the interests of stability, security and cooperation in Europe, the rights of the Russian-speaking population in the Baltic states.'[16] At meetings with EU representatives the Russian delegation regularly raises the question of what they see as the discrimination against the Russian-speaking minority and press the EU to use its influence to improve the situation. This 'Europeanisation' of the issue has generally been seen as helpful and the assumption seems to be that 'the entry of the Baltic states into the EU . . . would ensure better treatment for Russian speaking minorities in these countries.'[17] Certainly the EU is extremely anxious to avoid the nightmare scenario of a future Russian government 'coming to the assistance' of its compatriots in an EU member state and will continue to press for more inclusive citizenship laws and positive steps to encourage the full integration of the minorities into society.

Issues raised by enlargement

The official Russian response to the proposed EU enlargement has therefore generally been favourable and even Communist Party leader Gennadii Zyuganov told a group of Members of the European Parliament that 'The enlargement of the EU towards the east is a positive and very important element. It is commendable that the EU can gain more influence and play a more important role in Europe and in the international arena in general.'[18] However, it would probably be unwise to assume that the current favourable consensus will continue unchallenged as the date for the first accessions gets closer. While EU enlargement will almost certainly bring new opportunities for some individuals, enterprises and regions it may also pose risks to others. The likely ensuing domestic debate, if it does finally materialise, will inevitably spill over into the wider question of Russia's relations with the EU itself and perhaps with the outside world more generally. There are already fears that the impact of enlargement could be detrimental to Russian interests in several areas, specifically in trade and economic relations, the imposition of more stringent border controls and the future of the oblast of Kaliningrad which will be a Russian exclave in the European Union itself. Resolving these issues to the satisfaction of both parties prior to enlargement will be essential if they are not to threaten the development of the strategic partnership.

Trade

One of Russia's main concerns is that enlargement might have an adverse effect on its trade with the central and east European countries (CEECs) themselves and possibly also with the EU as a whole if the new members displace Russian exports as a result of the competitive advantage they will have from operating within the single market. Once they are EU members the CEECs will be able to take advantage of the 'four freedoms' of goods, capital, services and labour within the single market[19] while the Common External Tariff (CET) will apply to their trade with third parties. Russia has already expressed concern about the possible loss of markets as a result of the CEECs extending the EU's trade preferences to developing countries that are competing with Russian exports. The application of the CET to Russia itself is not likely to be a major problem as EU tariffs are generally low and in many cases lower than those currently applied by the CEECs and energy and other primary products which account for a high proportion of Russia's exports are zero-rated. Nevertheless, it has been a long-standing Russian objective to secure access to the EU market on the same terms as the CEECs and in the negotiations for the PCA they pressed hard for the inclusion of an 'evolutionary clause' with a commitment 'to examine together in the year 1998 whether circumstances allow the beginning of negotiations on the establishment of a free trade area' (Article 3). In the wake of the Russian financial crisis that year, the issue had to be postponed but it is likely to come back onto the agenda before the next enlargement.

Potentially much more damaging to Russia's trade with the enlarged EU are non-tariff barriers in the form of overt quantitative restrictions such as quotas and anti-dumping measures and the more subtle obstacles arising from the single market legislative norms on technical standards, product certification et cetera. When the CEECs join the EU, their trade with Russia will be conducted within the legal framework of the PCA which despite Russia's protests during the negotiations permits the continued use of quotas and contingent protection. There are also a number of separate agreements for sensitive goods such as textiles, steel and nuclear materials which also restrict access to the EU market and would of course be applicable for trade with the new member states. Russia is therefore pressing for an urgent review of what it regards as the EU's unwarranted protectionism arising from its reluctance to afford it full market-economy status. Anti-dumping in particular has been identified by the Russian Government as one of the key issues that it intends to raise in relation to enlargement.

Even more serious potentially, but probably more difficult to resolve, will be the consequences for Russia's trade arising from the adoption by the CEECs of the EU's *acquis communautaire* which includes literally hundreds of laws governing the single market. Already as part of their pre-accession programmes the CEECs are adopting EU technical standards and the Russian authorities are concerned that many Russian products, including machinery, pharmaceuticals and foodstuffs, will no longer be able to be sold there.[20] Although they seem to hope that they will be able to negotiate special arrangements to reduce the potential damage, in the long term Russia's own economic legislation will need to be harmonised with the EU *acquis* if a lot of Russian goods are not going effectively to be barred from the vast single market on their doorstep. Article 55 of the PCA commits Russia 'to endeavour to ensure that its legislation shall be gradually made compatible with that of the community' in respect of most aspects of the economic environment but it is difficult to envisage the current Duma being very enthusiastic about the task.

There are therefore a number of complex issues relating to the economic implications of the EUs enlargement that seem likely to dominate EU-Russian meetings in the coming years. At the summit on 22 October, 1999 the Russian delegation presented a list of fifteen areas where they believe their trade could be damaged by the accession of the CEECs and they certainly hope to be able to extract significant concessions or compensation from the EU. Both parties recognise the vital importance of good economic relations and increased trade as the surest foundation on which to build closer political cooperation. Over the past decade the EU has become by far the most important of Russia's trading partners and if enlargement did not cause significant trade diversion, about fifty per cent of its trade would be with the enlarged Union. In the Joint Statement issued after the 29 May, 2000 summit a more positive note was adopted than previously with a commitment that their 'joint aim is to mobilise the potential that EU enlargement will offer for increasing trade both between the enlarging European Union and Russia, and between Russia and the candidate countries.'

The expansion of the single market and the rising living standards in the new member states could offer new opportunities for enterprising Russian entrepreneurs and President Putin seems to be encouraging a more outward-looking business culture. However, there are significant sectors of the Russian economy that are much more likely to press for increased protectionism to shield domestic producers from EU competition. There is also considerable nervousness in the Russian business community that the dramatic westward reorientation of the CEECs' trade that has taken place since the abolition of the Council for Mutual Economic Assistance (CMEA) will receive a further boost by their accession to the EU. There are painful memories of the costs to the Russia economy of Finland's accession to the EU in 1995 and fears that the impact of the next enlargement could be even more serious. The greatest problem facing policy-makers in both Brussels and Moscow seems to be the lack of sufficient economic analysis of the probable effect of EU enlargement on the Russian economy in general and trade with the EU in particular. A special committee of experts is currently preparing a report under the PCA framework so hopefully at future meetings possible problems can be identified and discussed more constructively and be less based on speculation fuelled by alarmist reports in the media.

Borders

Since Finland's accession to the EU in 1995 Russia and the EU have shared a long common border and the impact on their relationship has generally been positive, with their commitment to the Northern Dimension initiative a clear reflection of the increased awareness of the importance of regional cooperation. The accession of Estonia, Latvia, Lithuania and Poland (the latter two border Kaliningrad) will further extend the common border but there are concerns that the consequences may not be so positive. Paradoxically, while the accession of the CEECs will bring the EU physically even closer to Russia, the EU's requirement that the new members adopt the Schengen regime of strict border controls will psychologically increase her sense of being apart from the rest of Europe.

The problem arises from the fact that the EU's internal security agenda depends on ensuring that its external border is vigorously policed to regulate who and what is allowed to enter the Union.[21] It has therefore required the applicant states to tighten their border controls even prior to accession to try to stem what it sees as the tide of illegal immigrants, traffickers in drugs, persons and nuclear material, money launderers and other international criminals permeating the eastern frontier. The Russian authorities are not adverse in principle to measures designed to reduce the level of organised international crime but unfortunately many of them also have the effect of imposing new restrictions on the legitimate movement of people and goods. For example, there is considerable resentment at the actual or planned introduction of visas for travel between the CEECs and Russia which it is claimed will inhibit both tourism and business travel between neighbours and is seen by the general public in Russia as an inexplicably retrograde step in the 'new Europe'. This is particularly sensitive in relation to the Baltic states, partly because of the Kaliningrad problem discussed in the following section, but also because it will increase the sense of 'apartness' of the Russian-speaking minorities who will understandably feel that they are being even more cut off from their families and friends who only ten years ago lived in the same country. Russia has also criticised the introduction of visas by the Czech Republic and Poland which it claims will damage business generally and tourism in particular. Furthermore, there are long delays at the border crossings that impose costly delays on the transport of goods and have already largely destroyed the informal small-scale cross-border trade that was characteristic of the early 1990s.

If EU enlargement is not to be perceived as creating new barriers across Europe, a 'paper curtain' of visa and custom formalities where once there was the 'iron curtain',[22] ways will need to be found to guarantee the security of the EU's external border without obstructing the legitimate movement of people and goods. Some of the practical irritations of measures like visas could be alleviated by improving the bureaucratic procedures to make the process as efficient and inexpensive as possible. For example, if the visa applications could be handled by EU agencies based in all the major Russian cities rather than the individual consulates of each member state it would seem much simpler for Russian citizens but of course such a move would be highly controversial for some EU members. In the longer term, if the EU and Russia could agree to introduce a visa-free regime, then obviously the problem in relation to the central and east European states would be resolved. But in the short-term, it is likely to be seen by ordinary Russians as one of the most obvious, and negative, consequences of EU enlargement, increasing their sense of isolation from the rest of Europe.

The danger that the new borders will draw a sharp line between insiders and outsiders is recognised as one of the most difficult issues arising from the eastern enlargement and has serious ramifications for the EU's relations with many other states apart from Russia.[23] One of the most constructive responses to the problem has been to encourage cross-border cooperation on specific projects and this approach is being adopted to try to alleviate some of Russia's sense of exclusion. One of the main objectives of the Northern Dimension is to extend the concept of the 'Euro-region' by seeking to engage north-west Russia in cooperative projects and initiatives that span the borders and in a practical way at least partly reduce their sharpness.

Kaliningrad

Probably nowhere in Europe are the problems considered in the previous section felt more acutely than in the oblast of Kaliningrad, seemingly destined to be a small Russian exclave geographically situated *inside* the European Union but with all the practical and psychological problems of being an *outsider*. Unless there is some exceptionally lateral thinking about the nature of its borders in both Moscow and Brussels, it risks assuming the role of a 'double periphery', on the fringes of both the EU and Russia.[24] Its geo-strategic position and ice-free port made it one of the most important Soviet military bases and it remains a largely militarised zone which heightens the political sensitivity of its future for both Russia and the EU.

Since the break up of the Soviet Union it has been completely cut off from the rest of Russia and special transit rights across Lithuania have had to be negotiated for both its residents, many of whom are military personnel, and energy and other vital supplies. One of the most difficult problems posed by Lithuania's accession to the EU is whether those transit rights can be maintained or whether the Lithuanian/Kaliningrad border will be as robust as the other external borders of the Union. It would certainly be a unique situation if sealed trains carrying Russian soldiers and military equipment continue regularly to travel across what is soon to become EU territory. However, it does seem to be recognised that it is vitally important to be sensitive to Russia's interests if the overall security position in the region is not to be compromised. The Russian Government has indicated that it might be appropriate to conclude 'a special agreement with the EU in safeguarding the interests of the Kaliningrad region as an entity of the Russian Federation in the process of EU expansion.'[25] It has specifically asked that a more favourable visa regime should be offered to Kaliningraders than would normally apply under the Schengen *acquis* so that they would not have to apply for visas in order to travel overland to other parts of the Russian Federation. With the decision at the Helsinki European Council in December 1999 to open formal accession negotiations with Lithuania, there is an increased sense of urgency to resolve the outstanding issues.

However, the Kaliningrad 'problem' is not just a question of visas and transit rights. Much more fundamental is the direction of its future development and its role in the Baltic region. There had been hopes that it could be transformed from a military garrison into a thriving economic zone taking advantage of its position as a Baltic Sea state with easy access to the European market. In the mid 1990s there was much optimistic talk of it becoming the Hong Kong of the north and providing a bridge between Russia and the EU market. [26] The reality today, however, is that its economy is stagnant, its infrastructure decaying and the gap in living standards between its population and the rest of the Baltic region widening. The only dynamic economic sector is organised crime and the local administration is both corrupt and inept.[27] In the EU, the greatest security risks emanating from Kaliningrad are seen to stem not from its position as a military base but as a hub of chronic socioeconomic instability and high levels of criminal activity. The prospect of acquiring such a neighbour as a result of enlargement is clearly not welcome.

The Russian Government seems to lack a clear policy on Kaliningrad, although that is true of its policies towards the regions generally. However, in the *Medium-Term Strategy* document it talks about Kaliningrad's 'transformation into Russia's pilot region within the framework of the Euro-Russian cooperation in the 21st century.'[28] There has to date been no further elaboration as to what this might mean in practice but it does mean that Russia is willing to concede that Kaliningrad is a shared problem, itself quite surprising given Russia's sensitivity generally about interference in its internal affairs. Also significant in the context of this study is the fact that it has been prepared to place Kaliningrad on the agenda of the Northern Dimension and seems to see its integration into the Euro-regional programmes as its best hope for avoiding isolation as a consequence of EU enlargement. Kaliningrad therefore seems likely to be the subject of quite intense EU-Russian interaction for the foreseeable future, with the potential for it to enhance cooperation but also the risk that it could be the cause of serious tensions.

The Future Relationship between Russia and the EU

It took nearly a decade since the collapse of communism for either the EU or Russia to develop anything even approaching a clear view of the kind of long-term relationship they hope to establish with the other. In part, of course, this is because both have been preoccupied with their heavy internal agendas but the prospect of the eastern enlargement has introduced a greater sense of urgency to the need to define their positions and clarify their goals. The importance the EU member states now ascribe to relations with Russia was demonstrated by their decision to make it the subject of their first use of the new policy instrument of the 'common strategy' introduced by the Amsterdam Treaty to strengthen its common foreign and security policy. The fact that the Russians responded almost immediately by producing a strategy document of their own was even more indicative of the new status afforded the relationship as previously there had been no known official Russian document defining the country's policy towards the EU.[29]

Although the two documents were developed independently there were informal exchanges of views and an unofficial draft copy of the Russian paper was circulated to EU Member states. After the *Common Strategy of the European Union on Russia* had been adopted at the Cologne European Council in June 1999, the Russian paper was considerably expanded and refined and at the EU-Russia summit in October 1999 the then Prime Minister Putin presented their *Medium-Term Strategy for Development of Relations between the EU and Russia*. There is therefore an unusually close relationship between the two documents not only in terms of their timing but also their content. Although there are obviously considerable differences in emphasis and style, what is most striking is the degree of commonality in terms of the overall goals and objectives. In the preceding discussion there have been numerous references to specific provisions in the two strategy documents so this final section will focus on the overall shape of their future relationship.

The *Common Strategy* opens with a statement of its 'Vision of the EU for its Partnership with Russia':

> A stable, democratic and prosperous Russia, firmly anchored in a united Europe free of new dividing lines, is essential to lasting peace on the continent. The issues which the whole continent faces can be resolved only through ever closer cooperation between Russia and the European Union. The European Union welcomes Russia's return to its rightful place in the European family in a spirit of friendship, cooperation, fair accommodation of interests and on the foundations of shared values enshrined in the common heritage of European civilisation.

Russia's Strategy contains no such 'vision' and instead emphasises that it 'is primarily aimed at ensuring national interests and enhancing the role and image of Russia in Europe and the world' but it is clear that it shares to a great extent the EU's analysis of its proper place in Europe. It also echoes the EU's view that the goal is 'the construction of a united Europe without dividing lines' while, as noted previously, ruling out its accession to the EU, at least for the period under review. Both documents therefore are implicitly seeking to answer the question posed at the beginning of the article, as to how Russia can be part of the process of European integration without aspiring to EU membership. They also seem to present similar answers: Russia must be integrated into a 'wider area of cooperation in Europe' creating 'a common economic and social area' particularly through the achievement of the free trade area and the approximation of Russian legislation and standards as envisaged in the PCA.[30] Similarly, the Russian strategy sees one of the key objectives to be 'to develop an advanced pan-European economic and legal infrastructure' and also stresses the importance of the free trade area and the approximation of economic legislation and standards.

The concept is close to that of the European Economic Area (EEA) that was developed in the early 1990s to integrate the EFTAn states into the single market but the scope of the cooperation is to extend across all three EU pillars, with particular importance attached to cooperation in foreign and security policy and justice and home affairs. It is therefore a much more overtly political integration model than the EEA with cooperation envisaged in such 'high politics' areas as police and judicial cooperation to combat organised crime[31] and illegal immigration, arms control, peace-keeping and crisis management as well as transport, energy supply, nuclear safety and the environment. Of particular interest to Russia is the possibility of more active cooperation in the security field as a result of the EU's development of a 'defence identity'. It has already responded positively to suggestions that it might be invited to participate in EU-led military operations to undertake 'Petersberg tasks' such as peace-keeping and humanitarian rescue missions. It is also interested in developing regular contact with the new defence institutions the EU is currently establishing as part of its Common European Security and Defence Policy initiative.

This ambitious and innovatory model of integration is to be based on the concept of a 'strategic partnership' between the EU and Russia as equals and reflects the extent to which Russia has come to recognise the EU as a political as well as economic actor. Their strategy document states that 'the development of a strategic partnership between Russia and the European Union will be reflected in active interaction between the parties to achieve major collective objectives of mutual interest and to solve European and world problems.'[32] The EU also believes that 'Russia and the Union have strategic interests and exercise particular responsibilities in the maintenance of stability and security in Europe, and in other parts of the world.'[33] How precisely this partnership will be organised, however, has yet to be worked out. The *Common Strategy* suggests that it will be developed within the framework of a 'permanent policy and security dialogue' but it remains to be seen whether this will be institutionalised in some new high-level body or incorporated within the existing PCA arrangements. The EU's Secretary-General of the Council/ High Representative for the CFSP, currently Javier Solana, is expected to play a key role but clearly the whole plan is still at an embryonic stage. Whether in fact the fine words and good intentions can be translated into an effective instrument for ensuring that Russia is fully integrated into Europe remains to be seen.

Conclusion: isolation or integration of Russia?

One of the obvious consequences of the next enlargement of the European Union is that its own centre of gravity will shift dramatically eastwards. Its new geo-political position will make Russia not only seem much closer but also much more important to the security and well-being of the Union itself.

The central and east European new members are also expected to have a special interest in the future of Russia and will bring a substantial body of expertise and experience to the development of relations with her. There is a clear recognition in EU circles that enlargement must be balanced by a significant upgrading of its relationship with Russia if it is not to create a new fault-line across the continent. An influential European Parliament report in 1998 acknowledged that 'devising an EU strategy for relations with the new Russia is a challenge' but urged that a way must be found 'to anchor Russia firmly in Europe on an equal footing and in a spirit of partnership.'[34] The *Common Strategy* is an attempt to meet that challenge and so far Russia's response has been positive. Its own *Medium-Term Strategy* also identifies a large number of specific areas where joint initiatives could help to create positive interdependence and potentially a complex network of cooperation could be developed across the continent. Both documents envisage that the partnership will be evolutionary, with the EU specifically hoping for 'ever closer cooperation' and the Russians hoping that a new framework agreement on the strategic partnership can be developed to replace the PCA.

However, considerable uncertainty remains as to whether the ambitious goals of the two strategies will be achieved. Obviously it will be important that the specific potential problems posed by the accession of the CEECs are resolved as quickly as possible. The best foundation for the development of the strategic partnership would be a steady growth in trade and other economic activities so that Russia gained a stake in European integration by sharing in the expected growth in prosperity and economic stability. However, there is only a limited amount that the EU can do to ensure that this happens. The most important condition for Russia's successful integration is that it should develop into a stable democratic society with a properly functioning market economy operating under the rule of law. The greatest danger of isolation would come if the reforms were to falter and Russia turned its back on the rest of Europe and retreated into protectionism and insularity.

Although President Putin remains somewhat of an enigma, his election has so far created a more stable political environment and the Russian economy is showing signs of recovery with a growth rate of over three per cent. He has impressed western leaders with his commitment to achieve Russia's full integration into the international economy and seems generally quite favourably disposed towards the EU. The conditions are therefore reasonably favourable for progress to be made in translating the high aspirations of the 'strategic partnership' concept into an effective new model of European integration that can meet the legitimate expectations of Russia. If EU enlargement is going to have a positive impact on the long-term stability and security of Europe, it will therefore be important to seize the opportunity to ensure that relations with Russia are substantially strengthened before it takes place.

University of Kent at Canterbury

jackie@gower.dircon.co.uk

Notes

[1] See European Parliament Resolution on the Commission communication, 'The future of relations between the EU and Russia' and the action plan 'The EU and Russia: the future relationship', *Official Journal*, C138, 4 May 1998 which warns against the creation of a new fault line across Europe and M. Light, S. White and J. Löwenhardt, 'A wider Europe: the view from Moscow and Kyiv', *International Affairs*, 76(1) 2000, pp. 77-99, for the argument that enlargement will inevitably create 'outsider states'.

[2] *Medium Term Strategy for Development of Relations between the Russian Federation and the European Union (2000-2010)*. An unofficial translation is available on the Finnish presidency web-site, URL:http://www.presidency.finland.fi. Please note that all the quotes used in the article have been taken *verbatim* from this unofficial translation and they are sometimes rather awkwardly phrased.

[3] *Financial Times*, July 1997.

[4] The European Council at Copenhagen in June 1993 set out the political and economic conditions that applicant states would be required to meet before membership. They include the stability of institutions guaranteeing democracy, the rule of law and human rights, the existence of a market economy and the capacity to take on the obligations of membership. There is general agreement that Russia is a long way off meeting them.

[5] The conceptual issues arise from the lack of any alternative model of integration in Europe today with the overwhelming dominance of the EU. For a fuller discussion, see J. Gower, 'The EU and Russia: The Challenge of Integration without Accession' in J. Gower and J. Redmond (eds), *Enlarging the European Union: The Way Forward*, (Aldershot: Ashgate, 2000), pp. 163-76.

[6] 'Common Strategy of the European Union on Russia', *Presidency Conclusions: Cologne European Council of the European Union*, (Annex II, Brussels: Council of the European Union, 1999); *Medium-Term Strategy*.

7   The Council and Commission Agreement on Partnership and Co-operation be-
    tween the European Communities and their Member States and the Russian
    Federation, *Official Journal of the European Communities,* OJ L 327, 28 November
    1997.

8   M. Light et al., *The Wider Europe,* p. 81.

9   *Medium-Term Strategy,* Point 5.1.

10 I. Leshoukov, *Beyond Satisfaction: Russia's Perspectives on European Integration* Zentrum
    für Europäische Integrationsforschung, Discussion Paper C26, 1998, p. 22. He com-
    ments that Russians welcome every European initiative which they interpret as
    'a project to counter American domination.'

11 V. Saveliev, 'USA-EU-Russia', *International Affairs,* Moscow, 43(6) 1997.

12 Quoted by S. Taylor, in 'Union seeks to use summit to influence Russian reforms',
    European Voice, 25-30 May 2000, p. 8.

13 Y. Borko, 'The New Intra-European Relations and Russia', in M. Maresceau (ed),
    Enlarging the European Union: Relations between the EU and Central and Eastern Europe
    (London: Longman, 1997), p. 380.

14 V. Baranovsky, 'Russia: a part of Europe or apart from Europe?', *International Affairs,*
    76(3) 2000, p. 450.

15 For a fuller discussion of these issues see J. Gower, 'The Baltic States: Bridge or
    Barrier to the East' in M. Smith and G. Timmins (eds), *Uncertain Europe: A Security
    Order for the 21st Century?,* (London: Routledge, forthcoming).

16 *Medium Term Strategy,* Point 5.2.

17 This is the view of Dimitrii Danilov, head of military-political studies at the Institute
    of Europe in Moscow. See his 'A piece of the partnership', *Transitions,* April 1998.

18 Danilov, 'A piece of the partnership'.

19 The change will not necessarily be dramatic as already under the Europe Agreements
    most CEEC exports of manufactured goods enter the EU market free of tariffs and
    there will almost certainly be transitional arrangements for agriculture for some
    years after accession, as indeed will probably be the case for free movement of
    people.

20 European Parliament Secretariat Working Party Task Force 'Enlargement', Briefing
    No. 14/Rev. 2, *Russia and the Enlargement of the European Union.*

21 See H. Grabbe, 'The sharp edges of Europe: extending Schengen eastwards',
    Internatioanl Affairs, 76(3) 2000, pp. 519-36 for a discussion of the growing tension
    between the internal and external security policies of the EU in relation to the
    eastern enlargement.

22 A report on the introduction of visa regimes in Poland, the Czech Republic and
    Slovenia appeared in *Pravda* on 5 February 1998 entitled 'Iron Curtain Redux'
    which concluded that 'the new "continental order" is actually leading to the *de*

facto resurrection of the Iron Curtain, except that this time it's much farther east than it was during the cold war.'

[23]   See W. Wallace, 'From the Atlantic to the Bug, from the Arctic to the Tigris? The transformation of the EU and NATO', International *Affairs*, 76(3) 2000, and G. Amato and J. Batt, 'The long-term implications of EU enlargement: the nature of the new border', Final report of the Reflection Group, (Florence, European University Institute, 1999).

[24]   For a very forthright appraisal of the current situation see P. Joenniemi, S. Dewar and L.D. Fairlie, *The Kaliningrad Puzzle - A Russian Region within the European Union*, Karlskrona (The Baltic Institute of Sweden and Mariehamn, The Åland Islands Peace Institute, 2000).

[25]   *Medium-Term Strategy*, Point 8.3.

[26]   A. Sergounin, 'The Russia Dimension' in H. Mouritzen (ed), *Bordering Russia: Theory and Prospects for Europe's Baltic Rim*, (Aldershot: Ashgate, 1998), p. 45.

[27]   G. Herd, 'Competing for Kaliningrad', *The World Today*, 55(11) 1999, pp. 8-9.

[28]   Medium Term Strategy, Point 8.3.

[29]   Leshoukov, *Beyond Satisfaction*, p. 5.

[30]   *Common Strategy*, Part I, point 2.

[31]   A major EU-Russia conference was held under the Finnish Presidency in December 1999 on promoting cooperation in combating organised crime and discussed proposals for an ambitious Action Plan and recommendations for closer cooperation between Europol and the Russian police. The large Russian delegation included some very senior officials indicating the high priority Russia affords to efforts to deal with the scourge of international crime.

[32]   *Medium-Term Strategy*, point 1.2.

[33]   *Common Strategy*, Part I, point 3.

[34]   Report on the Commission communication entitled 'The future of relations between the European Union and Russia' and the action plan 'The European Union and Russia: the future relationship', Rapporteur Mrs Catherine Lalumière, 12 February 1998. European Parliament Document A4-0060/98.

Martin Dangerfield

Subregional Cooperation in Central and Eastern Europe: Support or Substitute for the 'Return to Europe'?

ABSTRACT

This article considers whether there is any scope for multilateral subregional cooperation initiatives involving Central and East European (CEE) states possibly to become something more than mere supplements to the EU accession endeavour. Given the ongoing uncertainties about where the real limits of EU expansion lie, and the at best long-term membership prognosis of even some of the current candidate states, this question is not entirely theoretical. The first part of the article argues that with the exception of the Central European Free Trade Agreement (CEFTA) none of the current subregional groupings qualify as even hypothetical alternatives to the EU and, accordingly, the rest of the article concentrates on CEFTA. The main verdict is that while CEFTA cooperation has been an important component of the EU pre-accession process, the constraints to both CEFTA's further internal and external development are such that it is unlikely to move to a redefined role in the future.

Introduction

All of the central and east European (CEE) European Union (EU) membership candidates have been involved in one or more of the numerous multilateral sub-regional cooperation initiatives which have emerged in post-Cold War Europe.[1] Despite the general limitations to subregional cooperation in the context of the main business of EU and NATO expansion and clear differences in the effectiveness of particular groupings, many analysts have drawn attention to their low profile but nevertheless useful contributions to not only security and integration in the new Europe but also to the EU pre-accession process.[2] Given the complicated, tortuous and potentially exclusive nature of the EU accession endeavour, it may seem somewhat surprising that in CEE policy-making circles none of the various subregional cooperation initiatives have at any time been viewed as potential alternatives to EU membership. This article aims to clarify the potential of the current subregional cooperation vehicles in that respect.

It should first be said that as regards the leading cluster of EU candidates the idea of alternatives to the EU is now all but irrelevant, since the main debate is clearly to do with when rather than if they will join, and whether it will be in the framework of a modestly reformed EU or whether an alternative model of integration for the EU (multi-speed Europe, flexible geometry etc.) will have prevailed.[3] Yet for the more outlying CEE countries, particularly the laggards in the group of current EU candidates and those so far without EU associate membership, the likelihood of a very long wait for EU membership and the prospect of disruptions in relations with the fast-track accession candidates, means that the question of subregional cooperation as an alternative to EU membership is at least due some serious reflection. It is also the case that the Stability and Association Agreements (SAAs) being prepared for the non-associated Balkan states make reference to the absolute necessity to commit to subregional cooperation, and the text of the SAAs also refer to dimensions of cooperation (free movement of labour, services and capital) which equate with the higher echelons of the economic integration processes.[4] Clearly then, subregional cooperation involving CEE states is in one way or another connected to some of the big issues of the day and therefore a deeper knowledge and understanding of this process, especially with regard to those initiatives which are most closely linked to the EU accession process, is highly relevant for ongoing dilemmas connected to the future of both the EU and European integration in general. Is subregional cooperation inevitably restricted to the role of supporting EU accession efforts or are existing, or yet to be formed initiatives, capable of going beyond that and becoming alternative vehicles for genuine integration?

The first section of the article identifies the main subregional groupings which have emerged since the end of communism and briefly surveys the generic 'soft' security effects which have been set out in the literature. It then proceeds to distinguish between the various groupings according to the nature of their relationship with the EU enlargement process so as to establish which groupings should be included in the debate over supplement or substitute for EU membership. The conclusion is that at present the Central European Free Trade Agreement (CEFTA) is the only genuine contender in this respect. Accordingly, the second part of the article discusses the various ways in which CEFTA has been an instrument for EU pre-accession, including the impact on market (re-)integration in the CEFTA economic space, its political role and other aspects of CEFTA's 'training ground/fitness centre' functions. The third part considers various longer-term scenarios for CEFTA, including the possibility of it evolving into a vehicle for extending the broader European integration process to the more outlying, lesser-engaged (by the EU) CEE states and thereby providing a bridge between core and periphery in the European integration process or even developing into some kind of substitute for membership of the EU in the event that certain CEE countries remain excluded from the latter. Since the conclusion is that CEFTA is unlikely to evolve according to either of these scenarios, the main emphasis is on the various constraints on CEFTA's further development.

I Subregional Cooperation in Post Cold-War Europe

The various subregional groups which have emerged in post-Cold War Europe (collectively termed the 'Barents-Black Sea' set in some quarters and the subregional components of the 'Baltic-Black Sea Region' in others)[5] and their membership configurations are listed in Table 1. They include: the Barents Euro-Arctic Council (BEAC); the Baltic Free Trade Area (BFTA); Black Sea Economic Cooperation (BSEC); Georgia, Ukraine, Uzbekistan, Azerbaijan and Moldova (GUUAM); the Central European Initiative (CEI); the Central European Free Trade Agreement (CEFTA); the Visegrad Group; and the South European Cooperation Initiative (SECI).

The main studies of the significance of these groupings tend to focus on their contributions to security, usually stressing that this does not concern traditional notions of security cooperation (military alliances, arms control agreements and so on) but is more to do with more subtle, less 'hard' security functions. Bailes, for example, wrote that

> [t]he largest contribution all these groups make to security is probably at the unexpressed, existential level: the mere fact that their members belong somewhere, that they understand each other, that they can talk about their worries in the *corridors*, that they have telephone numbers to dial in a crisis. Beyond this, all the groupings under study have made some strides (whether they recognise it or not) in *soft security*, by easing human and economic exchanges across frontiers and thus helping to build wider social foundations for stability and understanding.[6]

The security functions of the subregional cooperation are also linked to the wider integration processes in that it has been asserted that not only can the existence and activities of subregional groupings help offset potential damage to relations between 'ins' and 'outs' of the EU expansion but also support EU accession ambitions and processes more actively.[7] The idea that evidence of ability to cooperate successfully at the subregional level (which usually results in relevant improvements in mutual political relations) enhances the participants' membership credentials for the EU is something that in principle applies to all the different groupings. Over and above this rather basic effect, more direct contributions may be possible if suitably cognate groupings agree to 'adopt a joint *pre-accession strategy* and work together to try out, or approach by stages, the standards and mechanisms of the *target* integrated group.'[8] Indeed, from the EU perspective it has been the pre-accession rather than security functions which are the basis of the EU's support for subregional groups in CEE. At a major conference on subregional cooperation held in Bucharest in October 1996, G. Bertrand (at the time representing the Planning Cell, DG1A of the European Commission) elaborated the importance of subregional groupings as follows:[9]

- they were a very practical means of integration, creating interdependence and solidarity.
- they fostered cooperative behaviour and reduced tensions.
- trans-border cooperation fostered homogeneous economic development within states, making good use NGO and private sector development.

- these groups strengthened economic ties between the EU members and their neighbours and among non-member states.
- they offered practical experience of the modalities of voluntary multilateral cooperation.
- they helped create a political/economic continuum throughout Europe, warding off any new two-way divide.

It is neither in the scope nor the purpose of this paper to discuss the details or assess the broader impact of all the subregional initiatives set out in Table 1, especially since this has already been given substantial coverage elsewhere.[10] Rather, the objective here is to differentiate between the groupings in terms of the strength of links with the EU enlargement process in order to establish which of them have the status of genuine and meaningful components of the EU pre-accession strategy, and also to identify candidates for inclusion in a debate on subregional cooperation as a possible alternative to EU membership. One method for recognising subregional groupings which have the appropriate profiles involves distinguishing between them according to the following classification criteria: (A) 'hard' vs. 'soft' cooperation agendas; (B) membership configurations, with special emphasis on involvement of non-CEE states; (C) membership rules and conditions. Within these categories we can differentiate as follows:

A1: Groups which have broad-based cooperation programmes, that is more loosely defined cooperation agendas

or

A2: Groups which have a more strictly defined agenda, that is 'harder' cooperation usually based on international agreements or treaties.

B1: Groups which combine CEE' and 'western' states, usually including both EU and non-EU members

or

B2 Groups which are 'CEE/CEE' combinations and are purely collaborations without EU states' involvement

Table 1: Subregional Groupings in the New Europe

BARENTS EURO-ARCTIC COUNCIL (BEAC), established 1993:

Denmark	European Commission
Finland	Iceland
Norway	Russia
Sweden	

COUNCIL OF BALTIC SEA STATES (CBSS), established 1992:

Denmark	Estonia
European Commission	Finland
Germany	Iceland
Latvia	Lithuania
Norway	Poland
Russia	Sweden

BALTIC FREE TRADE AREA (BFTA), established 1994:

Estonia	Latvia
Lithuania	

BLACK SEA ECONOMIC COOPERATION (BSEC), established 1992:

Albania	Armenia
Azerbaijan	Bulgaria
Georgia	Greece
Moldova	Romania
Russia	Turkey
Ukraine	

GUUAM, established 1997:

Azerbaijan	Georgia
Moldova	Ukraine
Uzbekistan	

CENTRAL EUROPEAN INITIATIVE (CEI), established 1989:

Albania	Austria
Belarus	Bosnia-Herzegovina
Bulgaria	Croatia
Czech Republic	Hungary
Italy	Moldova
Poland	Romania
Slovakia	Slovenia
FYR of Macedonia	Ukraine

CENTRAL EUROPEAN FREE TRADE AREA (CEFTA), established 1993:

Bulgaria	Czech Republic
Hungary	Poland
Romania	Slovakia
Slovenia	

VISEGRAD GROUP, established 1990:

Czech Republic	Hungary
Poland	Slovakia

SOUTH EUROPEAN COOPERATION INITIATIVE (SECI), established 1996:

Albania	Bosnia-Herzegovina
Bulgaria	Croatia
Czech Republic	Greece
Hungary	Moldova
Romania	Slovenia
FYR of Macedonia	

Sources: A. Cottey (ed), *Multi-Layered Integration: The Subregional Dimension*, Summary of the Inter-Governmental Conference held in Bucharest on 7-8 October 1996, (Warsaw: Institute for East West Studies, 1996), p. 33; Dwan, *Building Security*, pp. 217-252.

C1 Groups which do not rule out membership of any other subregional, regional or even global organisations or associations, and which do not have rigid membership criteria beyond basic political credentials

or

C2 Groups which are closed to members of the EU and which themselves must legally cease to exist when all members have acceded to the EU and which have rigid membership criteria which go well beyond the basic democracy condition

It seems reasonable to conclude that groupings which have the least concrete links to the EU enlargement process have characteristics A1, B1 and C1. B road - based cooperation agendas are less likely to be oriented towards specific EU accession requirements/tasks, especially as the various groups which correspond with this criteria (CEI, BSEC, BEAC, CBSS) are also type B1 too, and include non-associated CEE and former Soviet republics which clearly restricts the scope for EU pre-accession related activities. These A1/B1 groups also tend to be C1 which even further diminishes the cohesiveness of the group as far as prospects in wider integration frameworks are concerned. We should remember that many of the type A1/B1/C1 subregional groups do not in any case identify themselves as pre-accession instruments except in the very broadest sense already referred to. Thus, of the subregional groupings present in post-cold war Europe, the links with the EU accession process are clearly most pronounced for BFTA and CEFTA, which both have characteristics A2, B2 and C2. The Visegrad Group has clear links also, but falls shorter than CEFTA or BFTA because of the looser agenda, absence of any legalistic basis, and also because any enlargement of the Visegrad Group is currently ruled out by the member states.[11] Even though the level of economic cooperation in BFTA has in some respects (e.g. formation of a customs union, full liberalisation of agricultural trade) gone beyond that of CEFTA, BFTA is not normally discussed as an organisation which could develop a wider role in the European integration process. It is a market of some 7.5 million people against the 98 million people covered by CEFTA and has no enlargement agenda or prospects. In fact until recently, Latvia and Lithuania were attempting to join CEFTA. This seems to lead to the conclusion that CEFTA is the only current subregional group in the Barents-Black Sea zone which could be discussed in terms of an alternative to EU integration. The rest of the paper concentrates on showing that while CEFTA has been an important and underestimated pre-accession instrument for its current members, there are clear limitations in terms of any development beyond that role.

2   The Central European Free Trade Agreement (CEFTA)

2.1   *Aims and objectives of CEFTA*

CEFTA is a tariff and quota free zone for trade in industrial products between the Czech Republic, Hungary, Poland, Slovakia (the four founder countries), Slovenia, Romania and Bulgaria (which acceded in 1995, 1997 and 1999 respectively). The transition period to completely free industrial trade is scheduled to be completed by January 2002.[12] Though the attempt to completely liberalise agricultural trade has stalled, preferential conditions for intra-CEFTA agricultural trade have been established. CEFTA also includes provision to tackle certain non-tariff barriers. Articles 23 and 24 of the Cracow Treaty refer to the harmonisation of state aid regulations and opening public procurement markets respectively, for example, and the move to mutual recognition of test results and certificates for agricultural and food products is an ongoing project in CEFTA. Progress and problems in the implementation of CEFTA are overseen by the CEFTA Joint Committee, which is made up of the Ministers with responsibility for foreign economic relations and which has regular annual meetings.[13]

The original CEFTA treaty contained no provision for enlargement though any inclinations toward exclusivity the Visegrad four may have had soon evaporated. The proliferation of Europe Agreements, recurring trade deficit problems, the consequent pressure to expand exports, specific subregional political considerations, and the realisation that CEFTA was the kind of subregional cooperation which supported rather than compromised EU accession ambitions, were among the factors which led to the early agreement on a formula to open CEFTA to new members. The 1995 (Brno) summit meeting of CEFTA prime ministers approved the necessary amendment to the CEFTA treaty which states that CEFTA is open to any European country which belongs to the World Trade Organisation (WTO), has bilateral free trade agreements with the each of the existing CEFTA countries already in place, and associate membership or a free trade agreement with the EU. Though the

CEFTA programme of cooperation has virtually been completed and it looks set to lose its core members in three to four years time, further enlargement remains on the agenda. The declaration of the most recent CEFTA summit, held in Warsaw on 15 November 2000, stated that the 'Prime Ministers reconfirmed that CEFTA remains open and is ready to examine applications of countries fulfilling the necessary requirements.'[14] Countries which remain interested in CEFTA membership include Ukraine, Moldova, FYR Macedonia and Croatia, though none of them fully satisfies the CEFTA membership criteria as of yet.

2.3   Results of CEFTA cooperation

The outcomes of CEFTA cooperation can be placed into three categories. First, the extent to which intra-CEFTA trade has responded to the more open subregional market created by the liberalisation programme. Second, the political effects of CEFTA. Third, the contribution CEFTA participation has made to its member states' preparations for full EU membership.[15]

Intra-CEFTA trade

Table 2 covers the development of intra-CEFTA trade over the 1993-1999 period. It is clear that economic agents have responded and it is indisputable that CEFTA (in the context of the return to economic growth in the Visegrad countries which coincided with the introduction of CEFTA) has succeeded in its baseline task of fostering the recovery and intensification of the trade ties of the member countries. While all the member states have experienced consistent and strong growth in their exports to the CEFTA market, the best results in terms of trade surplus positions have been enjoyed by the Czech and Slovak Republics and, since 1996, Hungary.[16] Exports expanded faster than imports in the cases of the Czech Republic and Hungary over the five year period and this has also been true for Slovenia over its shorter participation in CEFTA, leading to a gradual narrowing of the latter's trade deficit with CEFTA to date. Poland has posted a consistent and widening deficit, though a modest reversal of this trend was achieved in 1999. Romania, also a deficit country but again with some improvement in 1999, experienced a huge (61 per cent) rise in imports from CEFTA and a modest (7 per cent) rise in exports during its first full year in CEFTA. Yet the overall trade deficit of

Romania deteriorated only slightly in 1998 - to \$0.2 bn from \$0.1 bn in 1997 - and the overall import value was constant at \$1.4 bn, suggesting that the growth in imports from CEFTA could well have been accounted for by trade diversion.[17] As a general point, to the extent that growth of intra-CEFTA trade has represented the reversal of an earlier trade diversion caused by the trade policies and problems of the early post-communist years, then the more the growth of intra-CEFTA trade has produced net gains for all parties and not just the surplus states. Further evidence of the dynamism of intra-CEFTA trade is illustrated by the fact that for the years 1995-1998 in the cases of all the CEFTA members growth of exports to the CEFTA area exceeded that of total exports (see Table 3).

Table 2: Intra-CEFTA Trade, 1993-1999, \$US Million

	1993	1994	1995	1996	1997	1998	1999	Index 1999/93 1993=100
CZECH REPUBLIC								
Total CEFTA:								
Export	3489	3258	4348	4944	4816	5199	4709	135
Import	2746	2718	3883	3886	3622	3657	3901	142
Excluding Slovakia:								
Export	655	925	1343	1824	1927	2392	n/a	365.
Import								
	497	594	900	1236	1369	1581	n/a	318*
HUNGARY								
Export	462	565	757	1163	1387	2039	1961	424
Import								
	655	900	982	1254	1378	1766	2025	309
POLAND								
Export	680	823	1245	1481	1659	2026	2227	328
Import	682	919	1624	2161	2585	2974	3070	450
ROMANIA								
Export				294	342	369	597	202**
Import				541	642	1040	928	171**

table (cont.)

	1993	1994	1995	1996	1997	1998	1999	Index 1999/93 1993=100
SLOVAKIA								
Total CEFTA:								
Export	2716	3057	3778	3656	3357	3397	3027	111
Import	2483	2226	2757	3225	2915	3122	2641	106
Excluding								
Czech Rep:								
Export	406.0	555.0	767.0	918.0	999.0	1233.0	n/a	304*
Import	208.0	268.0	424.0	543.0	563.0	732.0	n/a	352*
SLOVENIA								
Export			403	451	480	588	622	154***
Import			634	616	688	725	844	133***

Notes

* = Index 1998/1993, ** = Index 1999/1996, *** = Index 1999/95

Source: M. Dangerfield, 'Subregional Economic Cooperation in Central and Eastern Europe', paper presented at *European Odyssey: The EU in the New Millennium* - 4th biennial conference of European Community Studies Association-Canada (ECSA-C), Quebec City, Canada, July 31-August 2, 2000.

Political aspects of CEFTA cooperation

Though CEFTA is essentially a form of economic cooperation, its primary purpose can be seen as essentially political - as an exercise to help smooth the way for the participants' accession to the EU rather than an integration in its own right. A number of probably unanticipated secondary political advantages of CEFTA cooperation have also been evident. CEFTA has presented the opportunity for political leaders to meet and have bilateral as well as multilateral discussions at the annual summits.[18] In addition, the CEFTA factor has provided a good reason for CEFTA candidates to ensure that relations with CEFTA members stay friendly and has also provided a reason to tackle certain sources of dispute between particular parties.[19] Finally, for the CEFTA founders, CEFTA meetings were useful interim arrangements for top level political dialogue during the dormant phase of the Visegrad Group. In

Table 3: CEFTA States' Exports to CEFTA and Total Exports, 1995-1998
($US Values)

Previous year = 100

	Exports to CEFTA, 1995	Total Exports 1995	Exports to CEFTA 1996	Total Exports 1996	Exports to CEFTA 1997	Total Exports 1997	Exports to CEFTA 1998	Total Exports 1998
Czech R.*	145.2	110.3	135.8	101.2	105.7	101.0	124.1	115.7
Hungary	134.5	121.5	124.1	122.0	119.9	117.7	147.0	120.5
Poland	151.3	132.8	115.5	106.7	111.7	105.0	122.1	109.6
Romania	-	-	-	-	-	-	108.0	98.4
Slovakia*	138.2	119.0	119.7	102.3	108.8	102.2	123.4	129.3
Slovenia	-	-	117.7	99.9	103.9	99.1	122.6	108.1

* Excludes Czech/Slovak trade

Source: Dangerfield, *Subregional Economic Cooperation*, p. 64

this respect it has been noted by Handl that CEFTA 'contributed to increased political understanding during the years of Vaclav Klaus' 'separatist policy' pursued by the Czech government during the period 1992-1994'.[20] Certainly, until CEFTA's first expansion in 1996 the series of annual summits, which began in Poznan in November 1994, were Visegrad group meetings in all but name, and though the agenda was formally fixed to pure CEFTA business, the discussion often extended into other spheres. Eventually, the CEFTA summits proved to be an important factor in bringing about the reconvening of the Visegrad forum. The 1998 (Prague) session, when the Czech side suggested that CEFTA could 'develop some political dimensions along the lines of the Visegrad Accord'[21] clearly paved the way for the first meeting of 'Visegrad 2' in May 1999.

CEFTA and the EU accession process

Though the literature on eastward EU enlargement tends to disregard the role of subregional cooperation, many policy-makers within CEE have acknowledged the links between CEFTA cooperation and EU pre-accession endeavours. The idea that CEFTA functions as some kind of 'training ground/fitness centre' for EU accession has been an important factor in the motivations of countries which have joined CEFTA and for those who still wish to do so.

Following the signing of Bulgaria's CEFTA accession in Italy on 18 July 1998, for example, the Bulgarian Minister for Trade and Tourism, Valentin Vassilev, said that '(w)ith this accord, Bulgaria moves a step closer to membership in the EU.'[22]

As well as the important consideration of the EU conditionality that prospective members should take appropriate steps towards their mutual integration in advance of EU membership, the practical dimensions of the training ground/fitness centre functions of CEFTA include the following. First and foremost, the end of subregional trade discrimination has advanced the process of market integration which EU membership will entail anyway. Second, successful implementation of the basic trade liberalisation process may lead to attempts to upgrade the level of subregional integration if the participants decide to engage in more advanced EU-compatible cooperation. As well as the measures noted in 2.1 above, the question of free movement of capital, and liberalisation of trade in services have also featured on the CEFTA agenda. Third, the business of implementing the CEFTA provisions has also generated useful experience of intergovernmental cooperation. In sum there is a clear relationship, mainly indirect but nevertheless important, between CEFTA cooperation and further integration with the EU. The indirect influence reflects the fact that the EU essentially acts as the 'external integrator' for the CEE region and most of what happens at the subregional level is essentially a by-product of wider integration processes.

3   CEFTA Towards And Beyond The EU'S Eastward Expansion

3.1   *Internal Development of CEFTA*

As far as further development of CEFTA cooperation in the period towards the first stage of EU enlargement is concerned, integration can certainly continue to develop through trade growth and the alignment of the economic policy/regulatory framework which will continue as a result of the EU accession preparations. Other than that, there appears to be no prospect for any further serious integrationist innovations in the CEFTA framework. It has proved necessary to set aside key non-tariff barrier provisions of CEFTA, such as the harmonisation of state aid rules, for resolution in the EU context (the same applies to earlier intentions to liberalise capital movements and trade in services). There is also the issue of important unfinished CEFTA business, in particular the thorny problem of liberalisation of intra-CEFTA agricultural trade, which both crowds the agenda and, for certain CEFTA partners at least, creates negative attitudes. For example at the recent CEFTA summit, held in Warsaw on 15 November 2000, Hungarian premier Victor Urban stated that 'CEFTA has reached its limits. There are no effective ways to solve problems.'[23]

Apart from the question of intensification of intra-CEFTA economic cooperation what about further development in the political sense, particularly for coordination of EU accession negotiations? It is only really in the post-AGENDA 2000 period that accession-related problems needing collective action have become highlighted and common negotiating positions have been crystallising (on direct payment to CEE farmers for example) and a new more concrete subregional co-operation agenda towards the EU has emerged. CEFTA however, has not been playing a role in this respect.[24] Though all CEFTA partners are now in negotiations, they still remain divided between the Luxembourg and Helsinki groups and differentiated negotiating stages work against a common agenda which could be pursued through CEFTA. Reflecting this, the new subregional co-operation agenda is being pursued in other, more suitable subregional fora, including the reconvened Visegrád group and the regular co-ordination meetings of representatives of the Luxembourg 6. In the context of progress towards opening talks on the more contentious chapters of the 'acquis', the latter began showing signs of a shift towards some collective bargaining rather than just information sharing. For example in October 1999 a meeting of the Foreign Ministers of the Luxembourg 6 produced a collective letter to Romano Prodi requesting the acceleration of negotiations and it was reported that the meeting, held in Tallin represented 'the fast-track applicants' efforts to pool resources to strengthen their bargaining position. In particular the six are hoping to seek concessions over farming subsidies, and raise concerns over traditional trade ties with other eastern countries.'[25] CEFTA's strengths have been evident in the more indirect sphere of preparing for EU membership and the fact that first and second wave candidates have been able to cooperate in this particular pre-accession vehicle has been especially useful. Of course, the fact that even CEFTA has been unable to play any role in the EU accession negotiating process further highlights the relatively limited pre-accession functions of the other subregional groupings.

3.2   *Alternative Future Scenarios*

As far as the period after the first stage of the EU's eastward expansion is concerned, three potential scenarios can be considered. The first alternative is that CEFTA will simply wither away. In the absence of any further enlargement once the first group of CEFTA have withdrawn to take up full EU membership, CEFTA will reduce to a smaller free trade complex linked, as far as trade arrangements are concerned, to the expanded EU through Europe Agreements and to other CEE states by various bilateral free trade agreements. The diminished CEFTA would then either 'wither away' or remain in limbo due to serious delays in further waves of EU enlargement. The second alternative that has been floated around is that CEFTA may continue its role as a support for full EU membership but with an expanded line-up. In 1998, for instance, former Czech Trade and Industry Minister Karel Kuhnl suggested that 'after some of the CEFTA countries, including the Czech Republic, have joined the EU, CEFTA will remain a good starting point for its remaining countries in their efforts to enter the EU . . . these countries can practice rules for trade liberalisation, for example.'[26] The third scenario is also based on a reconfigured line-up but would involve CEFTA developing as an alternative to EU integration for CEE countries which proved unable to gain or dropped out of attempts to achieve EU membership.

3.3   *Constraints to the further development of CEFTA*

Problems of further enlargement of CEFTA

Scenarios two and three above could only possibly come about on the basis of further enlargement of CEFTA to its east and south, yet because of the close link between CEFTA membership and EU integration, this may not prove possible. Until recently, the countries acknowledged to be in the CEFTA accession queue (a status denoted by their Prime Ministers' attendance, as guests, at CEFTA summits) were Latvia, Lithuania, Croatia, FYR Macedonia and Ukraine. These days, the interest of Latvia and Lithuania has all but disappeared with their 'promotion' to EU candidates at the negotiating stage proper while Moldova came into the frame after declaring its interest in CEFTA membership in 1999. As noted in section 2.1 above, the most recent CEFTA summit declarations have confirmed that CEFTA remains open for enlargement provided candidate countries can meet the necessary conditions so the key question is when will the CEFTA candidates acquire the membership qualifications? As far as the WTO is concerned, while Croatia acceded in summer 2000, none of the other CEFTA aspirants are likely to be admitted in the very near future. Progress towards free trade with the EU has been accelerated so far only in the cases of FYR Macedonia and Croatia and there is the question of when this will actually materialise - with spring 2001 representing an optimistic schedule.[27] Then there is the CEFTA accession process itself to be completed, which entails putting in place the necessary bilateral free trade agreements with all CEFTA countries or ensuring that any existing trade liberalisation arrangements (e.g., Croatia and Slovenia, FYR Macedonia and Slovenia) conform with the CEFTA provisions. This could well turn out to be a lengthy process due to the number of partners involved and because there is plenty of potential for tricky negotiations, especially on agricultural trade. The fact that Croatian/Hungarian free trade agreement negotiations broke down in late 1999 because the Croatia side did not want to liberalise agricultural trade does not bode well for a fast conclusion of CEFTA accession talks.[28] Meanwhile, not only will CEFTA fully complete its transition to full removal of tariffs on industrial goods trade and implement those provisions covering non-tariff barriers which can be resolved at the CEFTA level (e.g. opening public procurement markets) but some of its members could also be on the verge of leaving CEFTA when new members are eventually ready to come in.

The final point to be made here is that the restrictions on CEFTA enlargement should not necessarily be interpreted negatively. As stated above, the deadline for completion of the free trade area is quite close (in fact certain pairs of countries, e.g., the Czech Republic and Slovenia, have already fully liberalised industrial trade) and new members would either have to adopt a very abrupt and most likely economically damaging opening to the CEFTA economic space or negotiate transition periods. Surely the establishment of a network of bilateral free trade agreements with the CEFTA countries free from the hindrance of the CEFTA rules is the most sensible and effective option at this late stage?

Possible formation of new subregional economic frameworks

Apart from the factors presently blocking further CEFTA enlargement, it may well be that some alternative subregional integration frameworks, perhaps based on the CEFTA model, will emerge. As noted earlier there is clear pres-

sure in this direction from the EU as the need to develop subregional cooperation is clearly going to be a condition of granting SAAs to relevant
Balkan/ex-Yugoslav states. Though the EU's perspective in this respect may
well turn out to be the most influential, calls for Balkan subregional economic
cooperation have come from other sources. Even before the ignition of the
Kosovo crisis the idea of the 'South East Europe Free Trade Area' (SEEFTA)
was being floated in the literature and in autumn 1999 George Soros called
for the Balkan states to come up with a 'plan of their own to win accession
(to the EU). The plan, he (Soros) said, should include a common Balkans customs union - which he had been advocating since June - and a common market interacting with the EU.'[29] Also, in October 1999 Radio Free Europe/Radio
Liberty reported that the Prime Ministers of the CIS countries met in Yalta
in order to 'discuss the introduction of a CIS free-trade zone. The participants
signed an agreement on reducing customs regulations and other deals oriented toward making the CIS a free-trade zone.'[30]

The limits of subregional cooperation

Whatever patterns of subregional economic cooperation develop in the coming years, the chances of any of the subregional cooperation initiatives in CEE
developing into a genuine alternative to integration in the EU are slim. For
one thing, the countries concerned would have to abandon their EU ambitions and so far, though the scepticism over the limits of EU expansion is
warranted, there is no real sign (especially post-Helsinki) of that happening
yet. The prospect becomes even more remote if we simply consider what the
process of developing beyond a free trade area would mean. The extra layers of integration would involve emulating the EC/EU since the mid-1980s
which represented, as Tsoukalis has written, 'a major qualitative change:
European integration is now largely about economic regulation, redistribution, and increasingly through the locking of exchange rates, macroeconomic
policies.'[31] Such developments would clearly be a long way down the line
even for the existing CEFTA members, let alone the slower reforming, economically weaker states that could make up the reconfigured CEFTA.

There is also the rather compelling argument that subregional cooperation
will always be second best when existing alongside wider integration processes.
According to the Hungarian scholar Andras Inotai it is only viable to attempt
to substitute subregional cooperation for engagement with a wider regional

integration framework if certain conditions prevail. First, the necessary material conditions have to be present, that is the 'development anchor (modernisation anchor) should be located within the sub-region'.[32] Second, the existence of 'an overwhelming external threat may force countries to cooperate'[33] though in this case the cooperation will be second-best and will disentangle when the external pressure disappears. Third, the subregional cooperation may represent some kind of independent preparation for membership of a wider regional integration scheme and will be viable as long as the cooperation entails adjustment to the rules of the larger integration. None of these would be relevant for a rump CEFTA looking to develop an alternative integration to the EU. Inotai also makes the important and connected argument that it is only in the context of full membership of the more developed and integrated regional framework that subregional integration can reach its full potential - that is for CEE states the main gains at the subregional level will come after accession to the EU as important barriers to deeper integration are removed and key financial resources to support infrastructure developments become available. On the prospects for what is presently intra-CEFTA and intra-BFTA trade, for example, '(t)he case of Portugal and Spain (and indirectly, the earlier case of the Benelux countries) shows that EU membership gives a substantial boost to subregional trade flows . . . Intra-regional trade can be expected to grow faster than trade with the present EU members, to a proportion of 12-15 percent of the total . . . Among the factors behind this will be higher growth rates, booming investment (domestic and foreign), deeper intra-industry specialisation, economic-policy coordination, enhanced security (also in psychological terms), financial transfers, and the establishment of a more efficient subregional infrastructure.'[34] Inotai's assumptions concerning the range of benefits of EU membership may well be up for debate and the accessibility of the EU for the more peripheral east, south and south-east European states may not be a question of choice, but it seems difficult to argue that the countries concerned could independently achieve an effective and advanced form of integration.

Conclusions

So far CEFTA has proved to be a useful device for the rebuilding of economic ties in CEE, improving political understanding and generating greater subregional cohesion, all of which underpin the EU accession process. Given the positive results generated by CEFTA cooperation, the idea that its role could be transformed is worth exploring in the context of possibility that the problems of eastward enlargement of the EU may dictate a modest rather than extensive intake of new members. As well as the prospect of existing CEE candidates being left in what could be an unsustainable association status, the immense difficulty of activating any self-contained multilateral cooperation in the west Balkan subregion and lack of integration possibilities for certain ex-Soviet Republics (currently Ukraine and Moldova in particular) indicate that a more pan-European extension of existing successful subregional groups may be seen as a potential policy option at least worth exploring.

The main conclusions of this paper are, however, that the constraints to further enlargement of CEFTA, leave question marks over whether accession of new members to CEFTA makes any sense at this late stage in its development, and the limited integration potential of subregional groups in CEE all point to CEFTA proving unlikely to move to a redefined role in the future. The fact that subregional integration cannot compensate for an adequate and inclusive EU eastwards enlargement strategy does not however mean that EU policy towards subregional cooperation can safely be restricted to the standard formula of requiring candidate states to engage in mutual economic cooperation for pre-accession purposes. For one thing, taking selected CEE states into the EU still looks certain to seriously undermine subregional relations in CEE. While the moves to grant SAAs to the relevant west Balkan states will go some way to ensuring that the minimum requirement of maintaining low level integration ties such as free trade agreements is met, future free trade developments with CEE countries to the east of CEFTA still remain compromised and the extension of the Shengen area will also have serious widespread consequences. Another reason for a more imaginative approach to EU policy on subregional cooperation in CEE is connected to the many problems of establishing multilateral subregional economic cooperation, along CEFTA lines, in the west Balkans. Further attention and support to the looser subregional cooperation initiatives operating there (such as the CEI, BSEC and SECI) with an emphasis on increasing funding to enable upgrading and expanding their activities may be more productive than purely relying on

traditional prescriptions which may be premature for this especially complicated zone of Europe.

Martin Dangerfield
University of Wolverhampton
le1919@wlv.ac.uk

Notes

[1] In this article we are concerned with multilateral state-to-state level subregional
cooperation. Bilateral state-to-state cooperation, and sub-state bilateral/multilat-
eral (e.g. cross-border initiatives) are also part of the multi-level, multi-dimensional
subregional cooperation structures.

[2] See, for example: A. Cottey (ed) *Subregional Cooperation in the New Europe. Building
Security, Prosperity and Solidarity from the Barents to the Black Sea*, (Basingstoke:
Macmillan, 1999); R. Dwan, *Building Security in Europe's New Borderlands*, (New
York: M.E. Sharpe, 1999); M. Dangerfield, *Subregional Economic Cooperation in Central
and Eastern Europe* (Cheltenham: Edward Elgar, 2000).

[3] For the front-runner EU candidates, therefore, the main questions regarding subregional cooperation therefore concern (a) the extent to which they can further
develop their mutual cooperation in the context of their EU accession preparations
and (b) the implications of the accession requirements for their relations with those
CEE whose progress on the EU front is less developed.

[4] To risk a gross understatement, such objectives are somewhat overambitious
for the group of countries concerned. Nevertheless, as the comments made by
Christopher Patten during a conference on the Balkan Stability Pact conference
held in Brussels on 29 March 2000 affirmed, the well-established precedent that
subregional cooperation must proceed in tandem with the upgrading of relations
with the EU will apply to the west Balkans too. He confirmed that the EU was
committed to speeding up trade liberalisation with non-associated Balkan countries but (*Financial Times*, 30 March 2000) added that the region's countries had to
trade more freely with each other and with other eastern European countries on
the road to EU membership.

[5] See Cottey (ed) *Subregional Cooperation*, and T. Danko, 'Perspectives of the Economic
cooperation of Ukraine with the states of the Baltic-Black Sea Region', paper presented at the Second Convention of the Central and East European International
Studies Association, Warsaw, 15-18 June 2000, mimeo, Kharkov State Polytechnic
University, 2000.

[6] A. Bailes, 'Subregional organisations: the Cinderellas of European security', *NATO*

Review, 45 (2) 1997, pp. 27-31 (via: http://www.mfa.ee/nato/docu/review/articles/9702-8.htm), p. 3.

7   The emphasis here is on the EU accession endeavour. Some of the points about subregional cooperation made here are also relevant for NATO expansions also.

8   Bailes, 'Subregional organisations', p. 3.

9   Cottey, *Multi-Layered Integration*, p. 21.

10 Again, see Cottey (ed) *Subregional Cooperation and* Dwan, *Building Security.* See also P. Dunay, 'Regional cooperation: much ado about nothing?', paper presented to the 3rd EPRC/ISA Conference, Vienna, 16-19 September, 1998, mimeo, Geneva Centre for Security Policy, 1998.

11 For an account of the progress of the Visegrad group since its revival in May 1999 see V. Handl, 'Visegrad: Chances for Revival', paper presented at the conference *Subregional Dimensions of the European Union Eastward Enlargement Process,* University of Wolverhampton, 23 June 2000.

12 It should be noted that for the original CEFTA states and Slovenia most industrial goods became duty and quota free at the beginning of 1997 following a series of amendments to CEFTA which advanced the liberalisation schedule for most goods by four years. However, a small percentage of products, the so-called 'lists of exceptions' remained subject to the original transition period which was to end in 2001 in most cases and 2002 for imports of automobiles and certain automobile components into Poland. The newer members of CEFTA were obliged to comply with the original CEFTA liberalisation schedule. See Dangerfield, *Subregional Economic Cooperation* for more detail of the CEFTA trade liberalisation programme.

13 CEFTA operates a rotating presidency and one of the main duties of the current holder CEFTA chair is to organise and host the regular meeting of the CEFTA Joint committee and annual Summit of CEFTA Prime Ministers. The CEFTA presidency was held by Poland in 2000, and passed to Romania in 2001.

14 *Declaration of the Prime Ministers of the CEFTA Countries, Warsaw, the Republic of Poland, November 15, 2000,* p. 3. (Author's copy kindly supplied by the Slovak Ministry of Economy.)

15 Here I offer only a brief summary of the results of CEFTA. Readers requiring more substantial coverage should consult Dangerfield, *Subregional Economic Cooperation.*

16 The data for the Czech and Slovak republics does not include their mutual trade. On Hungary, though a slump in agricultural exports affected its 1999 position negatively, the underlying trend in Hungary's intra-CEFTA trade has been in the direction of a steady shift from deficit to surplus country, underwritten of course by Hungary's position as the most dynamic export economy in CEFTA and leading recipient of export-oriented foreign direct investment.

[17] Data on overall imports and trade deficit of Romania in 1998 taken from *Business Central Europe*, June 1999.

[18] For example for large parts of the period in which Vaclav Klaus and Vladimir Meciar were Czech and Slovak Premiers respectively, CEFTA summits were the only forum in which the two actually met.

[19] The usual example of this has been the need for acceding CEFTA members to settle long-standing (usually socialist-era) debts with the existing members. This is a relevant part of Croatia's efforts to join CEFTA too - during Croatian Premier Ivica Racan's visit to Prague in early June 2000 the issue of CEFTA membership was discussed along with the question of resuming talks (suspended by the Czech side in 1998) on the necessary bilateral free trade agreement and the need to resolve (Czech News Agency, 8 June 2000) 'clearance of debt between the two countries.'

[20] Handl, *Visegrad: Chances*, p. 6.

[21] *Radio Free Europe/Radio Liberty (RFE/RL) Newsline*, 14 September 1998.

[22] *Warsaw Voice*, 6 July 1998, on-line version, via: http://www.warsaw.voice.com.pl.

[23] 'East European leaders press for quick EU entry', *Central Europe Online Daily News*, 17 November 2000, via: www.centraleurope.com/news.php3?id=221059.

[24] In principle, CEFTA could certainly have played a more active role in relations with the EU in its earlier phase. However, apart from the refusal of the Czech side to engage in subregional political co-operation and the drift in Slovakia's position, one of the main problems was that, until the post-AGENDA 2000 period at least, the instincts of the CEE countries were essentially competitive rather that co-operative as they sought pole position in the EU enlargement process.

[25] *Financial Times*, 12 October 1999.

[26] *Central European Business Weekly*, 26 June - 2 July 1998.

[27] See 'Nurturing the spoils of peace', *Financial* Times, 12 June 2000.

[28] I am grateful to Tamas Reti, of the Institute for Economics, Budapest, for informing me of this development.

[29] *New Europe*, 20-26 September 1999. See also Soros' more recent article 'How to encourage the Balkans' *Financial Times*, 23 November 2000. The difficulties of putting in place such schemes should not be underestimated. To illustrate, speaking at a public debate on the EU's strategy towards the west Balkans, held in Brussels on 10 July 2000, Italian foreign minister Lamberto Dini (*Financial Times*, 11 July 2000) 'complained that Balkan countries "seem to resist" cooperation among themselves' while Luxembourg foreign minister Lydie Polfer (*Financial Times*, 11 July 2000) 'said "it was not obvious" that countries in the region had understood the responsibilities involved in drawing closer to the EU.'

[30] *Radio Free Europe/Radio Liberty (RFE/RL) Newsline*, 11 October 1999. It should be mentioned that this is not seen by many as a practical possibility because the CIS

countries are simply not yet ready to implement an effective free trade area. It does however, throw light on the difficult situation of Ukraine in terms of its further development of its external economic relations. Association with the EU remains elusive, the CEFTA door has closed (or at least the illusion that it was open has gone) and bilateral economic relations with the CEE-10 - except with Estonia and Lithuania for now - look unlikely to materialise, and Ukraine appears to have no viable avenues for subregional economic cooperation.

[31] L. Tsoukalis, *The New European Economy Revisited* (Oxford: Oxford University Press, 1997), p. 2.

[32] A. Inotai, *Correlations Between European Integration and Subregional Cooperation. Theoretical background, Experience and Policy Impacts,* Working Paper No. 87 of the Institute for World Economics (Budapest: Hungarian Academy of Sciences, 1997), p. 5.

[33] Inotai, *Correlations Between*, p. 5.

[34] Inotai, *Correlations Between*, p. 6.

Aleissa Vatta

The Enlargement of the European Union and Social Dialogue in Central and Eastern Europe

ABSTRACT

In the coming years, the European Union is likely to have new members among Central and Eastern European Countries (CEECs). Currently, most of them are going through a massive process of institutional and legislative reform, particularly related to the adoption of *the acquis communautaire*. Meanwhile, the advent of free markets and moves towards privatisation of industry have led to major changes in their economies. However, the involvement of social and economic interest groups in public policy-making seems to be rather irregular, if not totally ineffective. This article presents an account of the development and the current state of social dialogue among trades unions, employers' organisations and the governments of the candidate countries. It argues that the role of representative groups must be strengthened in order to ensure an effective implementation of the reform agendas. Moreover, a more regular resort to concertation could help to establish a working system of 'checks-and-balances' in the political systems of CEE.

Social dialogue and the CEECs

After the Helsinki Summit in December 1999, the former division between the first and the second round of countries due to join the European Union has been officially overcome. From the perspective of accession, the adoption of the social dialogue between the government and the social partners has been supported as an important instrument to implement the necessary reforms. This implies the active involvement of interest organisations in the policy-making process, with the possible formation of tripartite bodies. Such a mode of interest inter-mediation relies on a good degree of legitimisation and representativeness of trades unions and employers' organisations, and on a positive attitude from governments towards concertation.

The debate regarding the foundation of tripartite councils in the CEECs had already risen in the first years after 1989. The two main theoretical interpre-tations stressed, respectively, a possible transposition of the "German model" of industrial relations in the *Reformländer*, with local adaptations, and the hypothesis that tripartism would only be a temporary solution, necessary only at the most difficult and problematic stages of the transition.[1] Neocor-poratism was also often evoked as an adequate theoretical framework even although its premises were grounded in a study of Western consolidated democracies. Although neocorporatist concepts may be usefully applied to the study of tripartism in the area, the extension of research to the ten can-didate countries of Central and Eastern Europe, shows that country-specific aspects also deserve attention. Moreover, only recently has economic and social cohesion gained the primary attention of the European Commission. In the *Guidelines for the implementation of the Phare programme for the years 2000-2006*, published by the European Commission in 1999, the chapter on eco-nomic and social cohesion explicitly refers to the priority of developing and reinforcing institutional capability in the CEECs (*institution-building*). And this chapter is also included in the second priority of the Phare programme, *investment support*. In these documents, social and economic cohesion is con-sidered as fundamentally important for the implementation of the *acquis com-munautaire* and the preparation of the candidate countries for the participation in the European Union. Twinning initiatives are also encouraged, in the hope to improve the conditions of interest representation. For this purpose, Phare should be converted from technical assistance to accession support. Actually, as regards the Phare-financed partnership projects concerning non-govern-mental associations, in 1998 the Commission remarked on their scarce impact on CEECs' civil societies, even if the creation of new services has registered some progress. In order to get a clearer picture, it is necessary to look at the state of social dialogue in the CEECs during the last decade.

The Baltic States

In *Estonia,* trades Unions have been already regulated by law in 1989. Two of the three national confederations (the Estonian Trades Union Association, and the Estonian Association of Employees' Trades Unions) take part in tripartite negotiations which, at central level, are binding for all the actors. However, employers' interests representation is still not properly structured. This is due to the limited implementation of labour law and to the simultaneous weakness of trades unions (often not represented in private firms). The main employers' organisations participating in tripartite negotiations are the Confederation of Estonian Industry, which includes many public firms, and the Estonian Association of Small Firms. The government regularly meets representatives from the employers, trades unions, local administrations and farming organisations, in order to discuss political issues. However, a tripartite Economic and Social Council was only established in 1997, and social dialogue - especially with the employers - has not yet fully developed. Currently, the council promotes tripartite negotiations, checks the main macro-economic indicators and gives recommendations to the government. Through the social dialogue, some important issues - like social security reforms - have already been discussed, and further innovations are due for consideration in the near future. Further tripartite councils are also being planned to deal with local problems.[2]

In *Latvia,* the main social partners' organisations face severe problems. The largest trades unions' confederation (Lbas) has about 300,000 members (if we include the unemployed and retired), but suffers from financial restrictions and cannot cover strike expenses or finance protest initiatives.[3] Employers are represented by a national confederation which includes managers of public firms, and does not easily cooperate with the newly-founded Union of Private Employers. Disputes between the two organisations have weakened the National Tripartite Cooperation Council, which - though established in 1992 with consultation purposes - received a proper statute only in 1998. In spite of a number of measures taken to improve interest representation, bipartite relationships between the social partners are rather sporadic and there are no specific institutional channels at their disposal (apart from the mass media) to exert influence on the law-making process. However, a new organisational structure for the Council was approved in 1999, with the establishment of sub-councils for labour and social policy.[4]

In Lithuania, labour is rather fragmented. Following a 1991 act, about seventy autonomous trades unions were born, but only six to ten per cent of the labour force is unionised.[5] Together with the Chamber of Commerce, the Confederation of Lithuanian Industrialists (including public and privatised firms) and the Employers' Association (representing firms established after 1992) cooperate actively, but employers often search for more direct contacts with the public administration, with the risk of mismanagement and corruption.[6] Bipartite relationships and sectoral negotiations are weak. Trilateral commissions, established at national and local level for labour market management are rather ineffective.[7] The Tripartite Council may in the future be able to gain more power from a cooperation agreement which was signed in February 1999 by the government and the social partners. In this agreement the government committed itself to submit to the Council any project regarding social, economic and labour affairs before its official adoption, and to transmit the Council's opinions to Parliament. According to this agreement, by the end of every year an agreement should be signed about minimum and maximum hourly and monthly wages, and on any related subject.

In both Latvia and *Lithuania*, social dialogue still looks rather weak. Relationships between interest organisations are not consolidated, and their social and political impact is low. The attitude of governments to the reform processes noted above will be of vital importance for their success. The associative context appears more developed in Estonia, but the real effectiveness of the tripartite council remains in doubt. Collective bargaining is not perceived as a priority: in the private sector, trades unions' membership is about ten per cent of the labour force, and working conditions are considered as personal problems.[8]

Bulgaria

In this country the beginning of social dialogue has been complicated by governmental and economic crises.[9] A tripartite commission was initially established in 1989, in order to avoid a serious strike wave. Between 1989 and 1991 the first General Agreements were signed, in an effort to institutionalise collective bargaining. In comparison to other CEE countries, bargaining is still rather centralised, because trades unions reacted vigorously to the attempts (made by the government in the early 1990s) to decentralise bargaining to the works councils. Moreover, as a result of joint pressures on the government, bipartite relationships among trades unions and employers are quite intense. The tripartite National Commission for Interest Coordination, legally established in March 1991, under the leadership of a vice-prime minister, worked until 1992 for the reform of wages and the elaboration of a new labour code, which was enacted in the same year.[10] According to its statute, twenty three sectoral commissions and eventually regional commissions were to be set in place. As a matter of fact, the commission started enlarging its scope of intervention by examining bills and decrees on labour and welfare, extending its influence to financial, monetary and privatisation policies. In 1992, after the dismissal of tripartite bodies by the government, the social partners themselves adopted a new series of rules for national level concertation, but these were limited to working conditions and industrial relations. Only in 1993, following the provisions of the Labour Code, the commission - now called the National Council for Tripartite Cooperation, (with nine subcommissions) - was revamped and its mandate now included areas dealing with problems and reforms related to economic and social change, including the definition of minimum wages and the resolution of conflicts. Together with some new sectoral trades unions, the main labour organisations (officially recognised in 1998 as negotiating partners by the government), the Knsb (Confederation of Free Trades unions of Bulgaria) and *Podkrepa* (Support), were the first trades unions to be established after the collapse of Communism in 1989. The entrepreneurial side is rather fragmented and includes many state-led or semi-public firms. In 1997, seventy per cent of Bulgarian firms was under state control.[11] The Bulgarian Industrial Association was officially recognised in 1993 as a member of the tripartite commission, together with the Union of Private Enterprises (Ssig), the Bulgarian Chamber of Commerce, and the association "Renaissance".[12] Several other interest groups, like the Confederation of Industrialists, have been created to promote entrepreneurship. In 1995 the Association of Bulgarian Employers' Organisations began the process of bringing together large and small firms of the various organisations. However, autonomous bipartite agreements between the social partners are hampered by governmental predominance and organisational fragmentation on the employers' side.[13] At the subnational level, tripartite agreements rarely apply. In spite of official declarations, the government often disregards the consultation of social partners on the problems of economic reform. The European Commission has insisted on the need to improve and intensify social dialogue, in order to check the course of social and economic transformation.[14]

The Czech Republic

In its 1999 Regular Report, the European Commission rated as 'satisfactory' the situation of the tripartite dialogue at the central level in the Czech Republic, while bipartite negotiations between trades unions and employers' organisations lack adequate structures at sectoral and local level. However, experience shows that even central tripartite dialogue faces several difficulties. Both the current Czech and Slovak Rhsd's (national tripartite councils) derive from the Czechoslovak Rhsd, which was split after the Velvet Revolution in 1993. According to its 1997 statute, the Czech council maintains advisory functions. The plenary session meets every two months, with seven representatives for each partner; a board acts as executive body; and specific working groups, with no more than nine members, are assisted by an administrative secretariat. Originally, the most important purpose of the council had been to forge an annual General Agreement on economic and social policy. But the absence of a definite legal status and the frequent hostility from the government have weakened the council. Internal disputes (especially on wage policy), sporadic meetings, the neglect from the government (often represented by officials without any decision-making power) and institutional isolation (due to the lack of other similar structures) led to the absence of such agreements between 1995 and 1998.[15] Wage control is also very limited, since minimum wages and their corresponding levels in the public sector have been centrally negotiated only since 1996.[16] Other wage issues are discussed at sectoral and local level, without any guarantee of respect for the negotiated minimum. Consequently, control over wages and prices have been scarce and agreements within the council are of secondary importance in comparison with governmental decisions. Moreover, the concept of a 'social pact' is still associated in the minds of some as a legacy of the Communist era, and in light of recent social security reforms, such a pact is unlikely to emerge.[17]

The representativeness criteria adopted in the statute of the council are rather selective. In 1995 it was established that, in order to join the council, trades unions must be independent from parties, have a confederal structure, be active throughout the country, prove to have at least 300,000 members and be able to take part in collective negotiations at the sectoral and local level. Employers' organisations (which face difficulties especially at local level) must have a national coverage, count at least 100,000 employees in member firms (since 1997), and the majority of employees at sectoral level. These criteria should encourage a strong vertical integration of representation, enhancing the efficiency of the council. However, the negative attitude of state authorities has caused a remarkable distrust from the social partners about the social dialogue, and moves to put political pressure on the government and the parliament, considered as the real decision-making bodies.[18] In this view, bilateral negotiations between the social partners should be intensified, particularly at sectoral level, while the Rhsd should only act as a *forum* for the discussion of general issues, like integration in the EU (especially under the profile of social dialogue).[19] Recently, a more positive phase of social dialogue has taken place. The Social Democratic government, elected in 1998, has begun the process of submitting all relevant bills to the social partners before these are discussed in parliament. In 1999 the council discussed important social and economic issues (industrial restructuring, pension reform, lifting of state control on prices). Future reforms will show more clearly the attitude of the government and the consequent prospects for the activity of the council.

Hungary

Tripartite bodies already existed in Hungary before the end of Communism. The Council for the Reconciliation of Interests (Ét) had been founded in 1988 as part of a reform programme for the partial liberalisation of the economy. After its decisive intervention for the conclusion of the national transport strike in 1990, the Ét survived the political transition and received a new statute in 1991. According to it, the Ét should play an informative role, express its opinions and give recommendations on bills (especially on labour law) and resolve labour conflicts. It should also determine minimum wage levels and cooperate in public policy-making. Plenary sessions were complemented by the work of specific committees, and the government gave financial support to the social partners' secretariats.[20] Even though tripartite agreements were limited to annual agreements, and conflicts between the government and the social partners were quite common, the Ét has not remained isolated. In 1993, social security funds boards were established, in which delegates of employers and trades unions were included. The role of the social partners in public policy-making had been officially recognised, even though the pressure for economic stabilisation made social dialogue increasingly difficult, especially in fiscal and budget matters.[21]

The Ét included representatives from nine employers' organisations and six trades unions' confederations.[22] Representative fragmentation was partially solved by law in 1995, when the public functions held by the economic chambers were separated from interest representation.[23] In spite of verticalisation attempts, the right of general interest representation is still not officially legally proscribed for employers' organisations. This has led to a decrease in collective bargaining since 1991-92, and caused severe difficulties in establishing binding commitments.[24]

Among other tripartite bodies there is the Council for the Reconciliation of Interests in Public Services (Kiet), which since 1992 has been responsible for negotiations over labour relations and public sector bills. In 1997 the Commission for the Management of the Labour Market Fund was established in order to deal with employment policies and allocate the resources of the fund (based on contributions by both employers and employees). At county level, tripartite bodies will take charge of the decentralised operations of the fund. Since 1996 a Mediation and Arbitration Service (Mkéds) has been working on behalf of the government and the social partners, to solve conflicts of interest and keep social peace. The Ét during this period also participated in such work, sending six delegates to the Joint Consultative Committee, in cooperation with the Economic and Social Committee of the EU.[25]

Since 1998, social dialogue has faced increasing difficulties, mainly due to governmental intervention. The Ét, whose approval was necessary for governmental decisions on labour policy, was dissolved in 1999 and substituted by two different bodies, the National Labour Council and the Economic Council. The Kiet and the funds boards were also dissolved, as was the Ministry of Labour, whose duties are now divided among the Ministries of Education, Economics, and Social Affairs. Of the Ét's successor bodies, the National Labour Council has been involved in minimum wage bargaining, but income policy negotiations have been suspended. In the Economic Council, consultations on economic policy, take place not only between the government and the social partners, but also with representatives from chambers, multinationals and financial institutions. Whereas the Economic Council is supposed to meet twice a year, there are no specific provisions regarding all the other new councils. Between 1998 and 1999, the government also started revising the labour code, trying to transfer collective bargaining prerogatives from trades unions to works councils.[26] Since the latter are not allowed to start protest initiatives, (including strikes) and are not experienced in interest intermediation, these moves from the government have been interpreted as an attempt to weaken the trades unions and collective bargaining. Moreover, the changes in the framework of tripartite bodies have been made without consulting the social partners. The influence of the new bodies is rather circumscribed; fragmentation and a lack of regulation further damage them. In the new Social Council, which mainly includes 'third-sector' associations and NGOs, social partners' representatives are not even allowed to take part.

On the whole, the future of social dialogue in Hungary looks uncertain, both at the central and local levels. While the Economic and Social Committee of the EU has strongly criticised recent developments, the European Commission remarked that it is the problems of fragmentation and lack of resources, which undermine possible negotiations.[27]

Poland

After the abolition of the tax on excessive wage increases (*popiwek*), the Tripartite Commission for Economic and Social Affairs, established in 1994, was granted the right to determine maximum wage increases in the public sector, and in private firms with more than fifty employees. According to official policy, wage increases depend on forecasts of inflation and GDP, with monthly levels fixed on an annual basis.[28] In case the commission does not reach a unanimous agreement, the government takes the ultimate decision.[29]

As a matter of fact, the activity of the commission began in 1993, following the enactment of laws on representative organisations and conflict resolution (1991), and the Pact of Transformation of State Firms (1993), which was supposed to encourage privatisation. However, within the commission, relations between the social partners' was tense. *Solidarnosc* did not intend to negotiate with the other major trades union confederation Opzz, and its double role (as trades union and governmental party) led to intense debates.[30] This situation required separate negotiations among the different groups, made even more difficult by the divisions within the employers' side.[31] Since then, because of such rivalries, only the Confederation of Polish Employers has taken part in tripartite meetings, while the other business associations have preferred the channel of interest intermediation. Legally, employers' organisations are not entitled to the same general representation as trades unions.[32] The social dialogue is thus weakened by the limited participation of the employers. However, in spite of frequent conflicts, in the mid-1990s social dialogue has led to the establishment of social security funds, the amendment of the Labour Code (in 1994) and collective bargaining legislation.[33] The European Commission has repeatedly insisted on the need to reinforce such negotiations.[34] This has encouraged the foundation, in 1999, of a new employers' organisation, the Polish Confederation of Private Employers. It could improve the state of social dialogue, provided that it will be able to moderate the strong particularism of the entrepreneurial environment and the highly decentralised nature of industrial relations, which often leads to the exclusion of trades unions from any negotiation.[35]

The role of the state remains ambiguous, due to its strong presence in the economy.[36] Especially in some strategic sectors (like metalworking), the state is still involved in the ownership of firms, and this also has consequences for social dialogue. The functions of the tripartite commission are increasingly reduced to the definition of the terms of collective bargaining, and even here its recommendations are often neglected. In fact, state-owned firms can afford to turn a blind eye to such recommendations, by virtue of their privileged relationship with the public administration, while private firms tend to offer higher wages in order to attract workers.[37] And social dialogue has come up against a host of new difficulties following the withdrawal of the Opzz from the commission in April 1999. Consequently, the decisions of the commission are no longer binding on the government.[38]

Romania

In the early 1990s, bipartite and tripartite negotiations were rejected by both the government and the social partners in Romania. Trades unions were not consulted before the adoption of the new labour law in 1991, and amendments and changes - particularly on collective bargaining and mediation -

were introduced either by decree or by law, without any negotiation with the social partners.[39] Only in recent years has the government slowly begun co-operating with trades unions and employers.[40] However, the representation of interests is highly fragmented and, on the employers' side, is complicated by the delayed privatisation of state firms. At the sectoral level, representation is very weak and national agreements are poorly respected. Only in 1997 have new acts been introduced, concerning collective bargaining and the establishment of an Economic and Social Council. The council is the central institution for social dialogue. It is a consultative body, with twenty seven members (nine for each partner). The council has been given the right to express proposals and opinions on economic development, wage and labour issues, privatisation, social security, education and health. It can examine bills and play a mediating role, on request of the social partners. On several occa-sions, the council has met members of parliament and the government , and it has promoted the foundation of tripartite bodies at county level. Within the council, five trades unions confederations and eight employers' confed-erations are represented. About the latter, which have developed only recently, their degree of representativeness is hard to define. At the present time, it is impossible to evaluate the effectiveness of the council.[41]

Slovakia

To a certain extent, Slovakia is a special case, since social dialogue is regu-larly applied. In 1999 the Act on Tripartism officially regulated the Council for Economic and Social Accord. The government also formed a Consultative Committee on European Integration, involving the social partners.[42] However, this apparent institutionalisation of concertation deserves a more attentive consideration.

The tripartite council (Rhsd) corresponds to the equivalent Czech body; but, unlike the Czech Republic, Slovakia has been relatively open to tripartism. The government and the parliament have shown an interest in the views of the social partners, and recommendations of the council are 'morally bind-ing'.[43] The Rhsd is not only involved in wage policy, but also in social policy-making. Pensions and social security funds are also led by tripartite boards. A separate tripartite commission has been entitled to extend the terms of col-lective negotiations *erga omnes,* a rather exceptional practice in the CEECs.[44]

Annual General Agreements adopted by the Rhsd include provisions regarding employment and social policy and the ratification of international conventions. The Rhsd acts as a consultant of the government on social and economic issues, and examines the relative bills. The council has a plenary session, which meets at least quarterly, and a board; it is state-funded, but the social partners reimburse the expenses of their representatives.[45]

In principle, the Rhsd could be considered an 'official' body, supporting the parliament in the decision-making process. As a matter of fact, this was far from the case until the adoption of the Act on Tripartism in 1999. Up until 1999, unanimous agreements reached within the council could be rejected by the government on a whole series of economic and political issues without even consulting the social partners. Between 1997 and 1998, the government even tried to create a parallel economic and social council, including public firms managers, civil society groups and trades unions' representatives which did not belonging to the Koz. The activity of the Rhsd was blocked, and interest groups intensified their lobbying on the parliament. Only in 1999, after decisive protests from the Koz, has the social dialogue been relaunched with the adoption of the Act on Tripartism.

In the early 1990s the council proved useful in preventing massive social unrest, while in recent years its role has been strengthened as part of the country's bid for EU membership. However, the effectiveness of the Rhsd still depends on the goodwill of the government and the parliament to accept its recommendations. Possible reactions from the trades unions must also be taken into consideration.[46] The unions rejected any idea of a 'stability pact' (which they saw as a an attempt by the government to legitimise emergency economic provisions), and instead demanded the effective application of existing tripartite initiatives. While the government continues to play this double role of public actor and employer, the Act on Tripartism cannot ensure the compliance of Rhsd's agreements. The Act on Tripartism only declares that - in case of disagreement - the disputed matter will be discussed again in plenary session. Interference from the government, thus, cannot be ruled out. Moreover, employers often tend to avoid direct negotiations with the trades unions and prefer bargaining with the government.[47] Notwithstanding its ambiguities, Slovak tripartism could be enhanced by becoming really systematic, which would imply a stronger bipartite dialogue at the sectoral and local level coupled with a clearer delimination of the areas of governmental intervention.

Slovenia

According to the European Commission, the state of social dialogue can be defined as satisfactory in this country.[48] The two relevant bodies are the Economic and Social Council and the National Council. The former was established in 1994 by the government and the social partners in order to discuss problems and solutions regarding economic and social policy.[49] Each delegation has five members. Decisions are binding, but they must be unanimous and later approved by the first chamber of the parliament, the National Assembly. The council participates in the elaboration of bills and in consultations regarding social rights, employment, collective bargaining, fiscal policy, economic policy and planning, cooperation with international organisations, codetermination and labour law. Proposals, recommendations and opinions are transmitted to both the chambers of the parliament and made public. Every year, the council is entitled to negotiate the Social Agreement, which defines conditions and expectations regarding economic and social policy. The enforcement of the agreement is mandatory.[50] The agreement also establishes procedures and sanctions in case of labour conflicts. Trades unions and employers' organisations are also members of the boards of social security funds. Accordingly, tripartite negotiations are not limited to the council, even though bipartite social dialogue - at sectoral and enterprise level - still needs to be reinforced.

The second chamber of the parliament, the National Council which was founded in 1992, represents social and economic interests. Out of its forty members, four are trades unions' representatives and four are employers' representatives. However, this council can be an interesting target for lobbying.[51] It can submit bills, organise *referenda*, promote official inquiries and declare a suspensive veto to bills presented by the National Assembly, which must then be voted on again and supported by an absolute majority. Since the parliament is quite open to the demands of the social partners, it can compensate for the reluctance of the government to deal with such problems, and the lack of an effective legal framework for the Economic and Social Council, whose functions are still informally defined.[52]

Some tentative conclusions

The experience of the CEECs shows that economic and social cohesion can be maintained only by pursuing compromises between the urgency of economic development and the respect of social justice. Cooperation between governments and social partners appears to be particularly important under this profile. The crucial position of the government is confirmed everywhere. The resort to tripartism has often been favoured by central governments in order to safeguard social peace during the economic and legislative reform processes necessary for the prospective access to the EU. However, governmental attitudes often depend on short-term (e.g. electoral) evaluations, more than on long-term strategies. This is also due to institutional problems, related to the scarcity of competent personnel, the resistance of the bureaucracy (which largely remained the same as in the previous regime) and the controversies over the division of tasks among the new ministries. The social dialogue is extremely vulnerable to such considerations, particularly because it suffers from the problems affecting social partners' organisations. Not only do they have poor resources (in terms of membership), but they are also riven with cleavages. In most cases, 'new' and 'reformed' trades unions have been at loggerheads with one another in the first years of the transition, and their autonomy from political parties has frequently been called into question.[53] Independent employers' organisations are also still weakly legitimised. Some of them, especially the chambers of commerce, and craft or cooperatives' associations, 'renovated' themselves, while new business associations have been formed in order to defend the interests of private firms. However, in spite of the privatisation process, the property regime in many sectors is still under a mix of public and private control. Consequently, the representativeness of employers' organisations remains uncertain. Moreover, there is a clear distinction between employers' organisations (EO's) and business associations (BA's). Actually, only EO's get involved in social dialogue, while BA's interest representation is limited to the promotion of business activity. It is often hard to distinguish 'entrepreneurial' associations from other political and economic pressure groups.[54]

Both trades unions and employers' organisations face representativeness problems, especially at sectoral level.[55] In particular, large firms may directly apply to local or central political authorities, without any intermediation by representative organisations. Since a clear-cut separation between the state and the economy is still lacking, the limited success of tripartite bodies is not surprising. Moreover, party politics - often with a relevant degree of polarisation - is a powerful competitor of social dialogue. In recent years, social security reforms appeared on the political agenda in several countries, while previously they had been postponed in favour of economic policies of liberalisation and privatisation.[56] In the future, social policies could be facilitated by the social dialogue, supported by the EU: but the weakness of labour law and collective bargaining needs to be corrected. As long as the new democracies continue to undergo consolidation, they will have to face important issues, such as welfare reforms, environmental recovery, employment reconversion. In this sense, the neglect of concerted laws and official agreements by the governments is directly related to the limitations of bipartite dialogue. In the majority of the CEECs, social partners have not developed autonomous bilateral negotiations, on the contrary, their rivalries tend to reinforce the distance between them and the governments. The frequent isolation of tripartite structures also reflects the weakness of national civil societies, which can now freely elect their political representatives, but cannot effectively check the political behaviour of the élites.[57] Interest organisations may in the future find new strengths and social support in their effort to overcome particularism and to define more general interests. However, a certain stability of the context and the terms of negotiations is needed, and the EU could exert a positive influence here through the Phare programme. If the Commission demands a more regular and effective implementation of the social dialogue and its commitments, and consequently offers proper assistance, the democratisation process and the adoption of the *acquis communautaire* would both benefit as would the interest of the Union and of its future member states.

University of Trieste
e-mail: osdee@sp.univ.trieste.it

Notes

[1] Concerning these two theories, see H. Wiesenthal, 'Organised interests in contemporary East Central Europe: theoretical perspectives and tentative hypotheses', in A. Ágh and G. Ilonszki (eds), *Parliaments and Organised Interests: The Second Steps*, (Budapest: Hungarian Centre for Democracy Studies, 1996), pp. 40-58; P. Stykow, 'Organised interests in the transformation processes of Eastern Europe and Russia:

towards Corporatism?, paper presented at the 8th International Conference on Socio-Economics, SASE, University of Geneva, 12-14 July 1996; and W. Reutter, 'Tripartism without Corporatism: trades unions in Central and Eastern Europe', in A. Ágh and G. Ilonszki (eds), *Parliaments and Organised Interests: The Second Steps* (Budapest: Hungarian Centre for Democracy Studies, 1996), pp. 59-78.

[2] European Commission, *Regular Report from the Commission on Progress towards Accession - Estonia* (Bruxelles, 1998, 1999 and 2000).

[3] H. Smith-Sivertsen, 'Latvia', in O. Berglund, D. Hellén and F. Aarebrot (eds), *The Handbook of Political Change in Eastern Europe* (Cheltenham: Edward Elgar, 1998), pp. 89-121.

[4] Organisation for Economic Cooperation and Development, *S.I.G.M.A. (Support for Improvement in Governance and Management in Central and Eastern Europe) - Report on Latvia* (Paris: OECD, 1999); European Commission, *Regular Report from the Commission on Progress towards Accession - Latvia* (Bruxelles, 2000).

[5] Organisation for Economic Cooperation and Development, *S.I.G.M.A. - Report on Lithuania*, (Paris: OECD, 1999); European Commission, *Regular Report from the Commission on Progress towards Accession - Lithuania* (Brussels, 1998, 1999 and 2000).

[6] R. J. Krickus, 'Democratisation in Lithuania', in K. Dawisha and B. Parrott (eds), *The Consolidation of Democracy in East-Central Europe* (Cambridge: Cambridge University Press, 1997).

[7] However, the recent act on the regulation of individual labour disputes (February 2000) should enhance dialogue and consultation, at least at the local level.

[8] Organisation for Economic Cooperation and Development, *OECD Economic Survey - The Baltic States* (Paris: OECD, 2000).

[9] Bulgaria changed 7 executives between 1989 and 1997.

[10] The Labour Code allows the government to select associations participating in collective bargaining at national level. The criteria for participation at sectoral and firm level are rather demanding: having 50,000 members, coverage of at least 50 per cent of each sector, stable structures (for trades unions); 500 members, widespread diffusion in at least 60 per cent of the local departments, and stable national and local structures (for business associations). On the whole, the system developed a high degree of concentration, under the control of the government (see O. K. Pedersen, K. Ronit and J. Hausner, 'Emergence of new forms of asso-ciability and collective bargaining in post-socialist countries', *Emergo*, 1(2) 1994, pp. 6-30).

[11] G. Koleva, *Industrial relations institutions in transition economies: the case of Bulgaria*, paper presented at the 3rd Conference of the European Sociological Association, University of Essex, 27-30 August 1997.

[12] "Renaissance" (*Vazrazhdane*) is an association of employers who got their property back after 1989 (Koleva, 'Industrial Relations', p. 8).

[13] European Commission, *Regular Report from the Commission on Progress towards Accession - Bulgaria* (Bruxelles, 1998).

[14] European Commission, *Regular Report from the Commission on Progress towards Accession - Bulgaria* (Brussels, 1999).

[15] A. Pollert, *Transformation at Work* (London: Sage, 1999); J. Kleibl and Z. Dvoráková, 'Industrial relations in the Czech Republic', *Prague Economic Papers*, (3) 1999, pp. 220-232.

[16] D. Vaughan-Whitehead (ed.), *Paying the price: the wage crisis in Central and Eastern Europe* (London: Macmillan, 1998).

[17] J. E. M. Thirkell, K. Petkov and S. A. Vickerstaff, *The Transformation of Labour Relations: Restructuring and Privatisation in Eastern Europe and Russia* (Oxford: Oxford University Press, 1998).

[18] Organisation for Economic Cooperation and Development, *S.I.G.M.A - Report on the Czech Republic* (Paris: OECD, 2000).

[19] However, in recent years trades union representatives have denounced the attitude of the government to exploit the pure existence of the Rhsd 'for the sake' of the EU, to show the formal application of the social dialogue (see note 44).

[20] S. Kurtán, 'Sozialpartnerschaft in Ungarn?', in E. Tálos (ed.), *Sozialpartnerschaft. Kontinuität und Wandel eines Modells* (Vienna: Verlag für Sozialkritik, 1993), pp. 267-284.

[21] T. Cox, and B. Mason, *Social and Economic Transformation in East Central Europe* (Cheltenham: Edward Elgar, 1999).

[22] The nine employers' confederations were the Mmsz (Hungarian Employers' Association), the Mgyosz (National Federation of Hungarian Industrialists), the Amsz (National Association of Agricultural Employers), the Okisz (Hungarian Industrial Association), the Mosz (National Federation of Agricultural Cooperatives and Producers), the Afeosz (National Federation of Consumer Cooperatives), the Iposz (National Association of Artisans), the Kisosz (National Federation of Traders and Caterers) and the Vosz (National Association of Entrepreneurs). The six trades unions' confederations were the Aszsz (Confederation of Autonomous Trades unions), the Észt (Confederation of Professionals' Unions), the Mszosz (National Confederation of Hungarian Trades unions), the Mosz (National Association of Workers' Council), the Liga (Democratic League of Independent Trades unions) and the Szef (Trades union Cooperation Forum).

[23] Mmsz and Mgyosz joined in 1998 see L. Hethy, 'Hungary: industrial relations background', *European Industrial Relations Review*, (313) 2000, pp. 16-23. In 1999,

the nine employers' confederations founded a joint association for international issues, the Mmnsz (Hungarian Employers' Confederation for International Cooperation), which is now member of the Unice.

[24] Economic and Social Committee of the European Union, *Opinion of the Economic and Social Committee on Hungary on the road to accession* (Brussels, 1 March 2000).

[25] Between 1994 and 1998 the government used to consult the leaders of the confederations. Such consultations are currently interrupted.

[26] A similar attempt had already been made in 1992, without success. However, even if works' councils are compulsory in firms with more than fifty employees, there is no prescribed sanction or fine in cases where they are absent. See L. Hethy, *Under Pressure: Workers and trades unions in Hungary during the period of transformation 1989-1998* (Geneva: ILO Bureau for Workers'Activities, 1999).

[27] European Commission, *Regular Report from the Commission on Progress towards Accession - Hungary* (Brussels, 1999).

[28] Once established, maximum levels are transmitted by the commission to the government and subsequently published in the official gazette, the *Monitor Polski*.

[29] M. Kabaj, 'Searching for a New Results-oriented Wage Negotiation System in Poland', in D. Vaughan-Whitehead (ed.), *Paying the Price: the wage crisis in Central and Eastern Europe* (London: Macmillan, 1998), pp. 234-272.

[30] J. Hausner, 'Models of the System of Interest Representation in Post-Socialist Societies: the Case of Poland', in A. Ágh and G. Ilonszki (eds), *Parliaments and Organised Interests: The Second Steps* (Budapest: Hungarian Centre for Democracy Studies, 1996), pp. 102-120.

[31] Originally, the composition of the commission included four representatives for each of the following actors: the government, the Confederation of Polish Employers (Kpp), *Solidarnosc*, the Opzz, plus one member for other major trades unions (forming a fifth group). Each group had a vote. A future revision of voting rules is foreseeable, due to the subsequent developments regarding the density of representative organisations.

[32] Hausner, 'Models of the system', pp. 116-117.

[33] See Cox and Mason, *Social and Economic Transformation*, 1999; Organisation for Economic Cooperation and Development, *S.I.G.M.A. - Report on Poland* (Paris: OECD, 1999).

[34] European Commission, *Regular Reports from the Commission on Progress towards Accession - Poland* (Brussels, 1998 and 1999).

[35] The estimated membership of *Solidarnosc* for the year 2000 amounted to 1,200,000 members, of whom only 700,000 were supposed to pay their dues (see K. von Hammerstein, 'Stiller Abschied', *Der Spiegel*, (32) 2000, pp. 86-87).

[36] K. Jasiecki, 'Strength or weakness of Polish business associations in transition pol-

itics', in K. Jasiecki, U. Kurczewska and M. Zdziech, *The Art of Effective Lobbying* (Warsaw: Warsaw School of Economics, 2000).

[37] J. Kulpinska, *How the Polish Industrial Relations System is Working in the 1990s*, paper presented at the 4th Conference of the European Sociological Association, Amsterdam, 18-21 August 1999.

[38] Economic and Social Committee of the European Union, *Opinion of the Economic and Social Committee on Poland on the road to accession* (Brussels, 9 December 1999); European Commission, *Regular Report from the Commission on Progress towards Accession - Poland* (Brussels, 2000).

[39] Pedersen, Ronit and Hausner, 'Emergence of new forms', p. 21.

[40] Within the Office of the Government, the Department for Social Dialogue promotes the relationships between the government and the NGO's (OECD, *SIGMA Report - Romania*, 1998 and 1999).

[41] R. Langewiesche, *Romania and Bulgaria - In Quest of Development and Integration*, Report n. 61 (Brussels: European Trades union Institute, 1999).

[42] European Commission, *Regular Report from the Commission on Progress towards Accession - Slovakia* (Brussels: 1999).

[43] M. Cambálikova, 'The Emergence of Tripartism in Slovakia', in A. Ágh and G. Ilonszki (eds), *Parliaments and Organised Interests: The Second Steps* (Budapest: Hungarian Centre for Democracy Studies, 1996), pp. 190-211; B. Haller and C. Schaller, '"Marktwirtschaft ohne Adjektive" oder Sozialpartnerschaft? Versuche sozialpartnerschaftlicher Konfliktregelung in der Tschechischen und Slowakischen Republik 1990-1993', *SWS Rundschau*, 34(3) 1994, pp. 309-331.

[44] M. Myant, B. Slocock and S. Smith, 'Tripartism in the Czech and Slovak Republics', *Europe-Asia Studies*, 32(4) 2000, pp. 723-739.

[45] The Rhsd has twenty one members, seven for each partner. Governmental representatives include the vice-prime minister and the ministers of Finance, Economy, Labour and Social Affairs, Health, Agriculture and Transport. The Unitary Trades unions Confederation (Koz) has six representatives, the Confederation for Arts and Culture (Kuk) just one, while employers' delegates are appointed by the Federation of the Unions and Associations of Employers of the Slovak Republic (see D. Malová and D. Siváková, 'The National Council of the Slovak Republic: The Developments of a National Parliament', in A. Ágh and G. Ilonszki (eds.), *Parliaments and Organised Interests: The Second Steps* (Budapest: Hungarian Centre for Democracy Studies, 1996), pp. 342-365; Organisation for Economic Cooperation and Development, *S.I.G.M.A. - Report on Slovakia* (Paris: OECD, 1999). The president and the secretary of the council are appointed by the government. Official criteria of representativeness are the presence in most economic sectors, a density of at least 10 per cent (of the labour force for the employers) and the presence in

at least five regions of the country (Act on Tripartism, Article 2).

[46]   However, Haller and Schaller detected a certain heterogeneity among the sectors, and a remarkable distance between peak authorities and the rank-and-file. Moreover, discontent is caused by the exclusion of smaller organisations from tripartite negotiations.

[47]   Haller and Schaller, '"Marktwirtschaft', p. 325.

[48]   European Commission, *Regular Report from the Commission on Progress towards Accession - Slovenia* (Brussels, 1998, 1999 and 2000).

[49]   Organisation for Economic Cooperation and Development, *S.I.G.M.A. - Report on Slovenia*, (Paris: OECD, 1999).

[50]   Organisation for Economic Cooperation and Development, *OECD Economic Survey - Slovenia* (Paris: OECD, 1997).

[51]   D. Fink-Hafner, 'Organised interests in the policy-making process in Slovenia', *Journal of European Public Policy*, 5(2) 1998, pp. 285-302.

[52]   Z. Vodovnik, 'The Transformation of Industrial Relations in Slovenia', *South East European Review*, 1(1) 1998, pp. 89-102; D. Fink-Hafner, 'Organised Interests as Policy Actors in Slovenia', in A. Ágh and G. Ilonszki (eds), *Parliaments and Organised Interests: The Second Steps* (Budapest: Hungarian Centre for Democracy Studies, 1996), pp. 222-240; D. Fink-Hafner, *Europeanisation of Slovenian Politics - The Europeanisation of Interest Groups and the Parliamentary Policy-Making Process*, paper presented at the ECPR Joint Sessions of Workshops, Mannheim, 26-31 March 1999.

[53]   M. Frybes, 'La mise en place de nouvelles régulations dans le domaine des relations du travail dans les sociétés de l'après-communismes. Expériences et tentative de bilan', *Revue de l'IRES*, (special issue) *Relations professionelles en Europe centrale*, (26) 1998.

[54]   F. Miszlivets and J. Jensen, 'An Emerging Paradox - Civil Society from Above?', in D. Rueschemeyer, M. Rueschemeyer and B. Wittrock (eds), *Participation and Democracy East and West: Comparisons and Interpretations* (London - Armonk (N.Y.), M. E. Sharpe, 1998).

[55]   M. Morjé Howard, *Free not to participate: the weakness of civil society in post-communist Europe*, Studies in Public Policy n. 325 (University of Strathclyde, Centre for the Study of Public Policy, 2000).

[56]   Cox and Mason, *Social and Economic Transformation*, p. 103.

[57]   D. Rueschemeyer, M. Rueschemeyer and B. Wittrock (eds), *Participation and Democracy East and West: Comparisons and Interpretations* (London - Armonk (N.Y.): M.E. Sharpe, 1998); W. Merkel, *Civil Society and Democratic Consolidation in Eastern Europe*, Budapest Papers on Democratic Transition n. 255, (Budapest: Hungarian Centre for Democracy Studies, 1999).

Antoaneta Dimitrova* and Rilka Dragneva**

Bulgaria's Road to the European Union: Progress, Problems and Perspectives

ABSTRACT

In this article we evaluate Bulgaria's progress in preparing for accession to the European Union and the country's achievements and problems related to it. Following from the examination of the most salient aspects of the relationship between Bulgaria and the EU, we argue that perceptions of the country in the West have not caught up with the recent considerable achievements in the areas of law reform, economic transformation and democratization. In doing that, we highlight the establishment of democratic and constitutional stability, the lack of ethnic conflict, and the adoption of a comprehensive legal framework for administrative reform and enhanced border control, as well as the country's role as a factor for regional stability in the Balkans. We further argue that, in addition to the domestic progress in the fulfillment of the Copenhagen criteria, other factors, such as geopolitics, perception and advocacy, influence Bulgaria's place in the current order of accession. Finally, we discuss the interaction between domestic politics and European integration as a two level game and argue that the link between the country's transformation and its accession to the EU helps to speed up the pace of reforms but can lead to a backlash if accession is delayed indefinitely.

Introduction

'"Well, in *our* country", said Alice, still panting a little, "you'd generally get to somewhere else - if you ran very fast for a long time as we've been doing."

"A slow sort of country!" said the Queen. "Now, *here*, you see, it takes all the running *you* can do, to keep in the same place. If you want to get somewhere else, you must run at least twice as fast as that!"' (Lewis Carol, *Through the Looking Glass*).

During the last decade, the post-communist states in Central and Eastern Europe have been struggling with the multiple transformation of their economies, political systems and statehood. Their main aspiration has been to make these transformations irreversible by joining the European Union, a symbol of prosperity and democracy and the long awaited 'return to Europe'. The ten year reform efforts of these countries have been 'rewarded' by invitations to start accession negotiations with the European Union issued by the European Council in Luxembourg in December 1997 and in Helsinki in December 1999.

Having experimented with various approaches towards organising this unprecedented accession of thirteen potential candidates,[1] the EU has recently hinted that ten candidates will join together in a first wave and two, Bulgaria and Romania, a few years afterwards. The *de facto* differentiation between candidates from the second group and Bulgaria and Romania has been expressed in several statements, among others by the Commissioner for Enlargement Verheugen in an interview with the *"Frankfurter Allgemeine Zeitung"* on 20 October 2000, predicting that "up to 10 countries" could join the EU by 2005 and that the only candidates unlikely to be admitted by that date are Bulgaria and Romania.[2] From a Bulgarian perspective, this scenario appears puzzling, as Bulgaria has made considerable efforts to fulfil the requirements associated with the Copenhagen criteria. Recent progress, however, has been overshadowed by past difficulties, Bulgaria's negative image and geographical location in the most unpopular and troublesome corner of Europe, the Balkans.

Should we evaluate Bulgaria's current placement in the implicit order of accession as the inevitable result of the EU's application of the Copenhagen criteria, which for the first time in the history of the EU's enlargements have presented candidates with a set of 'objective' conditions for accession?[3] Or are other factors such as perception, geopolitics and the EU's tendency to deal with countries in groups[4] also playing a considerable role?

We argue that, nowadays, despite achieving both internal stability and good external relations with its neighbours, Bulgaria is still seen by the West (and the EU in particular) through the lens of its Balkan location. Like a quiet pupil stuck in a corner with troublemakers, Bulgaria has not always been able to receive credit for its successful transition to democracy evaluated by the few interested commentators as peaceful and stable.[5] In this article we attempt to show that Bulgaria's efforts to join the EU have led to considerable progress in the country's political, economic and legal transformation, but that perceptions of the country are still largely lagging behind these developments. To illustrate this, the article will discuss the achievements, but also some stumbling blocks along Bulgaria's road to the EU. The first part of the article highlights the most important developments in the process of Bulgaria's accession to the EU, divided into two periods, before and after the application for membership. The second part focuses on the main achievements and the problems in this process, seen from the perspective of Bulgaria. The third section discusses the domestic politics of accession in relation to Bulgarian public opinion and the politicisation of certain issues of European integration. We finally argue that placing Bulgaria at the end of the queue of viable candidates for accession to the EU is not entirely related to Bulgaria's inability to comply with the Copenhagen criteria. Given that the overarching goal of the enlargement process has been the achievement of peace and stability in Europe and especially in the Balkans, Bulgaria's considerable efforts to contribute to regional stability and overcome the legacy of the past should be better recognised and encouraged.

1. Goalposts of the accession process

1.1. *From association agreement to application for membership*

In 1992-1993 Bulgaria negotiated with the EU its Association or 'Europe' Agreement. It was signed in March 1993 and still remains the main legal basis of its relationship with the Union.[6] The negotiations of the Association Agreement brought home the limits of the EU commitment to liberalisation of trade and enlargement. It marked, in the words of the chief negotiator on the Bulgarian side Ilko Eskenazi, the 'chilling of euphoria' regarding Bulgaria's integration into the European structures.[7] In the first place, there was no commitment by the EU that Association will lead to membership - something

that changed shortly afterwards at the European Council in Copenhagen in
June 1993. Secondly, the EU took a protectionist stance[8] and was too cautious
in liberalising trade in goods in which an applicant country might have a
comparative advantage - the so called 'sensitive goods': textiles, ferrous met-
als and agricultural products and wine, which was left out of the Bulgarian
agreement altogether.[9] According to Eskenazi, 'It came to tough bargaining
as regards agricultural products and there were instances when the fate of
this extremely important political and economic agreement depended on quotas and duties covering 100 tons of cherries or cucumbers'.[10]

While the mandate given to the European Commission in negotiating the
Association Agreements was restrictive for all CEE candidates, problems arose
with two other issues which were new to Bulgaria. The first was the introduction of a sophisticated suspension clause which provided for a suspension of the agreement in case of violation of human rights and democratic
principles.[11] The 'Bulgarian clause' was included for the first time in Bulgaria's
Europe Agreement - the other Europe agreements did not contain such clauses.
It provided for a suspension (with the possibility of arbitration) of the agreement in case of a violation of human rights and democratic principles on the
part of Bulgaria. Since then such a clause is included as a standard one in
EU agreements and even in the renegotiated agreements with the Czech
Republic and Slovakia after the split of Czechoslovakia.[12] In the case of
Bulgaria, the EU never had to resort to the suspension clause which became
rather unimportant in the light of the more comprehensive criteria for membership specified in Copenhagen in June 1993.

The second problem had to do with the delay in the implementation of the
trade liberalisation part of the Agreement. Because of their mixed nature the
Association agreements had to be ratified by all EU member states, a relatively long process. Meanwhile, the EU uses Interim trade agreements to
speed up the liberalisation of trade. The implementation of the Bulgarian
Interim trade agreement, however, was delayed by an internal EU wrangle
about anti-dumping competencies for almost a year. Its coming into force
was linked to decisions on anti-dumping policies inside the EU. By linking
the issue of the EC trade defence instruments and their efficiency to the operation of the Bulgarian Interim Trade agreement, some EU member states

increased the costs of the lack of decision on this issue. In the words of Alan Mayhew, who was at the time co-ordinator of the PHARE programme, the holding up of the Bulgarian trade agreement was 'extremely embarrassing for the EU' and had nothing to do with Bulgaria which was 'an innocent victim of an internal and very important Community dispute'.[13] Acknowledging this, the EU later decided to speed up liberalisation and removal of quotas to the level of the other Associated countries as a compensation for the lost time. The delay created a lot of frustration among Bulgarian political elites, expressed by former president Zhelev who said 'Bulgaria has become a hostage in disputes between Community "liberals" and "protectionists."'[14]

The other main policy tool of the EU for Central and Eastern Europe, the PHARE programme, has been less problematic and its functioning has improved with time. Early problems with Bulgaria's absorption capacity for PHARE funds have decreased as political blockages have been eliminated and public administration reform has finally taken off the ground in 1996-1997. Total commitment from the EU to Bulgaria under PHARE has amounted to 747 million Euro in the period 1990-1998.[15]

The Association Agreement and the PHARE programme created, despite the problems discussed above, a basis for relations with the EU similar to that of the other CEECs. Bulgaria's own progress in economic transformation, however, was insufficient to allow for the advancement of these relations. Over the period 1993-1996 the country experienced stagnation in reforms, and the rapid turnover of various governments, increased the perception of corruption. After a brief period of attempts at radical economic transformation under the first non-communist government led by Philip Dimitrov, successive cabinets delayed structural reform and privatisation. Economic decline followed, culminating in a dramatic economic crisis at the end of 1996. Inflation was in triple figures, the banking system was virtually brought to a halt, and the over exporting of grain by the Socialist government left the country almost without bread. The situation tested every aspect of the newly established democratic institutions in Bulgaria but also considerably damaged Bulgaria's bid to enter the EU.

1.2. *From application to negotiations: Bulgaria's true transition since 1997*

No progress towards accession to the EU was possible until the economic crisis was resolved. This resolution came about through an unprecedented popular mobilisation, as a series of demonstrations against the Videnov government rocked the country in the early 1997. The protesters demanded urgent measures to end the economic crisis as well as early elections. Despite the large scale of the protests, they remained peaceful save for isolated incidents. Bulgaria proved to itself, if not to the world, that its democratic institutions guaranteed stability even in politically turbulent times. In contrast to neighbouring Serbia, the governing Bulgarian Socialists resisted the temptation to quash the demonstrations and continue to govern without public support, and following days of street protest they finally agreed to early elections. One of several factors which influenced them at this critical juncture was their avowed pro-European orientation.[16] Most importantly, respect for the new Bulgarian Constitution of July 1991 was shown by all parties, including the Socialists who were unwilling to lose power but never used unconstitutional means to retain it. Early elections held in June 1997 were won by the Union of Democratic Forces, which formed the first democratic government in Bulgaria likely to serve a full term of office.

During this period of political turmoil, Bulgaria applied officially to join the EU on 14 December 1995. The application was submitted by the Bulgarian Socialist Party government led by Zhan Videnov. The European Commission's opinion on this application was presented in the Agenda 2000 in June 1997. Given that the economic situation in Bulgaria had only just started to improve after the crisis at the end of 1996, the Commission did not evaluate Bulgaria as ready to start accession talks in this document. Bulgaria was put into the second group of candidates, mostly on the strength - or rather weakness - of its economic performance.

The opinion of the Commission, at the same time, mobilised domestic effort and served as a clear reference point in identifying concrete measures. In response, Bulgaria adopted a National Strategy for Accession to the EU in March 1998.[17] The preparation of the country was further assisted by the Accession Partnership concluded between Bulgaria and the EU in 1999. This newly introduced instrument aims at providing a unified framework for intensified accession preparation. Based on the Commission Progress Report, the Partnership identified short- and medium-term priorities and linked them to conditional instruments for financial and structural assistance.[18]

Among short term priorities outlined in the Partnership were: integration of the Roma minority; restructuring of the nuclear power station Kozloduy; intensification of the restructuring of the economy and speeding the (transparent) privatisation process; judicial and administrative reform; adoption of measures against corruption and illegal immigration. In response, Bulgaria developed its National Programme for the Adoption of the *Acquis* and took a number of specific actions to address the short and medium term priorities, which we discuss in more detail below.

Alongside the institutional aspects of the process, the Kosovo crisis, and the Bulgarian response to it, provided an important boost to Bulgaria's position in the enlargement process. During the NATO campaign of 1999 Bulgaria strongly supported NATO actions at the risk of alienating its neighbour Serbia, as well as part of its own population. The Bulgarian Parliament mandated the government to negotiate specific measures in the context of NATO's peace-keeping actions in the region.[19] In April 1999, the government submitted a motion to allow NATO passage through Bulgarian airspace and radio space. This motion was challenged in front of the Constitutional Court by a group of deputies, but the Court upheld Bulgaria's Euro-Atlantic commitment.[20] The government stayed its course even after a number of chance hits on Bulgarian territory extended the campaign's already controversial "collateral damages".[21] The government's firm allegiance to NATO was further underlined by their refusal to let Russian planes pass through Bulgarian air space on their way to Pristina airport.

Aware of the political price it was paying at home for its pro-Western stance in the conflict and the defiance of former ally Russia, the Kostov government became more vocal in pressing its case for integration in Euro-Atlantic structures and looked for a more credible perspective for Bulgaria's accession to the EU. The EU offered such a perspective as the European Council in Helsinki in December 1999 invited all the candidates from the second group to start negotiations. This was interpreted, not only as a political invitation, based on Bulgaria's support for NATO's actions in Kosovo, but also as an acknowledgement of the progress the country had made. Actual negotiations started in March 2000, when six chapters of the *acquis* were opened. The progress to date, summarised in Table 1 below, is evaluated as good, given Bulgaria's later start. The intention of the Swedish Presidency is to open another nine chapters between January and June 2001. The Bulgarian government is more ambitious in aiming to open fourteen chapters and keep the momentum of the negotiations. The technical side of the process of negotiations, opening and closing of chapters, however, is not the most important aspect of the enlargement process. We would argue that this process is still, above all, a transformation process of profound magnitude. As such, it is subject to challenges and problems, not all of them necessarily of domestic character.

Table 1: Progress of negotiations

Chapter	Status
4: Free movement of capital	Open
5: Company law	Open
12: Statistics	Provisionally closed
16: Small and medium-sized enterprises	Provisionally closed
17: Science and research	Provisionally closed
18: Education and training	Provisionally closed
19: Telecommunications and information technologies	Open
20: Culture and audio-visual policy	Provisionally closed
23: Consumers and health protection	Provisionally closed
26: External relations	Provisionally closed
27: Common foreign and security policy	Provisionally closed

2. Main issues and problems in Bulgaria's accession process

2.1. *Economic reform and stabilisation*

As noted already, the pattern of economic performance and reform has greatly influenced Bulgaria's accession prospects. Since the low point of 1996 (see Table 2) there have now been a number of positive developments in the economy. A main policy priority of the UDF government of Ivan Kostov was to achieve a reversal of the negative trends in the economy and later to create conditions for increased economic growth.

The main instrument for macroeconomic stabilisation was the currency board, introduced in the middle of 1997 with IMF support, pegging the Bulgarian currency to the German mark and, subsequently, to the Euro. Despite some dissenting voices over the political acceptability of the loss of independence in state finance, inherent to the currency board mechanism, the government succeeded in putting it in place. As Table 2 shows, the board was successful in helping to create lower inflation, a reduction in the budget deficit and public debt. Equally important, it helped to maintain standards of financial and banking discipline, to engage in a prudent fiscal policy, and increase currency reserves. Bank privatisation has advanced and competitiveness has improved due to some foreign bank penetration. Efforts have been made to set up credible capital markets and improve standards for transparency and disclosure.

Financial stabilisation was accompanied by a programme for comprehensive restructuring, privatisation and other measures to encourage private sector development. The process is still in progress, but some of the early results, demonstrated in Table 2, testify to the effects of the policy. Most importantly, a positive growth trend can already be observed. The value added by the private sector amounts to a significant part of it. There is an increase in investment in capital equipment as well as a growth in foreign direct investment flows.

Table 2: Economic performance

	1996	1999
Real GDP growth rate	-10.1	2.4
CPI inflation (average)	123.0	2.6
Budget balance (%GDP)	-15.3	-0.9
Foreign debt/exports ratio (%)	168.9	180.7*
Public debt (%GDP)	124.6	71.0*
Current account (%GDP)	0.9	-5.3
Trade with EU (%total)	37.6	52.0
Share of private sector (%)	45.0	65.3
FDI flows (%GDP)	1.1	6.3
Fixed investment (%GDP)	13.6	15.9
Unemployment (%)	13.7	17.0

* Estimate

Sources: European Commission, 2000 Regular Report; ING Barings, Report on EU Enlargement and Convergence, March 2000.

The general improvement in the economy, shown by the indicators above, has been noted by the European Commission in its yearly Progress Reports, although it concludes in the 2000 Report that Bulgaria does not yet have all the characteristics of a market economy. The outlook, however, is evaluated as good, given the continuation of structural reforms. Other external sources, such as the IMF, have similarly been cautiously optimistic. Upon the completion of IMF's Fourth Bulgaria Review in September 2000, Acting IMF Chairman Stanley Fischer noted that

> the Bulgarian authorities have continued to follow prudent fiscal and incomes policies and to advance in the process of structural reform . . . In 2000-01 GDP growth is expected to reach the highest rates in a decade. To sustain both rapid growth and the transition to a full market economy, the authorities need to continue their strong policy efforts on a wide front.[22]

Clearly there is still a long way to go in terms of improvements to the economy. The world of the real economy, down to individual households, is the ultimate test for achievement in reform. As Stanley Fischer noted after commending the efforts of the government, 'in the face of these real policy improvements, it is understandably frustrating that the benefits are not being felt more tangibly . . .'.[23] That is especially true in the face of persisting high level of unemployment, currently at about 17 per cent. It is also true that the observed economic improvement is not too remarkable relative to those of other transition economies. This, however, should be balanced with the immense progress made compared to the severity of the 1996 crisis. As MEP Elmar Brok observed in 1998, 'If I compare to that the figures for 1997 or 1996, what was achieved is close to a miracle'.[24]

Economic performance has not been determined by domestic factors alone. The pegging of the national currency to the Euro was a clear signal of the country's declared long-term economic re-orientation and was accompanied by growing trade re-orientation to the EU. The depreciation of the Euro, however, despite IMF hedging, has had an impact on Bulgaria's ability to finance external trade and to service its debts, as the larger part of them are denominated in US dollars. Another major negative factor was the Kosovo crisis which damaged trade relations in the region following the Yugoslav embargo.[25]

Thus, Bulgaria has already started sharing in the risks of economic integration and liberalisation.

Despite the commitment to an ambitious reform programme, a more visible improvement of the business environment in Bulgaria remains to be seen. The country's determination to complete the economy's transformation into a successful market economy, however, is likely to continue if supported by credible prospects for accession. In contrast to the economic transformation, the establishment of stable democratic institutions has ran more smoothly and more successfully than expected and evaluated as good already in the second Commission progress report in 1998.

2.2. Democratic stability

Overall evaluations of Bulgaria's progress in terms of fulfilling the political criterion in Copenhagen from the EU and from Bulgaria are positive. There is little doubt that despite the severe tests to which the newly established political institutions were subjected in the past few years, they have shown to be functioning democratic institutions, capable of preserving both the fragile new democracy and stability in the country.

The most important factor in terms of the creation of a stable system of democratic institutions has been the adoption of the new Constitution of 1991, which, despite some criticism at the time, has served as a pillar for the new democracy and ensured both stability and the integrity of the electoral process.[26] Elections have been regular, free and fair. The rule of law and the separation of power have been maintained, with the significant contribution of a new institution, the Constitutional Court. Constitutional Courts have been important in the development of most post communist countries. In Bulgaria, the Court not only proved to be a reliable guarantor of the principles of the Constitution and the rights of minorities, but also prevented pre-1997 policies aiming at the reversal of the reforms, and direct attacks on the independence of the judiciary.[27]

An important issue to be discussed in the context of Bulgarian democracy is minority rights. It cannot be stressed enough that overall, in terms of ethnic relations, Bulgaria has presented a peaceful *Balkan* alternative to the ethnic unrest and violent conflict elsewhere in the region. The peaceful resolution of ethnic problems post 1989 was not a small achievement given that the Turkish minority had been mobilised by the discriminatory communist campaign of the 1980s, which changed Turkish names to Bulgarian ones, claiming that Turks were Bulgarians who had been converted to Islam in the 14th century.[28] In contrast to the repressive 'name revival campaign', which was immediately condemned by all major political forces post 1989, no significant ethnic conflicts occurred after the fall of communism, and ethnic problems were resolved though debate in the political arena. This has been facilitated greatly by the fact that the Turkish population has had representation in Parliament through the Movement of Rights and Freedoms party which has gathered about eight per cent of the vote in most elections to date. In a landmark decision of 1991, the Constitutional Court defended the constitutionality of this party and upheld its right to stand in parliamentary elections, despite the ban (in Art. 11.4 of the Constitution) on parties created on a religious or ethnic basis.[29]

In contrast to the Turkish minority which has been well represented in the political arena, the most disadvantaged minority have been the Roma. They have suffered poverty, social exclusion, and in a number of documented cases, condemned by the European Court of Human Rights, acts of police brutality.[30] In the last few years, some more serious efforts have been made to ensure the integration of the Roma population, including the creation of the National Council for Ethnic Problems, which proposed a National Programme for Roma integration adopted in April 1999. Despite these efforts, more remains to be done for the improvement of the situation of the Roma, which is also being closely monitored by the EU.

Apart from the Roma, the Commission's most serious criticism with respect to the first Copenhagen criterion relates to the insufficient reform of the judiciary.[31] A number of factors account for this unfinished reform. One is that the judiciary proved to be a major battle-ground of transition politics. For example, as country reports on Bulgaria in the 1995-1996 issues of *East European Constitutional Review* show, the government of Zhan Videnov not only interfered with the independence of the judiciary by attempting to influence its composition, but also restricted its budget and use of premises. As a result, prior to 1997, most changes were limited to appointments and only touched upon the comprehensive institutional restructuring of the system required by the 1991 Constitution.[32] Similarly, the adoption of procedural laws to underpin its functioning was postponed. Major improvements of the Civil Litigation Code, for example, were introduced only in 1997. Since that date significant progress has been achieved in terms of completing the regulatory framework and addressing problems of administration, material support and recruitment - but the starting position has been quite low.

This slow reform of the judiciary reflects a more general problem typical of the early transition thinking dominated by neo-liberal approaches to transformation, namely focusing on liberalisation and privatisation and underestimating the role of institutions. The 'transition orthodoxy' with its emphasis on withdrawal of the state and 'self-enforcing' models of governance contributed to the neglect of judicial reform as a policy priority.[33]

Despite the remaining economic and political problems, it can be said that the transition to democracy in Bulgaria has been accomplished. This, however, does not mean the work of reformist elites is over in their attempt to achieve depth and quality to the Bulgarian democracy and to maintain the legitimacy and public support of the institutions.

A serious challenge is maintaining the rule of law, in the sense of strict adherence to a set of formal rules, at every level of society. The rule of law is achieved not only through the availability of written legislation. Bulgaria has managed to prove that it is able to cope with an impressive legislation drafting agenda. Nonetheless, like other post-communist countries, it still needs to promote a culture of law-abiding citizenship and to provide for the development of a new civic paradigm behind the process of formal transformation.[34]

One of the most visible manifestations of the underdeveloped civil culture and a factor undermining public trust in institutions, is corruption - although its exact levels are difficult to estimate. The most recent administrative reform, which has recently beedn adopted, aims to curb this phenomenon in the longer term.

2.3. *Administrative reform, efforts to fight corruption, immigration and asylum laws*

Bulgaria has recently made serious strides in its administrative reform, although this process has been difficult. First steps were made by the Videnov government in 1995. A strategy was adopted in 1996, but after the Videnov government resigned in the midst of the economic crisis in 1996, little was made of this strategy.[35] The main legal framework underpinning the reform was finally adopted by the Kostov government in 1998-2000.

The causes for the delay in adopting this basic legal framework for a professional and depoliticised administration must be laid at the feet of Bulgarian political elites, and external advisers. Domestically, several Bulgarian governments between 1990 and 1997, have replaced considerable numbers of top and middle level officials in the administration. This was presented as reform, but has often been the result of politically motivated decisions taken in an absence of clear dismissal criteria. On the other hand, external advice on reform did not focus on the role of the administration till the mid 1990s. Thus, a similar argument to those discussed with regard to the judiciary, applies to the problems of public administration reform.

The last few years have marked a new commitment to introducing the principles of professionalism and independence. The necessary regulatory framework was completed with the adoption of the Administration Act of November 1998 and the Civil Service Act of 1999, a number of secondary instruments, and the 1999 amendments to the 1991 Local Self-Rule and Local Administration Act. Explicit standards for discharging civil servants' functions were set up, underpinned by a system of disciplinary measures and oversight by the State Administrative Commission established in 2000. These standards are supplemented by a package of anti-corruption measures. They range from eliminating instances which might invite corruption, such as removal of a host of licensing regimes, to improved disclosure of interests, such as the 2000 Public Register Act requiring high officials to provide a declaration of their property and income, and to stricter imposition of sanctions and procedural guarantees as required by the 2000 Tax Procedure Code and the 2000 amendments to the Penal Code.

The latter measures have a particular importance with regard to the functioning of customs authorities and border police. Clearly, reforming these is also aimed at relieving EU fears of illegal immigration and commodities traffic. A further comprehensive set of legislative and administrative measures aimed to alleviate such fears was introduced after 1997. A new Law on Foreigners in Bulgaria was adopted in December 1998, specifying the rules and procedures for admission. The 1999 Law on Asylum Seekers incorporates the international law rules in that area. In addition, a new Law adopted in 1998 on Bulgarian Identity Documents, introduced new identity cards and passports which are less prone to fraud and falsification.

Regarding the task of administrative support for European integration, a new three level institutional framework was established in January 2000 as part of the National Programme for the Adoption of the *Acquis*. The new framework establishes central co-ordinating units and aims for stronger horizontal co-ordination between ministries, while at the same time preserving the important role the Ministry of Foreign Affairs has played so far in the process. Thirty-one working groups which have been set up in the ministries form the basis of the structure. Their work is co-ordinated by the new Department for European Integration and Relations with International Financial Institutions, which is directly attached to the Council of Ministers. The Prime Minister chairs the new Council for European Integration at ministerial level, which oversees the work of the Co-ordination Council for European Integration at deputy minister level. The institution responsible for Parliamentary oversight and draft legislation is the Parliamentary Committee for European Union Affairs.

Despite the creation of these structures and the progress in administrative reform in general, there are still doubts expressed by the European Commission regarding Bulgaria's horizontal co-ordination capacities and its general ability to implement the *acquis*. While the criticism regarding the delay in administrative reform is justified, general doubts regarding the ability of candidates to create the administrative capacity to implement the *acquis* adequately should be taken with a grain of salt. This is an area in which no fixed criteria exist, and even the Commission itself has not yet developed a comprehensive system for evaluating progress,[36] a gap which is only partially filled by the guidelines developed by the SIGMA group of the OECD. Thus, at least at present, progress is particularly susceptible to the perceptions and experiences of those evaluating it. We believe that especially in the light of the implementation deficit existing in current member states, the issue of lack of administrative capacity in Bulgaria or other candidates should not be exaggerated.

2.4. *A factor for regional stability*

The lack of violent domestic ethnic conflict or external disputes with its neighbours, as well as the proactive policy in regional groupings and initiatives, such as the Black Sea Co-operation, have made Bulgaria a factor for regional stability in the Balkans. It has improved relations with Turkey, not least due to its efforts to improve the situation of the Turkish minority in Bulgaria post 1989. It has become a member of CEFTA and the Stability Pact for South Eastern Europe. Its pro-active position in favour of all forms of regional integration has been consistent with the EU's efforts to maintain regional stability. Furthermore, as described above, the country has firmly maintained its pro-NATO orientation in foreign policy and supported NATO actions in Kosovo. Since then, it has been active in normalising relations with the new Yugoslav government.

Currently, however, Bulgaria's main concern is to ensure that regional forms of integration favoured in the Balkans do not replace its goal of becoming a EU member. The challenges which Bulgaria faces as part of the Balkans brings us to our discussion of a different category of factors influencing accession, factors such as geopolitics, advocacy and perception, for the most part beyond the country's control.

2.5. *Advocacy and perception*

Such factors are more difficult to pin down as they are not to be found in official documents and institutional evaluations. Nonetheless it is our argument that they play their role in the making of overarching political choices in this enlargement process. The first one, perception, is linked to the image of the Balkans. The designation 'Balkans' has come to bear multiple negative connotations - most recently as a result of the wars of former Yugoslavia. This is also seen in the construction of the idea of the Balkans as the 'other', a construct often posed to distinguish Central Europe from the Balkans and to perpetuate the myth that Central Europe is a part of (Western) Europe[37] - a process emancipatory for Poland or Hungary but damaging for Bulgaria or Romania. Perceptions of Bulgaria's 'otherness' were further reinforced by ideas of the cultural and political importance of the Roman Catholic - Orthodox divide for the development of democracy, ideas made popular by Samuel Huntington.[38] Zhelyu Zhelev, Bulgaria's first democratically elected President, tried somewhat in vain to combat such ideas by stating , 'The artificial division of the former socialist countries into "Byzantium European" and "Roman Catholic European" which has been promoted recently by some European politicians, revives a pattern of thinking dating back to the time of emperor Constantine'.[39]

The second set of factors, geopolitics and advocacy, relates to the fact that none of Bulgaria's neighbours has taken up the role of a champion of the country's accession, as Germany has done for Poland, Hungary and the Czech Republic or Sweden and Denmark for the Baltics. Although the European Commission tries to assure candidates of the objective nature of the process and to stress that progress according to the Copenhagen criteria and the EU's own readiness are the only variables influencing accession, some evidence suggests otherwise. As Friis points out, during the Madrid European Council in December 1995, former German Chancellor Kohl tried to push for a decision committing the EU to start negotiations with Poland, Hungary and the Czech Republic first.[40] Friis also describes the role of Sweden and Denmark in pushing the case for the Baltic states to join this group. Similarly, Alan Mayhew points out the historical links between France and Romania, which have led France to champion the interests of Romania in the enlargement process.[41] Bulgaria's only neighbour which is a current EU member, Greece, has not so far played such a role, as it has focused its lobbying efforts on Cyprus instead. Thus, as admitted privately by EU officials, Bulgaria almost alone among all candidates, lacks a strong champion among the current member states and this is a significant factor which may slow down its accession. Such a delay has its own dangers, which are linked to the Bulgarian electoral cycle and the challenges to domestic elites to maintain their public support for joining the EU. The following section examines the domestic politics of Bulgaria and the European issue.

3. Domestic politics and enlargement in Bulgaria

As Bulgaria moves closer to accession, with a self imposed target of joining in 2006, those who have been the greatest advocates of the process, political elites and the UDF government, are also those who have expressed the most reservations and criticism towards the EU. This apparent paradox can be resolved if we see the actions of the government as a two level game.[42] Similarly to politicians in the EU member states, the government justifies domestically unpopular reforms with EU requirements, while at the same time tries to push for accession in Brussels by pointing to domestic political difficulties associated with EU led reform. This strategy is an adequate response to EU's own strategy of promoting democracy through conditionality and enlarge-ment.[43] By establishing a firm link between the success of reforms and the success of enlargement, both strategies contain the risk of a backlash in the case of interminable delays in accession. This danger is evoked by those who insist on the EU keeping to a timetable of accession and fear the goalposts may be moved by the addition of further conditions by one or another member state. Given the implied assumption of Bulgaria's late accession, it is even more real for Bulgaria.

So far support for accession remains sufficiently strong among the electorate and all political parties. While it was the UDF government, led by Ivan Kostov, that made the decisive effort to bring the country to its current position in the accession talks, there is no major political party in Bulgaria which opposes European integration. The leadership of the Bulgarian Socialist Party, the main opposition party at the moment, has broken, at least officially, with pro-Russian orientations of the past and declared itself pro-EU and pro-NATO. It was a Socialist government which submitted Bulgaria's official application to join the EU.

Among the public, the levels of support for accession to the EU in Bulgaria are high, but this support is still rather shallow and not based on sufficient knowledge of the EU. According to a national representative survey from 10 December 1999 by the National Centre for Public Opinion research (NCPO), 77 per cent of Bulgarians would say 'Yes' to European integration and only 7 per cent 'No', but at the same time 30 per cent state that they don't feel and behave like 'Europeans'.

Two issues linked to the EU requirements in the process of accession have tested the support of the public and the commitment of political elites to European integration. The first one was the issue of the Bulgarian nuclear power station Kozloduy, whose old reactors 1-4 are due to be closed in the period 2003-2006 according to the current agreement between Bulgaria and the EU.[44] The adoption of a timetable for the gradual closure of the station, starting with its Chernobyl type reactors, was one of the main conditions set by the EU to Bulgaria in the run up to the Helsinki invitation to start negotiations.

The setting of such a condition, to Bulgaria and other candidate countries,[45] could be seen as an additional criterion in this enlargement process, since nuclear safety and standards are national policies for the existing EU member states. Furthermore, there is no uniform EU standard to which the applicant countries have to conform, although the Vienna European Council has asked the Commission to develop such criteria.[46] Nevertheless, the requirements to close important energy providers could be considered as discriminatory by the candidate countries. Not without reluctance, the Bulgarian government has agreed to adopt a timetable for closing one of the major sources of electricity supplies in the country, and sought funds for the reconstruction of the station.

The second, possibly the most politicised issue with regard to the EU to date, was the issue of freedom of movement restricted by the visas required for Bulgarians (and also Romanians) visiting EU member states, especially member states of the Schengen group. In contrast to Poland, Hungary, the Czech Republic and Slovakia, which had visa free travel for their citizens as soon as they signed Association agreements with the EU, Bulgaria and Romania were too late to have the restrictions on their citizens lifted, and became the target of immigration fears. The issue became highly politicised. Queuing for days in front of EU embassies and the slow and overly bureaucratic visa procedures made travel to the EU, not only a difficult but also a humiliating experience for Bulgarians. In 1997-2000, the Kostov government conducted a vigorous diplomatic campaign aiming to influence the EU Council of Justice and Internal Affairs Ministers to remove the visa regime for Bulgarians and harmonise it with the practice of the other candidates. The Kostov government and the Prime Minister himself argued that Bulgaria had fulfilled the requirements and conditions set by the EU[47] and that a refusal on the part of the EU to accept this would be discriminatory and would mean that Bulgaria was not perceived as part of Europe's geopolitical space.[48]

Similarly, public opinion polls conducted in the capital suggested that two thirds of Sofia citizens found that they were discriminated against by the EU. At the same time, 62 per cent of respondents were convinced that Bulgaria should continue working to fulfil the EU's' criteria for membership. EU fears of great waves of immigrants if the visas were removed seemed unfounded as 61 per cent of respondents declared that they never tried to emigrate and would not want to live and work abroad.[49]

The Council of Justice and Internal Affairs Ministers decided on 30 November 2000 to remove visa restrictions for Bulgarians.[50] The decision was greeted as a recognition of Bulgaria's efforts by all political parties in the country. However, some worrying aspects of the EU debate were represented by some member states requiring that the visa question should be solved for Bulgaria and Romania simultaneously, regardless of the progress either country had made in fulfilling EU requirements. This is indicative of the kind of problems which can arise by the EU's traditional approach to deal with countries in groups. Regarding, not only this issue but the entire enlargement process, Prime Minister Kostov expressed a wide-spread concern that Bulgaria's progress might be measured with the lowest common denominator of the integration effort of the countries of the region.[51]

Thus, the danger exists that Bulgaria's accession to the EU could be impeded by factors beyond its control.[52] The whole enlargement process may be considerably slowed down after the entry of the first group of candidates. We believe that in the face of such risks it is especially important for the EU to keep in focus the relative importance of the criteria and factors influencing enlargement and the initial rationale of enlargement - stability.

Conclusions

Our concluding discussion of the progress and problems of the enlargement process, as viewed from Bulgaria, does not differ much, on the whole, from the European Commission's evaluation in its Progress Report.[53] Our perspective on the whole process, however, is different. Among the four big areas singled out by the Copenhagen criteria, Bulgaria's comparative position to most countries in the second group is weakest in the economic sphere. The current ordering produced by the Commission's latest progress report also seems to be predominantly led by the economic criterion, although this has been denied by Commission officials.[54] We have to question, however, whether an accession led by economic considerations alone can best ensure stability in Central and Eastern Europe. Secondly, it is not clear whether candidates with comparable achievements situated in the Baltics or Central Europe would be similarly left behind.

We would argue against such a scenario: on the whole, Bulgaria has made remarkable progress in its transformation in the last three years, inspired by a hope for joining the EU. There has also been good progress in complying with the Copenhagen criteria, and a clear realisation that a lot remains to be done. Even though its progress has been noted by the Commission in its third yearly report, little has changed in terms of the perception, that Bulgaria is one of the candidates hopelessly stuck at the end of the queue for accession. While it is true that the government's self imposed target is accession in 2006-2007, this target cannot be achieved without continued public support, which in turn cannot be maintained without some positive signals from the EU. If no such signals are given, the possibility of the development of isolationist and Euro-sceptic discourses is only too real.[55] Keeping Bulgaria indefinitely in the queue for accession has the potential of not only diminishing the support for European integration in the country but, in an extreme scenario, of undoing some of the progress in the country's transformation.

This domestic argument in favour of a more pro-active attitude of the EU towards Bulgaria is supplemented by the international one. The disadvantage of Bulgaria's geopolitical position can be turned into an advantage by the EU if the country becomes a positive example for other countries in the region. So far Bulgaria has been a factor of stability in the Balkans and a positive example for the countries in the South Western Balkans, some of which are still in the grip of nationalism. The European Union would serve its goal of exporting stability in the Balkans well by admitting Bulgaria sooner rather than later.

Notes

* Leiden University, Department of Public Administration, e-mail: <u>Dimitrova@fsw.lei-</u><u>denuniv.nl</u>; **Leiden University, Faculty of Law, Institute of East European Law and Russian Studies, e-mail: R.O.Dragneva@law.leidenuniv.nl. Antoaneta Dimitrova would like to thank the Netherlands Organization for Scientific Research (NWO) for their financial support.

1 According to the Commission's initial proposal the Luxembourg European Council differentiated between the candidates which were divided into a first and a second group. The first group, consisting of Czech Republic , Poland, Hungary, Estonia, and Slovenia was deemed ready to start negotiations, whereas Bulgaria, Latvia, Lithuania, Romania, and Slovakia were evaluated as 'pre-in's, not ready to negotiate. The decisions of the Helsinki European Council in 1999 invited also the second group, plus Cyprus and Malta, to negotiate according to the so-called 'regatta principle'.

2 *Radio Free Europe/Radio Liberty Newsline,* 20 October 2000.

3 These are: (1) the stability of institutions guaranteeing democracy, the rule of law, human rights and respect for and protection of minorities; (2) the existence of a functioning market economy, capable of coping with competitive pressures and market forces within the Union; (3) the ability to take on the obligations of membership, including adherence to its aims of political, economic and monetary union. (Copenhagen European Council, Conclusions of the Presidency, *Bulletin of the European Union*). The European Council decisions in Madrid in 1994 have also added administrative capacity to implement the '*acquis* communautaire' as a condition.

4 C. Preston, *Enlargement and Integration in the European Union* (London: Routledge, 1997), p. 21.

5 According to Linz and Stepan, for example, Bulgaria overperformed democratically in its transition to democracy, especially given the near ideal type of totalitarian regime which the country had before 1989. See J. Linz and A. Stepan, *Problems of Democratic Transition and Consolidation: Southern Europe, South America and Post-Communist Europe* (Baltimore and London: The Johns Hopkins University Press, 1996), p. 342.

6 Association agreements of this type are mixed agreements containing provisions for liberalisation of trade and for political dialogue. The Agreement also contained provisions for harmonisation and created institutions such as the Association Council and the Joint Parliamentary Committee. These have had a beneficial effect in socialising politicians in the way in which the EU operates (see A. Dimitrova, 'The Role of the European Union in the Process of Democratization in Central and Eastern Europe: Lessons from Bulgaria and Slovakia.') *Doctoral Thesis* (University of Limerick, 1998), p. 213.

7   I. Eskenazi. 'Bulgarian Association with the EC' in *Bulgaria and the European Community*, 30 September - 1 October 1993, (Sofia: Center for European Studies, 1993).

8   H. Kramer 'The European Community's response to the "new Eastern Europe"' *Journal of Common Market Studies*, 31 (2), June 1993, pp. 213-244.

9   'It was after the European Agreement was endorsed that negotiations on wine started' see Eskenazi, 'Bulgarian Association', p. 52.

10 Eskenazi, 'Bulgarian Association', p. 52.

11 European Commission, Commission Communication, 'On the Inclusion of respect for democratic principles and human rights in agreements between the Community and third countries', COM (95) 216, Brussels: 1995.

12 Commission Communication of May 1995 (*On the inclusion of respect for democratic principles and human rights in agreements between the Community and third countries'*, COM (95) 216) required all agreements concluded by the Communities to include clauses allowing them to suspend the application of an agreement on partnership, association or co-operation, or to take other adequate measures in case of breach of human rights and democratic principles stipulated also in the preamble of the agreements.

13 A. Mayhew, Speech at the opening of the conference 'Bulgaria and the European Community' 30 September - 1 October 1993, Sofia. *Conference Papers* 1 (Sofia: Center for European Studies, 1993), p. 15.

14 Zhelev, Zhelyu, Speech at the opening of the conference, 'Bulgaria and the European Community', 30 September - 1 October 1993, Sofia. *Conference Papers* 1 (Sofia: Center for European Studies, 1993), p. 11; See also Eskenazi, 'Bulgarian Association', p. 44.

15 European Commission, *Enlargement as a Historic Opportunity* (Brussels, 1999).

16 A. Dimitrova, 'The Role of the European Union', p. 222.

17 The National Strategy is available on http://www.government.bg/eng/index.html.

18 Despite their role in assisting local reform efforts, there have been doubts expressed regarding the Accession Partnerships' legal status and the potential unilateral imposition of EU priorities through them. See Sedelmeier, U. and H. Wallace, 'Eastern Enlargement: Strategy or Second Thoughts?' in H. Wallace and W. Wallace (eds.), *Policy making in the European Union*, (4th ed.) (Oxford: Oxford University Press, 2000), p. 452.

19 'Declaration of 23 October 1998', published in *State Gazette*, No. 125, 1998.

20 'Decision of 3 May 1999', published in *State Gazette* No. 41/1999.

21 *Kapital*, 7 May ('Is there a Pilot in the Plane?') and 14 May 1999.

22 'IMF Completes Fourth Bulgaria Review an Approves US$ 68 Million Credit', *IMF News Brief*, No. 00/84 8 September 2000, at http://www.imf.org/external/np/sec/nb/2000/nb0084.htm visited 10 January 2000.

[23]   Stanley Fisher, 'The Lessons of Reform - Ten Years On, Lecture at the University for National and World Economy', May 2000, at http://www.imf.org/external/np/speeches/2000/052500.htm.

[24]   E. Brok, 'Europe Ahead of Its Political and Economic Reorganisation' (European Meetings, Centre for European Studies) see, http://www.cesbg.org/docs/brok.doc.

[25]   As Sedelmeier and Wallace point out, Bulgaria and Romania's fragile economies have been considerably damaged by the Yugoslav wars. See, U. Sedelmeie and H. Wallace, 'Eastern Enlargement: Strategy', p. 455.

[26]   T. Verheijen, *Constitutional Pillars for New Democracies* (Leiden: DSWO Press, 1995); V. Ganev, 'Bulgaria's Symphony of Hope'. *Journal of Democracy*, 8 (4), 1997, pp. 125-40. The text of the Constitution can be found at http://home.digesta.com/p/3110.asp.

[27]   H. Schwarz, *The Struggle for Constitutional Justice in Post-Communist Europe*. (London: The University of Chicago Press, 2000).

[28]   This campaign, initiated by Zhivkov and his interior minister Stoyanov, is currently the subject of reniewed debate in Bulgaria, aiming at bringing surviving participants to justice. See *RFE/RL* 'Endnote', 9 January 2001.

[29]   For an extended discussion see Country Profile, *East European Constitutional Review*, 1 (1), 1992, p. 11.

[30]   The latest case Nikolova versus Bulgaria (No. 31195/96) was decided in March 1999 and relates to violations of the role of the investigator and prosecutor in ordering detention and the scope of its court revision.

[31]   *European Commission, 2000 Regular Report*, pp. 16-17.

[32]   For an extended discussion of the characteristics of pre-1998 judicial system and the main issues in the process of its reform, see R. Dragneva, 'Legal Preconditions for Contractual Relations in the Transition to a Market Economy: the Case of Bulgaria', Institute of Development Studies Bulletin, volume 29(3) 1998.

[33]   Many examples can be given regarding policy choices in the area of privatisation and corporate governance, i.e. B. Black and R. Kraakman, 'A Self-Enforcing Model of Corporate Law', *Harvard Law Review*, 109, 1996, pp. 1911-1982.

[34]   One appreciates the slow speed of the changes in societal values and behaviour when reminded of the ideological and declaratory rather than regulatory role of law under communism, elaborated upon by F. Feher, A. Heller, and G. Markus, *Dictatorship over Needs* (Oxford: OUP, 1983), or V. Havel in his famous essay, *The Power of the Powerless* (English version published by Unwin Hyman, 1985).

[35]   J.J. Hesse, Y. Venna and T. Verhejien, *Strategy Options for Public Administration Reform in Central and Eastern Europe: An Assessment of the Current Situation and Recommendations for Future PHARE Strategy* (Oxford: Nuffield College, 1997).

[36]   Interview with Eneko Landaburu, Director General of DG Enlargement, 17 November 2000.

[37] The construction of the myth of 'central Europe' in opposition first to Russia and then to the Balkans has been documented carefully by Todorova, *Imagining the Balkans* (Oxford: Oxford University Press, 1997). Evidence of the construction of the myth of Central Europe is also to be found in Elster, Offe and Preuss, *Institutional Design in Post Communist Societies* (Cambridge: CUP, 1998), p. 46. They cite Miszlivetz who remarked that, 'Central Europe became a programme which allowed one to distinguish oneself from "the barbarians"'.

[38] S. Huntington, 'The Clash of Civilizations?' *Foreign Affairs*, 72, (3) Summer 1993, pp. 23-49.

[39] Z. Zhelev, Speech at the opening of the conference 'Bulgaria and the European Union' (Sofia: Centre for European Studies, 1993), p. 11.

[40] L. Friis, 'The End of the Beginning of Eastern Enlargement - Luxembourg Summit and Agenda Setting, *European Integration online Papers (EIoP)* 2 (7), 1997, p. 6, at http://eiop.or.at/eiop/texte/1998-007a.htm consulted at 27 November 2000.

[41] A. Mayhew, *Recreating Europe: The European Union's Policy Towards Central and Eastern Europe* (Cambridge: CUP, 1999).

[42] R. Putnam, 'Diplomacy and Domestic Politics: the Logic of Two Level Games' *International Organization*'; 42 (3), Summer 1988, pp. 427-460.

[43] L. Whitehead, 'The Enlargement of the European Union: A "Risky" Form of Democracy Promotion', *Central European Political Science Review*, 1 (1), September 2000, p. 17.

[44] European Parliament, Committee on the Environment, Public Health and Consumer Policy, 2000.

[45] Similar requirements were put to Slovakia, the Czech republic, Lithuania and Slovenia.

[46] European Parliament, 'Committee on the Environment'.

[47] Among others, the replacement of foreign travel passports with less fraud sensitive documents, the conclusion of re-admission agreements with EU member states, and so on.

[48] I. Kostov, 'Speech in Parliament' 10 November 2000 at http://www.government.bg/bg/cm/index.html; http://www.government.bg/eng/primeminister/index.html

[49] A survey representative for the city of Sofia, conducted by Alfa Research in the period of 7-9 November 2000 (*Kapital*, No. 45, November 2000).

[50] The decision is still subject to the European Parliament's approval.

[51] I. Kostov, statement reported by the *Bulgarian Telegraph Agency*, 20 November 2000.

[52] Another important factor which we do not address here is the EU's own preparation for enlargement and institutional reform which has been made a *de facto* pre-condition for enlargement. See, Sedelmeie and Wallace, 'Eastern Enlargement: Strategy', pp. 446-447).

53 Commission progress report.
54 Interview with Eneko Landaburu, Director General for Enlargement, 17 November 2000.
55 See the forthcoming study of discourses on democracy in Central and Eastern Europe, J. Dryzek and L. Holmes, *Postcommunist Democratization* (Cambridge: CUP, 2001).

David Phinnemore

Stuck in the 'Grey Zone'? - Fears and Frustrations in Romania's Quest for EU Membership*

ABSTRACT

Since 1990, concerns have been expressed in Romania that the EU and NATO have little intention of extending their membership to include Romania and look set to consign the country to a 'grey zone' of economic, political and social instability in southeastern Europe. In recent years these concerns have intensified as the EU has introduced renewed differentiation into its relations with central and eastern Europe (CEE) through its approach to enlargement. As a consequence, and with the west showing little interest in providing Romania with tangible rewards for its support in 1999 during the Kosovo crisis, frustration has emerged as a key characteristic of Romania's relations with the EU. The article examines the reasons behind the frustration and assesses the extent to which Romania should fear the possibility of being stuck in a 'grey zone'. Attention is drawn to the EU's attempts to promote inclusiveness in its approach to eastern enlargement and the reasons why Romania has arguably benefited from these. This is accompanied by an analysis of how Romania's position in the EU's accession process has evolved with attention being drawn to the conditionality used by the EU to justify Romania's position therein. The final part of the article examines a series of issues which are likely to figure in the development of Romania's membership prospects and which could result in frustration persisting as a hallmark of Romania's relations with the EU.

Introduction

Since the collapse of the Ceaucescu regime in December 1989, Romania has struggled to promote itself as country committed to, and deserving of, full integration into the European Union (EU). Although included in the pre-accession and accession processes launched by the EU, Romania is rarely regarded as being on a par with other applicant states from central and eastern Europe (CEE). For almost the entire period since 1989 it has been labelled a 'laggard', generally relegated to last position among the ten CEE states which the EU currently envisages admitting.[1]

Romanian discussions of the country's position in EU and NATO enlargement often refer therefore to the country occupying an unenviable position in some 'grey zone' between west and east.[2] From the perspective of European integration, this 'grey zone' is for states deemed to be peripheral to, but not wholly excluded from, the mainstream of developments. More specifically with regard to south-eastern Europe, the 'grey zone' is synonymous with the instability and uncertainty associated with, on the one hand, the former Yugoslavia and Albania, and on the other, the successor states to the Soviet Union. Furthermore, the 'grey zone' invokes notions of being stuck between Russian and American-European spheres of influence. Moreover, not being part of 'Europe' can imply eventual drift towards possible Russian domination.[3]

Concerns over Romania's future within Europe have prompted comment from, among others, Romania's President, Emil Constantinescu. During NATO's Washington summit in April 1999, he accused the west of adopting 'a kind yet indifferent attitude towards the south-eastern democracies' which induced 'a feeling of being marginalised'. This, he argued, was being used by the same forces of national-communism as had been overthrown in 1989. Hence the danger of also losing ground gained so far, of turning south-eastern Europe into a 'no man's land' dominated by 'various groups and obscure forces'.[4] Constantinescu's line of argument echoed that of a former Foreign Minister, Teodor Meleşcanu, six years previously in *NATO Review*. He called on the west to remember 'those of us in the Cold War's "forgotten" part of Europe'.[5] Such statements barely conceal fears that if Romania's calls on the EU and the west in general go unanswered; Romania will be left to the 'no man's land' of the 'grey zone'.

Analyses placing Romania in such a 'grey zone' are often inspired by Samuel Huntington's *The Clash of Civilizations and the Remaking of World Order*.[6] Here, in direct reference to the EU, Huntington advocates identification with western Christendom as a clear criterion for the admission of new members to western organisations. His definition of Europe excludes Romania from a Europe co-extensive with western civilisation. Such a position, Huntington maintains, was one 'which west Europeans, certainly in the 1990s, wanted to hear, which they overwhelmingly supported *sotto voce*, and which various intellectuals and political leaders had explicitly endorsed'.[7] Such comments understandably heightened fears that Romania was being deceived concerning the long-terms intentions of the EU and other western organisations to admit the country. Moreover, defining Europe's eastern border as running 'through Romania between Transylvania with its Catholic Hungarian population and the rest of the country',[8] raised fears among Romanians, particularly nationalists, that Huntington and western leaders supported Hungarian claims for a revision of the 1920 Treaty of Trianon and the reincorporating of Transylvania into Hungary.

The 'Balkan' label so often attached to Romania reinforces the perception that the country is being confined to some undesirable semi-periphery of Europe. It is not surprising therefore to find Romanian politicians as well as governmental officials and diplomats arguing forcibly in favour of Romania being accepted as part of east-central, if not central, Europe, and against the 'Balkan' tag.[9] While this has its opponents within Romania, it has met with some success within EU circles.[10] Romania is classified as a CEE state. However, the introduction in 1999 of 'western Balkans' in EU terminology to describe Albania, Macedonia, the Federal Republic of Yugoslavia and Croatia implies that Romania, by implication part of the 'eastern Balkans', is still perceived, if not publicly referred to, as a 'Balkan' state.

This article examines the origins and foci of the fears and frustrations expressed by Romanian leaders with regard to the EU, particularly since 1996. It then places the concerns voiced within the context of the EU's approach towards Romania, noting the extent to which Romania's own failures in meeting the criteria for accession to the EU have impacted on its membership prospects. The final section assesses the likelihood of frustration remaining a prominent feature of Romania's relations with the EU. In brief, the argument implicit in the article is that that Romania's integration to date with the EU places it outside the feared 'grey zone' and on a path that can lead to EU membership. Successful negotiation of the path is unlikely though to be free of frustration.

Frustration with the EU

Studies of the relations which have developed between the EU and central and eastern Europe since 1989 often pay only limited attention to Romania. This can be explained by the fact that Romania has never been among the front runners for accession to the EU. It has tended to lag behind other states in the region, notably the Czech Republic, Hungary and Poland. Equally, it has not been regarded as a strong partisan of integration. It may have been the third ex-Communist state to apply for EU membership, submitting its application on 22 June 1995, but this was more a reaction to the emerging dynamics of eastern enlargement and a desire not to be omitted from any accession process under development than the expression of a clear wish to accede to the EU in advance of other CEE states.[11] The situation has arguably changed since 1996, in particular after the coming to power of the more reformist coalition government led by the Democratic Convention of Romania (CDR). EU membership has been repeatedly held up alongside accession to the North Atlantic Treaty Organisation (NATO) as one of the two main goals of Romanian foreign policy. Giving prominence to this goal has not always brought the desired success. Indeed, frustration has often characterised Romanian responses to developments in the EU's approach towards eastern enlargement.

The Commission's 1997 Avis

A first example can be seen in the Romanian reaction to the publication in July 1997 of *Agenda 2000*, the Commission's blueprint for enlargement. This set of documents included the Commission's *avis* on Romania's preparedness for membership of the EU. It concluded that Romania was unprepared and should not therefore be invited to open accession negotiations. In fact, the Commission was quite damning. With regard to the economy, it concluded that Romania 'would face serious difficulties to cope with the competitive pressures and market forces within the Union in the medium-term'.

Progress in implementing the 1995 White Paper designed to help align the Romanian economy to the EU's single market had been limited. The Romanian government had 'neither transposed nor taken on the essential elements of the *acquis communautaire*.[12] As regards the political criteria, it is clear that the Commission expected progress under the new CDR-led government: '[c]urrent improvements following the arrival in power of a new government make it possible to conclude that Romania is on the way to satisfying the political criteria set by the European Council at Copenhagen'.[13] The conclusions regarding the economy conveyed a similar message: Romania 'has made progress recently towards improving the competitive capacity of its economy, notably by addressing major distortions such as low energy prices, by accelerating privatisation, and by beginning to liquidate loss-making state-owned farms.[14] Such conclusions meant that the Commission excluded Romania from the list of countries recommended for accession negotiations. This heralded a period of renewed differentiation in the EU's approach towards CEE states. Outside negotiations Romania was on the wrong side of this differentiation. Despite the election of a new reformist government, Romania seemed to be consigned to the 'grey zone'.

The publication of the Commission's *avis* was not greeted with particular enthusiasm in Romania. The Prime Minister, Victor Ciorbea, argued that the proposed approach to EU expansion - of proceeding in waves - could not be justified on the grounds that enlargement is a process of continuous integration. He then declared that the government would continue its political and diplomatic fight to ensure that Romania would be invited to negotiations.[15] This line was also argued by the foreign ministry. It noted that 'to separate the applicant countries for the opening of negotiations is counter productive, creating artificial and discriminatory frontiers, contrary to the principle of continuity of the process of enlargement of the EU'.[16] It did concede, however, that 'in its broad lines, the Commission's [*avis*] corresponds to the reality of today's Romania'. It was clearly feared that differentiation in the EU enlargement process would penalise Romania, influence public opinion negatively and slow down the rate of economic reform. Hence, in the months after the publication of the *avis*, a key element of Romania's policy towards the EU was a concerted effort to ensure that differentiation and discrimination within the accession process would be kept to a minimum.[17]

Luxembourg 1997 and the Launch of the Accession Process

The decision on whether to invite Romania to negotiate was not pre-determined by Agenda 2000 but would be taken by the Luxembourg Summit of the EU's European Council in December 1997. Prior to this member state governments were lobbied in an attempt to ensure that the European Council would launch an all-inclusive accession process. In November 1997 the Romanian government circulated a paper to all EU governments in which it argued that differentiation would distort trade, lead to discrimination between applicant countries in terms of financial transfers (the six countries of the 'first group' would obtain significantly more from the European budget in the period 2000-2005 that the other five), and cause a 'massive migration of foreign direct investment' to countries of the first group.[18] Fears that exclusion would have adverse economic implications clearly existed.

The outcome of the Luxembourg Summit helped assuage these fears. The European Council, while agreeing to proceed with negotiations with only five CEE countries (the Czech Republic, Estonia, Hungary, Poland and Slovenia), declared that the accession process would be 'all-inclusive'. An enhanced preaccession strategy 'intended to enable all the applicant states . . . eventually to become members' would be established involving new 'Accession Partnerships' with each CEE applicant. In addition, Romania and the other CEE countries not invited to open negotiations were promised a regular review of their progress in meeting the criteria for membership. A positive review might lead to the opening of accession negotiations. A further new development was the establishment of an annual European Conference.[19]

The response of the Romanian government to Luxembourg was enthusiastic. The Romanian Foreign Minister, Adrian Severin, argued that the decision to include all CEE applicants in the overall enlargement process was a 'fantastic opportunity for European integration'.[20] Even though Romania was not formally invited to negotiate, differentiation had been minimised. Hence, when launched on 30 March 1998, the EU's accession process was welcomed. Romania appeared to be both part of the accession process and moving closer towards EU membership. Participation in the European Conference in March 1998 and the signing of an Accession Partnership with the EU the following month confirmed Romania's involvement in accession process. Consignment to a 'grey zone' of instability on Europe's periphery appeared to have been avoided.

The Commission's 1998 Regular Report

Developments in late 1997 and in early 1998 temporarily assuaged concerns that Romania could become a victim of renewed differentiation in the EU's approach to the CEE applicants. These concerns soon re-emerged, however, once the Commission produced its first Regular Report on Romania's progress towards accession in November 1998. In refreshingly clear and direct language, the report concluded that 'Romania has made very little progress in the creation of a market economy and its capacity to cope with competitive pressure and market forces has worsened'. Improvements in meeting the economic criteria for membership were acknowledged. Although, reforms were deemed to have been 'far too hesitant and slow, complicated by legal and administrative uncertainty, as well as by frequent changes and delays in implementation'. The Commission warned that the 'economic situation in Romania is very serious. The new [Vasile] government must give absolute and urgent priority to restoring macroeconomic stability and establishing credibility in international financial markets'.[21] Its overall conclusion made no better reading: 'Romania meets the Copenhagen political criteria. Much remains to be done in rooting out corruption, improving the working of the courts and protecting individual liberties and rights of the Roma. Priority should also be given to reform of the public administration'. Despite progress made in transposition of key parts of the *acquis*, Romania has a long way to go in terms of additional legislative transposition, implementation and enforcement before the country will be able to assume the obligations of membership.[22]

Implicit in the Commission's conclusions was a clear sense of disappointment with the efforts of the post-1996 governments. This could hardly go unnoticed in Romania. Officially, the report was welcomed. The Romanian Minister for European Integration, Alexandru Herlea, acknowledged the 'difficult situation' in which the country found itself and argued that 'determined efforts to catch up lost time' must be made. The country's prime minister, Radu Vasile, also indicated few reservations about the reports essentially negative conclusions. Romanian radio quoted him as expressing no surprise

at the inclusion of 'negative aspects along with positive ones' and concluding that '(o)n the whole, [the report] can be viewed as an indication of support for Romania'.[23] All the same, the Commission's view that other CEE
applicants, notably Latvia, could be considered during 1999 for formal negotiations renewed concerns that Romania faced the prospect of being marginalised if not forgotten in the accession process. Frustration with the EU
was most openly expressed by President Emil Constantinescu in an interview with the Austrian newspaper, *Die Presse*. Here, he expressed his disappointment with the Austrian Presidency of the EU Council of Ministers,
adding that it 'is our tragic fate that this country always gives to others yet
never receives anything in return, not even thanks ... We have demanded
nothing from either NATO or the EU and note with regret that no one has
given us anything ... We have the feeling that the Iron Curtain still exists
even though it is now made out of silk or velvet'.[24]

As for the development of the EU's approach towards eastern enlargement,
Constantinescu described as 'absurd' the idea of dividing applicants up further.[25] The clear fear was that Romania's last position in the accession process
would be confirmed. The point was underlined at the April 1999 meeting of
the EU-Romania Association Council when Romania's representatives argued
in favour of the Helsinki Summit of the European Council in December 1999
opening accession negotiations with all CEE applicant states. Immediately
after the meeting, Romania's ambassador to the EU, Constantin Ene, confirmed
that the country was not yet ready for accession and did not expect membership in the near future. Opening negotiations would, however, send an
important political message that Romania was not being 'left outside'.[26] Ene's
comments were unlikely to fall on deaf ears. The Kosovo crisis was intensifying and Romania's strategic importance for the west was at last being
recognised.

Kosovo and the Response of the West

The Kosovo crisis certainly demanded a response from the EU. There was a
clear need to promote stability in south-eastern Europe and tying Romania
more firmly into the EU was regarded as one means by which to achieve this.
Moreover, there was a need to avoid sentiments of neglect intensifying in
Romania. For much of the previous nine months, the Romanian government,
president and parliament had been issuing statements and adopting deci-

sions in support of NATO in its dealings with Serbia. These extended to allowing NATO forces access to Romanian territory for actions against Milosevic.[27] In Romanian eyes, the statements and decisions had gone unrewarded. In particular, the Washington summit of NATO leaders in April 1999 had failed to deliver the desired and anticipated invitation to Romania to join the alliance.[28]

In the light of the NATO decision, criticism of the west became more outspoken. President Constantinescu described an admittance date some time beyond 2002 as 'an unjust and far-away prospect for our countries, which have assumed the same risks as other NATO countries'.[29] The sense of disappointment and indeed frustration was echoed three months later when Constantinescu criticised NATO and the EU of 'double standards' and for treating Romania unfairly given its support during the Kosovo crisis and the economic costs it was suffering as a consequence of the embargo on oil sales to Serbia: 'Every day, personalities from NATO and the EU come to Bucharest and tell us that during the (Kosovo) conflict we behaved like member states of NATO. But nobody offers us security guarantees or speaks about recovering our losses in respect of the embargo ... While we are patted on the back and congratulated, our losses mount day by day'.[30] Later in July 1999, Constantinescu was reported as accusing the west of 'indifference' to Romania.[31] Sympathy for this position came from the Romanian Foreign Minister, Andrei Pleşu who noted the 'accumulated frustration' among the population with the west which had shown that its priorities did not lay with former communist countries.[32] During the Kosovo conflict it was clear that popular attitudes and some leading media commentators were becoming increasingly hostile towards the west.[33] And with the EU's decision to create 'Stabilisation and Association Agreements' with states in the western Balkans, there were even fears that in the absence of an invitation to negotiate EU membership Romania's status could be relegated.[34]

The EU's Approach to Romania

Romanian frustration with the EU in particular and the west in general has been clearly expressed by the country's political leaders. Yet there is good reason to argue that Romania's position within the EU's accession process has actually advanced faster and further than would have been the case had the EU applied a strict interpretation of the Copenhagen criteria (according to which progress towards membership is supposed to be determined). Even the conclusion of the 1993 Europe Agreement and the granting of PHARE aid in 1990 arguably preceded eligibility given the concerns which existed over government policies and behaviour during the presidency of Ion Iliescu (1990-1996). Had the Moscow *coup* of August 1991 not jolted the then European Community into adopting a more accommodating approach to the integration aspirations of the CEE states, then Romania would undoubtedly have had to wait longer before negotiating its Europe Agreement.[35]

Since, the early 1990s, the development of Romania's relations with the EU have benefited from the EU's attempt prior to Agenda 2000 to reduce the emerging differentiation in its approach to the CEE states. Romania, for example was included in the 'structured relationship' and 'multilateral dialogue' launched by the European Council at Copenhagen in June 1993. It was also included in the 'pre-accession strategy' launched by the European Council eighteen months later at its Essen Summit and detailed in the Commission's 1995 White Paper on preparing CEE countries for integration into the Internal Market. It has also received 1.167 billion euros under the PHARE programme since 1990.[36]

Agenda 2000 and the Launch of the Accession Process

The sense that the EU has been generously inclusive in its approach to Romania is supported by the reaction of the Council of Ministers and the European Council to Agenda 2000. As noted, the Commission's 1997 *avis* did not recommend Romania for negotiations. Yet, in an attempt to minimise the renewed differentiation heralded by the opening of accession negotiations, an inclusive accession process was launched by the European Council at its Luxembourg summit in December 1997.[37] Only five CEE countries (the Czech Republic, Estonia, Hungary, Poland and Slovenia) would be invited to start formal membership negotiations. But Romania, along with the other four CEE applicants, would be included in an enhanced pre-accession strategy intended to enable all applicant states 'eventually to become members' and be offered an 'Accession Partnership'. This, along with the promised regular review of progress towards meeting the criteria for membership and the establishment of an annual European Conference maintained hopes that the renewed differentiation would be temporary. Eventually, Romania would join the EU. Indeed, with the launch of the accession process in March 1998 and the establishment of an Accession Partnership, Romania appeared to be moving closer towards EU membership.

From Luxembourg to the Commission's 1998 Regular Report

The outcome of the Luxembourg Summit of the European Council clearly suggested that the EU was willing to give Romania's post-1996 reformist government the opportunity to prove its reform credentials. Success in 1998 was therefore of great importance for the Ciorbea government. Within four months, however, Ciorbea had resigned from office as a consequence of coalition infighting and Romania had a new government under Radu Vasile. The change of leadership did not lead to a significant reversal of the slow down with the reform process, a fact not missed by the Commission. Even at the time of the Luxembourg European Council, the Commission was expressing concern at the Romanian government's capacity to fulfil the reform programme for industry and scepticism about the creation of an institutional framework for the transposition of EC legislation.[38] Similar concerns were being voiced by leading Romanian politicians. Ghiorghi Prisecaru, President of the Senate's Foreign Policy Commission and member of the Joint Parliamentary Commission with the European Parliament, warned in March 1998 that unless the government settled its difficulties and adopted reasonable measures with regard to reform, Romania would run the risk of missing 'the last carriage of the last train for . . . accession to the EU'.[39]

Such comments were followed in July 1998 by outspoken criticism from Günter Burghardt, head of the Commission's DG-1A, of the Romanian government for the slow pace of economic reform. In particular, Burghardt highlighted the negative impact on the reform process of political infighting, corruption and excessive bureaucracy. He added that Romania had the worst economic performance of any applicant for EU membership and commented that 'if things do not change, Romania risks being the only applicant country which instead of progressing, actually regresses'.[40] Such a warning was clearly serious. Hence, in August 1998, the Minister for European Integration, Alexandru Herlea, called for urgent steps in the areas of privatisation and public administration reform to ensure that Romania could maintain progress towards EU membership.[41]

The desired progress was almost impossible to achieve. Despite the change of prime minister earlier in the year, parliamentary support for the government remained far from stable. There were also tensions within the governing coalition about the speed of economic reform and the future of inter-ethnic relations within Romania.[42] On the former, the government in 1998 succeeded in losing two of the most prominent supporters of reform. In September Daniel Daianu resigned his post as Finance Minister. The following month Sorin Dimitru, the Privatisation Minister, followed suit. In responding to accusations that they had failed to implement reforms, each blamed other ministers and bureaucrats for the lack of progress.[43] Moreover, the government was being weakened by tensions over the establishment of a multi-cultural Hungarian- and German-language university in Transylvania. In the light of the government's difficulties and the slow progress with reform the Commission had little choice in its 1998 Regular Report other than to issue mild rebukes and encourage the Romanian government to speed up the reform process. Arguably though, there was little point in criticising the government too strongly for fear that its commitment to reform would waiver. The fact that Romania, unlike Latvia, was not named by the Commission as a possible candidate for recommendation in 1999 for negotiations provided sufficient warning that Romania's unofficial laggard status could be further confirmed if progress was not made.

Kosovo and the Accession Process

Implicit in the Commission's 1998 Regular Report was the fact that Romania was running the risk of falling behind in the accession process - if not dropping out of it altogether. The official jargon governing the process now divided the CEE applicants into 'ins' and 'pre-ins'. By early 1999, a new category was emerging. Romania was being referred to in some diplomatic circles as a 'pre-pre-in'. The domestic situation was also deteriorating. The miners' unrest of January and February 1999 did not instil confidence either at home or abroad, a point that the EU's declaration of support sent to the government in January 2000 could hardly conceal.[44]

Despite the seemingly bleak accession prospects that Romania faced in early 1999, the EU's response to the Kosovo crisis provided a welcome fillip to the country's position. Following a declaration by the EU Council of Ministers expressing appreciation for the country's support for the west's position in

Kosovo, the EU began re-evaluating its approach to enlargement to the apparent benefit of Romania.[45] In part, this resulted from member state governments voicing explicit support for an invitation to Romania to open accession negotiations. A key figure here was the UK Prime Minister, Tony Blair, who during his visit to Bucharest in May 1999 promised UK support in obtaining an invitation to negotiate from the European Council at Helsinki in December.[46] His position was soon supported by the Dutch. The re-evaluation by the EU of its approach to enlargement was also driven by the new Commission President, Romano Prodi, who advocated not only a more high profile EU presence in south-eastern Europe within the context of the Stability Pact launched in July 1999, but also a stronger EU commitment to enlargement.[47] With Prodi taking office in October 1999, the prospects of Romania receiving an invitation from the European Council at Helsinki to negotiate accession rose.

The Commission's 1999 Regular Report

The boost provided by the Kosovo crisis however could not mask Romania's lack of preparedness for EU membership. This was made clear by the Commission in October 1999 when it published its second regular report on Romania. On the positive side, this noted that Romania still fulfilled the Copenhagen political criteria. However, concerns were expressed with regard to the crisis in the country's childcare institutions, the government's increased use of ordinances to enact legislation, the independence and efficiency of the judiciary, progress in the fight against corruption, and improvements in the situation of the Roma.[48] These concerns were nothing when compared to the conclusions regarding the economy. As the Commission noted, 'Romania cannot be considered as a functioning market economy and it is not able to cope with competitive pressure and market forces within the Union in the medium term'.[49] The report then proceeded to define the areas of economic policy and activity where further attention and reform were needed. This constituted an almost endless list of socio-economic shortcomings, covering everything from privatisation to trade to financial regulation. Concern over the progress with reform was evident and underlined in the Commission's summary of the reports:

> All candidates except Slovakia, Lithuania, Bulgaria and Romania are considered to be functioning market economies . . . The economic situation in

Romania is very worrying and sustained efforts will be needed to put a functioning market economy in place . . . Romania [does] not meet either economic criterion. Regrettably, the situation in Romania has, at best, stabilised compared with last year.

There are however exceptions. The situation of over 100,000 children in institutionalised care in Romania has seriously deteriorated, with the Government failing to act in time to ensure that adequate funding was provided for the children. This is an issue of human rights and the Romanian Government needs to continue to give it the political priority which it urgently requires.

Romania have a mixed record in legislative approximation, with good progress in certain areas offset by delays in others . . . The capacities of the administration and the judiciary in Romania remain weak.[50]

The predominantly negative tone of the Commission's reports was arguably unprecedented. Romania's progress with economic reform had been poor and the country was clearly not ready for EU membership. All the same, the political expediency generated by Kosovo and the desire for a more inclusive enlargement process led the Commission to forego a strict application of conditionality in determining developments within the accession process and to recommend that the EU open negotiations with Romania in 2000. There were, however, two conditions which would have to be met before an invitation could be offered: the Romanian authorities would have to provide adequate budgetary resources for and implement structural reform of childcare institutions before the end of 1999; and adopt appropriate measures to stabilise the macroeconomic situation in the country.[51]

Towards Helsinki and beyond

The immediate concern of the Romanian government in the light of the Commission's 1999 reports was to ensure that the European Council would endorse the Commission's recommendations and propose the launch of negotiations. To this end, priority was given to meeting the conditions laid down by the Commission.[52] On the issue of childcare institutions, there was clearly a sense of disquiet within official circles at its presence. President Constantinescu, for example, criticised reports in the international media about conditions in orphanages arguing that the situation was overstated.[53] Nevertheless, extra funds totalling fifty-five million euros were allocated and a National Agency for the Protection of Children's Rights was set up. This then adopted a strategy for improving the position of the institutionalised children.[54] With regard to the macroeconomic situation in Romania, progress was required in two areas: the continued successful implementation of existing short-term adjustment programmes agreed with the International Monetary Fund, the World Bank and the EU; and the establishment of a medium-term economic strategy covering at least three years which is geared to EU accession and approved by the government.[55] On the second of these, the unprecedented step was taken of proposing the establishment of a task group involving Commission, IMF and World Bank representatives to work out with the relevant Romanian authorities a medium-term economic strategy for the country. For some within Romania, including former Prime Minister Nicolae Văcăroiu, the suggestion smacked of external interference. Yet for critics of government performances regarding the economy, it was welcomed.[56] Steps in the direction of establishing a policy began almost immediately.

With the government addressing the conditions laid down, attention turned to the position of the EU member state governments in advance of the European Council meeting in Helsinki. Public support for the Commission's position came from the French government which insisted that Romania should not be marginalised 'with extra conditions (and that) negotiations should be opened'.[57] Indeed there were no real indications from the member states that any of them would oppose the Commission's proposal.[58] Only a failure on the part of the Romanian government to deliver progress on the two conditions seemed likely to upset the prospects for the Helsinki Summit. Romanian domestic politics suggested otherwise. In the lead-up to the European Council meeting, the coalition partners in Romania's government only just managed to keep their differences over the incumbent Prime Minister under wraps. Almost as soon as the Helsinki Summit had issued its communiqué, government infighting intensified resulting in the departure of Vasile and the appointment of Mugur Isarescu, the former governor of the National Bank, as prime minister on 16 December 1999.[59]

Helsinki and the Launch of Negotiations

Despite the Commission's conclusions in its 1999 Regular Report as well as continued concerns over the economy and the childcare institutions, the European Council at Helsinki provided the Romanian government with the

short-term goal it so desperately sought. It announced that accession negotiations with Romania would be opened in early March 2000. Not surprisingly, the announcement was welcomed by Romania's leaders. President
Constantinescu mused on the frustrations of being outside ongoing negotiations noting 'uncertainty of having to make sacrifices without knowing what
we would achieve'. He concluded, '(w)e can now see the light at the end of
the tunnel'.[60]

The Helsinki decision to launch negotiations appeared to signal not only a
stronger commitment on the part of the EU to admitting Romania, but also
evidence of a more pro-active approach towards the country. In January 2000,
Commissioners Prodi and Verheugen paid a visit to Romania, meeting the
entire cabinet of the new Prime Minister, Mugur Isarescu, as well as President
Constantinescu.[61] Later the same month, the Commission proposed removing Romania and Bulgaria from the list of countries whose citizens required
visas to enter the EU - and this was adopted on 26 January 2000.[62] One of
the main events of 2000, however, was the formal opening on 15 February
of the intergovernmental conference governing the accession negotiations.
This was followed on 28 March by a first round of substantive negotiations.
These two events elevated Romania from the status of 'pre-in' to 'new-in'
and appeared to lock the country into an irreversible process leading to EU
membership.[63]

A Future of Frustration?

The opening of accession negotiations in early spring 2000 was clearly welcome. There is good reason to believe, however, that the decisions taken by
the European Council at Helsinki in December 1999 and the subsequent
launch of accession negotiations will not see an end to Romania's sense of
frustration with the EU. The Helsinki decision represented little more than
a change in EU tactics designed to promote a more inclusive image to the
accession process. With only five of the thirty-one chapters being opened initially, fewer than in any other negotiating state and fewer than initially envisaged by the Commission, the start of talks arguably had little practical
significance for the EU.[64] As for Romanian fears that the country might be
slipping into the 'grey zone', there can be no certainty that these will be
assuaged in the coming years. Numerous obstacles will have to be overcome

before progress towards accession, let alone accession itself, can take place. At least five issues are of relevance to any discussion of whether fear and frustration will gain renewed prominence in Romanian debates over the prospects for membership once the relief at starting EU accession negotiations has subsided.

One is the commitment of Romanian governments to - and their capacity for - establishing the macroeconomic stability required by the EU if negotiations are to proceed. Officially, the Romanian government believes that EU membership can be achieved by 2007. This is the personal conviction of the country's foreign minister, Petre Roman, and a position publicly shared by the country's chief negotiator, Aurel Ciobanu Dordea.[65] The attachment to the 2007 date can be explained by the adoption in March 2000 by the Romanian government of a medium-term economic strategy for 2001-2004. This had the support of all thirteen political parties represented in the national parliament as well as employers and trade unions, and is designed to create macroeconomic stability by 2004.[66] Its implementation and success will condition negotiations. The Commission's reaction to the strategy was diplomatic, Verheugen indicating that it was 'satisfactory' but adding later that the 'one important question [remaining] is [whether] the country [is] able to implement the strategy or not?'.[67] The Commission clearly remained concerned over the state of the Romanian economy. A report presented to the Council of Ministers on 20 March 2000 drew particular attention to the continued absence of substantial and genuine structural reforms.[68] The following day, the EU-Romania Association Council noted that 'further efforts are needed for the realisation of the short-term Accession Partnership priorities which have only partially been met'.[69] Not surprisingly, the Commission does not share the Romanian optimism that the country could join the EU in 2007.[70] Reform has not come easily in Romania. Among the reasons for this are the lack of political will to force it through and the inertia and opposition within the administration.[71] Yet the implementation of economic reform and the creation of macroeconomic stability are vital if further progress is to be made towards EU membership. Romania's record to date does not inspire confidence.

This leads to a second issue likely to impact on Romania's accession prospects: the outcome of the 2000 general and presidential elections. At present, there seems little likelihood of the incumbent reformist government retaining power.

Opinion polls consistently predict victory for the former president, Ion Iliescu, and his Party of Social Democracy in Romania (PDSR). As for the CDR, its prospects - and with them seemingly the best chance for reform along the lines required by the EU - are not encouraging. Failure to deliver economic and governmental stability and an improvement in the standard of living of Romanians has led to support for the CDR more than halving since taking office. This leads to the question of how a return to Iliescu and the PDSR will affect Romania's progress in accession negotiations with the EU. Officially, the PDSR views integration into the EU and other Euro-Atlantic structures as 'the fundamental strategic objective of Romanian foreign policy'.[72] Yet many observers reflecting on the 1990-1997 period when Iliescu and the PDSR were in power question the PDSR's commitment to the norms and values which act as prerequisites for integration with the EU. Hence there are concerns that an Iliescu-led Romania risks international isolation, much as it did in the early 1990s.[73] Arguably, Iliescu and the PDSR, have learnt from their period in opposition the advantage of actively seeking to meet EU entry criteria. All the same, concerns continue to be expressed about Iliescu's alleged indifference to corruption.[74] Iliescu and the PDSR are also finding it difficult to shrug off the populist-nationalist image evident in 1990-1997. In February 2000, Verheugen indirectly compared the PDSR to Jörg Haider's Freedom Party in Austria indicating that he would expect the EU's member states to 'react in a similar way' if such a populist and nationalist party participated in a government in a candidate country.[75] Indeed, analysts also question whether the PDSR would adopt a more assertive nationalist approach in its dealings with the EU.[76] Likewise, there are concerns over how relations with Hungary will develop if there is a change of government. Senior PDSR members remain suspicious of, if not hostile to, Hungarian interests in Transylvania.[77] This could result in a deterioration of relations and by implication a less favourable view of Romania's eligibility for membership. A PDSR-led executive would face numerous challenges in ensuring that it can keep Romania on target for accession to the EU.

The challenge of meeting the EU's accession criteria features prominently in a third issue which could lead to further expressions of frustration on the part of Romania: the prerequisites of membership. At present, Romania is obliged to meet the requirements of the existing *acquis communautaire*. This is already proving difficult as the Commission's regular reports have noted.

In early 2000, it was the focus of international attention as the apparent inadequacy of Romanian standards and enforcement procedures in the environmental field contributed to the damage in Hungary and along the Danube resulting from the cyanide spillage in Baia Mare and the later spillage of zinc- and lead-laden water from Baia Borsa. Once accession negotiations turn to the environment, the emphasis will be on Romania proving its capacity to prevent and respond to environmental disasters beyond announcements of a ten-year plan aimed at closing down plants capable of causing ecological accidents.[78] Romanian officials have already voiced fears that the country's membership prospects would be set back unless measures are taken to prevent further environmental disasters and spills.[79] Moreover, the *acquis communautaire* is evolving and entering new areas, notably under the new Article 13 of the Treaty of Rome, to include non-discrimination based on sex, racial origin, religion or belief, disability, age or sexual orientation. As such legislation enters the *acquis communautaire*, it will provide the EU with the opportunity to make yet further requirements of Romania. With so many obligations, question marks could be raised over the extent to which political and popular support for membership within Romania will persist, particularly if negotiations drag on and insufficient concessions and derogations are granted. There is a fear that opposition to the EU may well increase just as it has in Poland and the Czech Republic.[80]

A fourth and linked issue is whether the EU will continue to want to admit, assuming it already does, Romania to its membership. Recent analyses of the EU's approach towards eastern enlargement refer to a seemingly strong commitment on the part of the EU to the process.[81] While such analyses may explain why the EU has become more committed to enlargement, there is no guarantee that the EU will not shift its position again. Certainly, the disparity between the EU's words and actions with regard to the Stability Pact for south-eastern Europe has raised concerns about its commitment to the area.[82] The situation is recognised by the EU as being unsatisfactory.[83] The EU may in March 2000 have revived its enthusiasm for the Stability Pact and agreed to provide more financial support. However, cynicism about its commitment remains. Initially, following the Kosovo crisis in 1999, interest in south-eastern Europe was high. Since then it has slipped down the EU's agenda. The implication is that Romania and the region are at best of marginal concern to the EU.

A fifth issue is popular support within the EU for Romania's application. Currently, there is generally noticeably less enthusiasm for Romanian membership than for nearly all other CEE applicants. Only Slovenia's application is viewed less favourably by people in the EU. As can be seen in Table 1, opposition has on average overtaken support within the EU. Popular support may be high in Greece, but this is counterbalanced by very low and declining support levels in, for example, Austria.

Table 1: Romanian Membership of the EU and EU Public Opinion

	In favour			Against		
	EU	Greece	Austria	EU	Greece	Austria
September 1998	39	56	18	37	28	64
March 1999	37	58	15	40	32	67
July 1999	33	58	10	43	26	71
April 2000	34	54	14	42	28	69

Sources: Eurobarometer, 49, September 1998, B.45; *Eurobarometer*, 50, March 1999, B.63. *Eurobarometer*, 51, July 1999, B.50; *Eurobarometer*, 52, April 2000, B.45.

These declining support levels are discouraging and could easily deteriorate further with popular concerns over environmental pollution and increased numbers of Romanian migrants. Similarly, they could become important factors in determining the policies of national governments towards EU enlargement. What is significant here is that states are only admitted to the EU on the basis of a unanimous vote among existing member states. One member state government responsive to a domestic electorate opposed to Romanian accession can easily slow down accession negotiations and frustrate an applicant's membership ambitions.

Conclusion

These issues clearly cast doubt over whether Romania will accede to the EU within the foreseeable future. Foreign Minister Roman's target date of 2007 appears optimistic. Moreover, there are other issues which remain unresolved but which will impinge on the EU's capacity to admit Romania even if Romanian governments do succeed in implementing reform and meet the criteria for EU membership. Entry will also depend on, for example, adequate reform of the EU's institutions; the EU's experiences of admitting the first wave of CEE countries; the EU's budgetary capacity. Officially, there is a strong commitment to bring the country in to the EU. Yet with the Romanian government's capacity to implement reform and the *acquis communautaire* in doubt, the implications of a change of government in the 2000 elections uncertain, and the capacity and desire of the EU to enlarge to include Romania open to question, it is certainly possible, indeed probable, that Romania will remain frustrated in its quest for EU Membership. The country's current position in the accession process provides an opportunity to dispel inaccurate notions that Romania is stuck in some half-forgotten, half-abandoned southeastern European 'grey zone'. Yet if the negotiations do not lead to membership, whether swiftly or in the longer-term, fears and frustrations concerning Romania's future within the European integration process will surely mount. The challenge for the EU and for Romania will be to ensure that these do not lead to any reversal in the integration achieved and to the prospect of membership being abandoned.

Queen's University, Belfast
D.Phinnemore@qub.ac.uk

Notes

* This is a revised version of a paper presented at the 5th UACES Research Conference, Central European University, Budapest, 6-8 April 2000.

[1] The 'laggard' label persists even with the opening of negotiations in March 2000. See 'The Eastern Laggard Joins the Other EU Candidates', *European Report*, 22 March 2000, pp. 9-10.

[2] See, for example I.M. Pașcu, 'Destin sau conjunctură', *Sfera Politicii*, 63 (1998), pp. 10-15; M. Zulean, 'Interesele americane în Eurasia, *Sfera Politicii*, 63 (1998), pp. 16-19; A. Lazescu, 'România între Kosovo și Kremlin', *22*(20) 1999; 'Sa ne rugăm pentru inca un razboi?', Adevărul, 15 October 1999.

[3] Concerns over Romania's position in Europe are evident in the recent controversy surrounding discussions in 1993-1996 between Romanian and Russian officials over the possible installation of a telephone 'hotline' linking Bucharest and Moscow. See *RFE/RL Newsline*, 21 March 2000; *Reuters*, 28 March 2000.

[4] E. Constantinescu, 'South-Eastern Europe in the Third Millennium', *Romanian Journal of International Affairs* 5(2-3) 1999, pp. 6-12, p. 9. This is the transcript of a speech delivered to the Council on Foreign Relations in New York on 23 April 1999.

186   David Phinnemore

5   T. Meleşcanu, 'Security in Central Europe: A Positive-Sum-Game', *NATO Review* 41(5) 1993, pp. 12-18, p. 1.

6   See, for example, the comments of Adrian Năstase, as discussed in 'The salt block', *Evenimentul zilei*, 14 October 1999 (via *EvZ Online's English Version* available at www.expres.ro/press/evzilei/english/, accessed on 15 October 1999).

7   S. Huntington, *The Clash of Civilizations and the Remaking of World Order* (New York: Simon and Schuster, 1996), p. 159. Huntington draws on comments made by Michael Howard, Pierre Behar, Max Jacobson and Max Beloff.

8   Huntington, *The Clash of Civilizations*, p. 158.

9   See, for example, E. Zamfirescu, 'Reflections on Narrow Post-Cold War Defini-tions of Central Europe', *Central European Issues* 2(1) 1996, pp. 167-92; Meleşcanu, 'Security in Central Europe', I. Iliescu, *Aufbruch nach Europa: Rumänien - Revolution und Reform 1989 bis 1994* (Köln: Böhlau, 1995), pp. 264-66.

10 A. Pippidi, 'Deconstructing the Balkans', *Politica Externă*, 3 (7-8) 1999-2000, pp. 19-28.

11 See D. Phinnemore, 'Romania and the EU in the 1990s: avoiding exclusion or seek-ing inclusion?', Paper Presented at the British-Romanian Historical Colloquium, Cluj, Romania, 24-26 June 1999.

12 EC Commission, *Commission Opinion on Romania's Application for Membership of the European Union*, DOC/97/18, Brussels, 15 July 1997, conclusion, europa.eu.int/comm/dg1a/enlarge/agenda2000_en/op_romania/contents.htm.

13 EC Commission, *Commission Opinion*, C.1.

14 EC Commission, *Commission Opinion*, C.2.

15 Cited in G. Avery and F. Cameron, *The Enlargement of the European Union* (Sheffield: Sheffield Academic Press, 1998), p. 123.

16 Avery and Cameron, *The Enlargement*, p. 123.

17 For a critical analysis of the government's campaign, see V. Stan, *România şi Eşcul Campaniei pentru Vest* (Bucureşti: Editura Universităţii din Bucureşti, 1999).

18 Avery and Cameron, *The Enlargement*, p. 124.

19 Council of the European Union, *Presidency Conclusions - Luxembourg European Council* (Brussels: Council of the European Union General Secretariat, December 1997), point 5.

20 *RFE/RL Newsline*, 15 December 1997.

21 EC Commission, *Regular Report on Progress towards Accession: Romania*, Brussels, 4 November, 1998, B.2.4, www.europa.eu.int/comm/dg1a/enlarge/report_11_98_en/romania/. Radu Vasile replaced Victor Ciorbea as Prime Minister in April 1998.

22 EC Commission, *Regular Report on Progress . . . 1998* C. For a reiteration of EU con-cerns over the slow progress of reform, see 'Fifth Meeting of the Association Council between the European Union and Romania - Joint Press Release', *EU/Romania -*

Association Council - Press Release, UE-RO 1809/99 (Presse 124), Luxembourg, 27 April 1999, point 2.

23 *RFE/RL Newsline*, 5 November 1998.

24 '"Österreich hat vergessen, daß es nicht das letzte westliche Land ist, sondern mitten in Europa liegt"', *Die Presse*, 23 November 1998, www.diepress.at, accessed on 20 September 1999).

25 For this and a critical analysis of the Romanian government's reaction to the EU's position in 1998, see V. Stan, 'Cu spatele la Europa . . .', *Sfera Politicii*, 65 1998, pp. 16-20.

26 B. O'Rourke, 'Endnote: EU, East European Candidates Review Progress', *RFE/RL Newsline*, 6 May 1999.

27 In October 1998, the Romania parliament approved a government decision to allow NATO forces limited access 'for emergency and unforeseen situations' to the country's air space in the case of military intervention by the alliance in Yugoslavia. This was followed in early April with considerable logistical and political support to NATO in its attempts to resolve the crisis in Kosovo. Not only did the government risk popular disapproval in backing NATO's bombing of Serbian targets but Parliament also approved a NATO request for unlimited use of Romanian airspace. On the policies pursued by the Romanian government during the Kosovo crisis, see T. Gallagher, 'Romania, NATO and Kosovo: Right Instincts, Wrong Tactics', *Politica Externă*, 3(7-8) 1999-2000, pp. 84-95.

28 At their Madrid Summit in July 1997, NATO leaders had inferred that Romania along with Slovenia would be next in line for membership and that membership invitations could be extended at NATO's 50th Anniversary Summit in 1999.

29 *RFE/RL Newsline*, 27 April 1999. Also *Monitorul On-Line*, 27 April 1999.

30 Cited in an article by T. Gallagher, *International Herald Tribune*, 23 July 1999; See also *RFE/RL Newsline*, 14 July 1999; *RFE/RL Newsline*, 15 July 1999.

31 See 'Un gouvernement divisé qui a du mal à sortir de dizaines d'années de dictature communiste', *Le Monde* (édition électronique), 28 août 1999, www.lemonde.fr, accessed on 28 September 1999.

32 'La Roumanie est responsable de son histoire', *Le Temps*, 11 août, 1999, domino. kappa.ro/mae/presa, accessed on 21 September, 1999.

33 See S. Fati, 'Kosovo: interesul naţional şi propaganda anti occidentală', *Sfera Politicii*, 70, 1999, pp. 23-28; C. Săftoiu, 'Războiului în presă', *Sfera Politicii*, 70, 1999, pp. 23-29.

34 *European Voice*, 20 May 2000.

35 See D. Phinnemore, 'Romania and Euro-Atlantic Integration since 1989: A Decade of Frustration?' in D. Light and D. Phinnemore (eds), *Post-Communist Romania: Coming to Terms with Transition* (London: Macmillan, forthcoming).

[36] 'EU funding won't flow in any sooner than 2001'. *România Liberă* (English Edition), 13 March 2000.

[37] L. Friis, 'The End of the Beginning of Eastern Enlargement - Luxembourg Summit and Agenda Setting', *European Integration On-line Papers*, 2(7) 1998, eiop.or.at/eiop/texte/1998-007a.htm.

[38] 'EC not very happy with government's restructuring programme', *România Liberă* (English Edition), January 1998, www.romanialibera.com/7ENG/224v03.htm, accessed on 10 June 1998.

[39] 'European Parliamentarians: negative perception of political crisis in Romania', *Romanian Business Journal*, 7 March 1998, p. 3.

[40] *RFE/RL Newsline*, 13 July 1998; 'Who'll give me a dollar?', *Business Central Europe*, October 1998.

[41] 'P.D.-P.N.T.C.D. wars: president sees European integration minister', *România Liberă* (English Edition), 10 August 1998.

[42] *Financial Times* (Survey), 28 September 1998.

[43] *Financial Times*, 20 October 1998.

[44] *Declaration by the Presidency on behalf of the European Union on Romania*, Press Release 5452/99 (Brussels: Council of the European Union General Secretariat, 22 January 1999).

[45] *Council Declaration on Romania and Bulgaria*, Press Release 7561/99 (Brussels: Council of the European Union General Secretariat, 25 April 1999).

[46] Speech by the Prime Minister, Tony Blair, to the Romanian Parliament, Bucharest, Romania, Tuesday 4 May 1999, www.fco.gov.uk/news/speechtext.asp? 2366, accessed on 4 May 1999.

[47] See the Speech by Romano Prodi, President-designate of the European Commission, to the European Parliament Strasbourg, 14 September 1999, SPEECH/99/114, europa.eu.int/rapid/start/cgi/guesten.ksh? p_action.gettxt=gt&doc=SPEECH/99/114|0|RAPID&lg=EN. See also 'New Agenda', *Business Central Europe*, October 1999.

[48] EC Commission, *Regular Report from the Commission on Romania's Progress towards Accession*, (Brussels: 13 October 1999), p. 77.

[49] EC Commission, *Regular Report*, p. 77.

[50] *Commission sets out an ambitious accession strategy and proposes to open accession negotiations with six more candidate countries*, IP/99/751, Brussels, 13 October 1999.

[51] EC Commission, *Composite Paper: Regular Report from the Commission on Progress towards Accession by each of the Candidate Countries*, Brussels, 13 October 1999, point VI.

[52] Department of European Integration, *Immediate measures of the Government of Romania in the perspective of opening the negotiations for accession to the European Union*, October 1999 (via email).

53 *RFE/RL Newsline* 27 October 1999; 'Romanian News Round-up', *Central Europe Review*, 1 November 1999, www.ce-review.org/99/19/romanianews19.html.

54 The importance of addressing the childcare issue was underlined by the new Commissioner for enlargement, Günter Verheugen, during his visit to Bucharest in late October 1999. See 'EU wants to be sure Romania will go on with the process of accession no matter what', *Nine O'Clock*, 29 October 1999, www.nineoclock.ro/ARHIVA/ARCH.html, accessed on 13 November 1999.

55 EC Commission, *European Commission expresses strong confidence that negotiations with Romania will start in 2000*, IP/99/810, Brussels, 28 October 1999.

56 See 'The protest of the disabled lion-hearted', *Evenimentul zilei*, 2 November 1999 (via *EvZ Online's English Version* available at www.expres.ro/press/evzilei/english/, accessed on 3 November 1999).

57 'EU Reassures Romania, Bulgaria Over Invitation', *Central Europe Online*, 16 November, 1999, www. centraleurope.com/news.php3?id=110039&text.

58 E-F. Pătru, 'România şi summit-ul de la Helsinki - între aşteptări şi provocări', *Sfera Politicii*, 77 2000, pp. 4-7.

59 'Romania PM-Designate Aims for EU Accession', *Central Europe Online*, 22 December 1999 (via www. centraleurope.com/news.php3?id=119640&text, accessed on 22 December 1999). A change of Foreign Minister also took place. Andrei Pleşu was replaced by Petre Roman, Prime Minister in Romania's first post-Ceauşescu government (1989-1991).

60 Cited in 'Union comes of age in Helsinki', *European Voice*, 16 December, 1999.

61 'Visite du président de la Commission européenne', *Adevărul*, 14 January 2000 (translation into French from *Le Courrier des Balkans* via email from www.bok.net/balkans/).

62 *Reuters*, 27 January 2000. The immediate reaction of the member states did not suggest rapid adoption. See 'Le long chemin de l'abolition des visas', *Adevărul*, 30 January 2000 (translation into French from *Le Courrier des Balkans* via email from www.bok.net/balkans/).

63 See the comments of Constantin Ene on the value of negotiations in 'Poate in aceasta iarna UE va crapa portile pentru România', *România Liberă*, 28 September 1999, www.romanialibera.com/1POL/ 28c5prom.htm.

64 The five chapters were those widely regarded as the easiest on which progress could be made: foreign relations, common foreign and security policy, small- and medium-sized enterprises, research and development, and education and training. Indeed, they were soon closed by the end of May 2000. The Commission recommended that eight chapters be opened with all 'new-ins'. See *The enlargement negotiations after Helsinki*, Memo/00/6, Brussels, 8 February 2000.

65 *Reuters*, 3 February, 2000; *Reuters*, 23 February 2000. Previously, Dordea had argued

that it would be realistic to envisage the completion of negotiations in ten years' time. See E-F. Pătru, 'România și summit-ul de la Helsinki - între așteptări și provocări', *Sfera Politicii*, 77, 2000, pp. 4-7.

[66] 'Petre Roman plaide la cause roumaine en Europe', *Le Soir*, 27 March 2000 (via www.lesoir.be/ AARTICLES/A_0043F7.html). The medium-term economic strategy envisages a budgetary deficit of no more than three per cent of GDP; economic growth of 4-6 per cent per annum; single figure inflation of nine per cent by 2004; and a reduction in unemployment from its current thirteen per cent to nine per cent within four years. The *National Medium-Term development Strategy of the Romanian Economy* (Bucharest: The Government of Romania, 16 March 2000) is available via http://servernt1.exec.gov.ro/die/en/straten.htm.

[67] *Reuters*, 21 March 2000; *Reuters*, 15 May 2000.

[68] 'La Roumanie frappe à la porte de l'Union européenne', *Curentul*, 21 March 2000 (translation into French from Le Courrier des Balkans via www.bok.net/balkans/).

[69] 'Sixth meeting of the Association Council between the European Union and Romania', *Joint Press Release* UE-RO 1805/00 (Presse 84), Brussels, 21 March 2000.

[70] See the remarks of Günter Verheugen and others Commission officials in *RFE/RL Newsline*, 16 February 2000.

[71] Note the conclusions of one academic report which observed that elites in Romania can display 'reluctance and sometimes a resentful attitude towards pressure to accelerate economic transformation and adapt political institutions and practices . . . to meet the demands of EU entry', in J. Batt (Rapporteur), *The Long-Term Implications of EU Enlargement: Culture and National Identity* (Florence: European University Institute - Robert Schuman Centre Policy Paper 99/1, 1999), p. 7.

[72] *The Political Programme of the Social Democracy Party of Romania* (PDSR: Bucharest, June 1997), point VIII.D.

[73] See, for example, the comment of Karl Grobe that under the PDSR ' "Europe" will move from almost graspable proximity into the unattainable distance' in 'Unfertige Gesellschaft', *Frankfurter Rundschau*, 19 June 2000.

[74] See the concerns expressed by the US Commission on Security and Cooperation in Europe in 'Concern About Possible Iliescu Presidency's Impact on Crime and Corruption in Romania Valid', *CSCE News Release* (Washington D.C.), 28 March 2000. See also Iliescu's alleged role in the Adrian Costea money-laundering affair, as reported in *RFE/RL Newsline* in May-June 2000.

[75] *Reuters*, 11 February 2000. In response to the remarks, Iliescu wrote to Verheugen seeing clarification.

[76] Gallagher, 'Romania, NATO and Kosovo', pp. 84-95.

[77] See the thinly veiled comments of the former Romanian Foreign Minister, Adrian Năstase in A. Năstase, 'Rethinking Borders at the End of the Century - a doctrine

for destabilising Europe', *Romanian Journal of International Affairs*, 5 (4) 1999, pp. 57-61.

78 *Reuters*, 21 March 2000.

79 See the comments of Aurel Ciobanu Dordea, as cited in *Stability Pact Watch*, 2 (6), 4 April, 2000.

80 Pătru, 'România și summit-ul de la Helsinki'.

81 See, for example, K.M. Fierke and A. Wiener, 'Constructing institutional interests: EU and NATO enlargement', *Journal of European Public Policy*, 6(5) 1999, pp. 721-42; U. Sedelmeier, 'East of Amsterdam: The Implications of the Amsterdam Treaty for Eastern Enlargement', in K. Neunreither and A. Wiener (eds), *European Integration After Amsterdam: Institutional Dynamics and Prospects for Democracy* (Oxford: Oxford University Press, 2000), pp. 218-37.

82 'Testing times ahead for EU's Balkan Strategy', *European Voice*, 20 January 2000; *RFE/RL Newsline*, 24 January 2000; 'Balkans wait in vain for eastern funds', *The Guardian*, 14 March 2000.

83 See the comments of the Commissioner responsible, Chris Patten, on the pact's first year and the EU's bureaucratic procedures and patchy expenditure record in 'Brussels reaffirms its commitment to rebuild Balkans', *Guardian Weekly*, 16 March 2000.

Lenka Anna Rovna

The Enlargement of the European Union: The Case of the Czech Republic

ABSTRACT

Since 1989 the countries of Central and Eastern Europe have experienced major changes in their political and economic structures. The most important one from the political point of view is the transition from an authoritarian system to a multi-party parliamentary democracy, and from an economic perspective, from a centrally planned economy towards a market economy. In foreign policy these countries proclaimed the popular slogan 'Back to Europe'. And Europe and the EU have both played crucial roles in furthering democratisation and modernisation in the region. Following the pre-accession strategy for full membership in the EU, the Czech Republic is now closer to becoming a functioning and stable democracy with a prosperous market economy, and a modern effective state. However, the post-Communist transition to democracy in the Czech Republic has also suffered a number of drawbacks. Problematic voucher privatization, the as yet unfinished transformation of big companies, the absence of a clear legal framework, and the lack of the reform of civil service, are the most pressing problems still to be solved.

Introduction

After 1989 the countries of Central and Eastern Europe went through several significant processes. The most important one, from the political point of view, was the transition from an authoritarian system towards a multi-party parliamentary democracy, and from an economic perspective, from a centrally planned economy towards a market economy. In foreign policy these countries proclaimed the popular slogan 'Back to Europe', which for most of these states meant joining the North Atlantic Treaty and the European Community. The transition of the former Communist countries towards democracy soon became a major research topic of political scientists, economists, historians, and sociologists, and even spurred the creation of a new sub-discipline - 'transitology'.[1]

The second most important process in Central and Eastern Europe is *accession* to the European Union, a process, which started later, and has many dimensions. In fact the process of accession was only begun after the Copenhagen summit in 1993, when the member states of the EU decided to open the door to their Central and Eastern European neighbours. These two processes: the transition and the accession, at times went hand in hand, but at other times they diverged to the detriment of both.

These transitions have led to dramatic and fundamental change in these countries, after their experience of fifty years of totalitarianism and authoritarianism under Soviet dominance. Most of these states had only a very limited experience of democratic development in the inter-war period. Czechoslovakia from this point of view was one of the more happier one, as it was one of the few states in the region which maintained a semi-democratic form of governance. Unlike the other Central and East European states Czechoslovakia was able to draw succor from its more positive past and to develop a political culture which is now supportive of democracy. This positive inheritance, never fully lost in the Soviet period, has played a major role in strengthening civil society and promoting a democratic political culture. Indeed, the influence of the past encompasses almost every aspect of life (e.g., the respect and the protection of human rights, the behavior of political parties, the creation of a legal framework, implementation of laws connected with the reform of the civil service). Another important aspects of the transformation process is economic reform - which, in the Czech case, is also firmly grounded in law.

The accession process, with its clear criteria for entry to the EU has played a positive role in helping countries 'to navigate' through the stormy waters of the transition process, thereby speeding up their economic and political transitions. This article examines how politics within the EU has impacted on developments in the Czech Republic, and in particular, the democratisation of Czech society.

Europe and the Czechs

The independent Republic of Czechoslovakia was formed in 1918 and served as an example of a quasi-democratic state until 1938 when the Munich agreement allowed Hitler to annex parts of the country. With the split and formation of an independent Slovakia in March 1939, Hitler was soon able to occupy the rest of Bohemia and Moravia. After the Second World War, Czechoslovakia was faced with the momentous task of rebuilding the state. Ruthenium was lost to the Soviet Union, German citizens were expelled, and Jews and Romas perished in Nazi concentration camps. Once again Czechs and Slovaks were faced with the task of forging a political union and reviving the heritage of Mazaryk.

In 1948 a Communist coup placed Czechoslovakia in the Soviet bloc. Under Communism the image of Europe was perceived through the prism of class struggle. For the communist establishment, Europe represented an enemy, the other side of an Iron Curtain. For dissidents and many citizens it represented hope. The hope became a reality in 1989 with the collapse of Communism. For Vaclev Havel, 'the return to Europe' meant a renewed stress on values such as respect for civil rights and freedoms, political and economic pluralism, parliamentary democracy, decentralization of local government and self-government.[2] Europe was understood as an idea, as a moral defender of the principles of humanity and democracy. Whenever in their history Czechs referred in a broad sense to 'Europe' or 'European', these were synonyms for moral, humane and democratic values.

According to criteria developed by Jean Blondel, the Czech Republic can be characterized as a relatively stable multiparty political system based on parliamentary democracy.[3] Free elections have been held on a regular basis and there has been a peaceful turnover of governments without any political earthquakes.[4]

Dankwart Rustow's ideas on the transition to democracy, especially those referring to the last stage of the development of democracy, when democracy becomes the way of life of a society is especially important.[5] For Rustow it takes one complete generation to 'finalise' the transition to democracy.[6] The difficulty of the transition is described well by Blondel,

> The overall picture at the level of the population as a whole is therefore one of attitudinal support for liberal democracy. The support which has more the characteristics of a gesture than of a way of life; while many appreciate the freedoms which they have gained, they are not truly engaged in the democratic process, perhaps not surprisingly given the history of the countries concerned.[7]

Transition towards Democracy

Martin Potůček points out that,

> ... not only Czech society, but also Czech political representation in many ways has not yet crossed the shadows of the past. Political slogans stating, that our country has completed the transition towards a market economy and a standard European democracy, have been generated by the propagandist needs of the moment rather than the realistic evaluation of the actual situation.[8]

And he further stresses that the weakness of the Czech state and its negative impact on many aspects of society; the growth of criminality, the inability of the legislature to maintain control over the privatisation process, to bring an end to corruption, and deal with conflicts between public and private interests. The unfinished reforms of health care, social care and the alarming situation in education are further examples of weak state capacity.[9]

It is also necessary not to underestimate the other danger in new democracies

> ... a number of scandals have affected the political elite and the government: this has happened most recently in the Czech Republic, Slovenia and Estonia. This does not of course render these countries unique, given what occurs in many parts of Western Europe and elsewhere in the world. However, repeated scandals may well erode the already rather passive popular support for democracy in these countries.[10]

Relatively stable, but fragile democracies, with many remnants from the Communist past are still open to corruption, to a non-effective civil service, divided society etc.[11] The transition process is far from being finished. This is not only a quantitative process measured by the number of elections, or political parties, but also a qualitative process. The aim is that democracy should become 'a way of life'.

There are several domestic factors which play a key role in promoting democracy - such as economic prosperity, the constitutional and legislative framework, the development of civil society, a non-profit and non-governmental sector, the development of 'normally' functioning and well structured political parties, and the presence of a stable and relatively consolidated political elite with no influential anti-system forces.[12] All these entities are in general internal domestic factors.

Referring to the Czech case we have to mention a very important internal factor - the economic aspect. After originally being considered a success story, the Czech Republic more recently has suffered a slump in economic growth, and it has yet to complete its economic reform programme.[13] The state still supports large inefficient industrial enterprises (lame ducks), and voucher privatisation has proved to be a failure. The lack of foreign investment has led to the bankruptcies of many enterprises. The proud 'captains of Czech industry' did not end up in prison due to loopholes in the judicial system.

After the recession in 1997-99, recent development show a marked improvement. According to the *Economist* GDP grew by 4.4 per cent and industrial production 6.5 per cent, in the summer of 2000.[14] Unemployment, which previously was less than 4 per cent grew dramatically and the Minister of Labor and Social Affairs Vladimír Špidla was correct in his estimation that it would reach eleven per cent in 2000. Faster implementation of modern technologies, which seems to be necessary for the economic reform will lead to yet more unemployment. How society is going to cope with this unprecedented situation is not yet clear.[15] All of these internal factors play an important role in the democratic transition. However, several mistakes and slow downs, especially in the period up to 1998, led to a situation whereby the internal domestic transformation process was out of tune with the bid to join the European Union and the demands of the accession process.

The Role of the EU

Besides the internal factor Jean Blondel also emphasized the role of external factors, which may play a quite positive and stabilizing role.[16] The most important and stabilizing factor for the development of democracy and a prosperous economy seems to be the identification with Western values, which are expressed institutionally by joining of NATO and EU. The D-day for joining NATO was March 12, 1999. As the *Economist* noted,

> Central Europe's long-term destination is not in doubt, even if its time of arrival is. Its closeness to the EU has already helped it to weather the recent financial storms. But it could become a worry if the EU economy takes a further turn for the worse. Poles, Hungarians and Czechs alike are looking west, anxiously.[17]

It is more than obvious that the EU plays a very important role in the fourth stage [using Rustow's theory] of the development of democracy in Central European countries, the stage when democracy becomes 'the way of life', not only a 'gesture'.[18]

The official diplomatic relations between Czechoslovakia and the European Community were established in September 1988, in December the 'Trade Agreement' on industrial products was signed. After the fall of Communism in May 1990, 'A Trade and Cooperation Agreement' was concluded and an Association Agreement known as 'Europe Agreement' was signed on December 15, 1991. After the breakup of Czechoslovakia, a new European Agreement was ratified with the Czech Republic on October 4, 1993, the provisions of which included a liberalization of trade,[19] intensive political dialogue, economic and technical cooperation, cultural contacts, support for newly established industrial branches.[20]

For Central and Eastern European countries, a very important decision was taken at the European Council in Copenhagen in June 1993 when two conceptions of the development of EU, 'widening' or 'deepening' were first discussed. The EU concluded that the associated countries in Central and Eastern Europe that so desire should become members of the Union. The accession could take place when the states fulfilled the economic and political criteria for membership including adherence to the aims of political, economic and monetary union.[21]

At the Essen Summit in 1994, the EU put forward a strategy for associated countries - the 'The Pre-Accession Strategy'. The main tools here were European Agreements which offered the associated countries, trade concessions and other advantages; 'Structured Dialogue' which helps the associated countries to become familiar with EU institutions and the decision-making process, and the Phare Programme providing them with grants which targeted the reform process.[22]

'The White Paper', which was approved at the session of the European Council in Cannes in summer 1995 set out the legislation which candidate countries would have to implement to meet the *acquis communautaire*.[23] The European Council in Madrid in December 1995 referred to the need, in context of the pre-accession strategy, 'to create the conditions for the gradual, harmonious integration of the applicant countries . . .'[24]

To meet EU criteria, the Czech government established in November 1994 the Government Committee for European Integration, headed by Prime Minister Václav Klaus, (the other member were Ministers of Finance, Industry and Trade, Agriculture and Foreign Affairs). The Deputy Minister of Foreign Affairs chairs the Working Committee. A year later the Czech government approved and published the timetable for the accession in its document, 'Priorities for the Implementation of the White Paper in the Czech Republic'. In this paper there was a call for further changes in the administrative structure, the administration of the environment, changes to direct and indirect taxation, laws on personal data protection and social policy.[25]

During the last five years great progress has been made in the development of mutual relations between the Czech Republic and the European Union. Exports from the Czech Republic to EU countries grew from 4.9 to 11.7 billion ECU and imports from 6.1 to 15.8 billion ECU. The Czech Republic improved its trade relationship with the EU, which now represents 60 per cent of its trade exchange.[26]

The change in the relationship, and a new quality of relations was also expressed in the participation of the Czech Republic in programmes of the EU, such as Socrates, Leonardo Da Vinci, Kaleidoskop, Mattheus. The implementation of ISPA and Sapard are intended for structural assistance in the pre-accession period. In 1990-1997 the Czech Republic received a contribution of 493 million ECU under the PHARE programme for the support of reforms in all sectors (protection of the environment, support of enterprises, harmonization of law, social policy, cross border cooperation etc.).[27]

Applying for the EU membership

In January 1996 the Czech Republic submitted its application to join the EU and was invited, by the European Council in December 1997, to be one of the first six countries to start negotiations.[28] Screening started in April 1998 with the first six countries.[29] 'Screening is the first phase of discussion on accession to the Union, prior to the negotiation itself. European Communities' legislation has been divided into thirty one chapters; during screening individual legal norms are examined in multilateral and bilateral discussions. Legal analyses are also carried out and Czech legislation is scrutinized with regard to its compatibility with EU norms.[30] The screening process was supposed to be finished in the summer of 1999.[31]

'The Regular Report from the Commission on the Czech Republic's Progress towards Accession' was published in November 1998.[32] The Report documented how the Czech Republic was progressing in the light of the Copenhagen criteria, and especially the rate at which it was adopting the Union acquis.[33]

The EU as an external factor influencing the transition to democracy played a crucial and direct role. It was somewhat of a blow to Czech politicians and Czech society to read in EU Political Criteria: 'The Accession Partnership with the Czech Republic' mentions as medium term priorities,

> further work on the integration of the Roma; strengthening of laws which guarantee press freedom; further attention to ensuring equal access to public services.[34] The evaluation was far from satisfactory. The Commission stated further that: 'The change in Government has not resulted in any major shift in the country's policy towards the European Union'.[35]

The critical tone of the Report continued: 'There has been virtually no progress in public administration reform since July 1997.'[36] This is not only the wish of the Commission. A functioning civil service is considered to be one of the most important pre-condition for a functioning of democracy, a factor guaranteeing the functioning of the market economy [for instance the control of capital markets, economic competition, work of financial offices etc.], a factor of institutional cooperation at all levels of the internal market, and a key condition for the adoption of *acquis communautaire*.[37]

The Czech Republic was also criticised over its handling of human rights. The General Evaluation stated that:

> Developments in the Czech Republic confirm the opinion that the Czech Republic fulfils the Copenhagen political criteria. Nonetheless the Czech Republic needs to devote continuing attention to the reform of the judiciary, to fighting corruption more effectively and to improving the situation of the Roma.[38]

The new minority government, which came to power in June 1998, had a much more open policy of support for joining the EU and the European card was its first priority. The European dimension was no longer considered a question of foreign policy and now became under the new regime, a domestic issue. The transformation process and the *accession* process now walked (with some minor exceptions) hand in hand.

A year later in October 1999 the European Commission published a new annual report 'The Regular Report of the European Commission on the Czech Republic for 1999. The Progress in the Accession.'[39] It was of course quite hard to overcome the heritage of the past, and it was not surprising therefore, that in the introduction the Commission stated that the Czech Republic's progress was very unbalanced. Positive developments had occurred in the economic field. Imports from the EU to the Czech Republic had grown from 11.8 to 14.7 billion EURO. Exports from the Czech Republic grew by 11 per cent.[40]

The *Pre-Accession* aid was done through *PHARE*. Thirty per cent of this was used for the strengthening of the institutions that were involved in the implementation of the *acquis*. Seventy percent were directed to the investments needed to restructure the economy, and to support economic and social cohesion.

The PHARE budget for the Czech Republic in 1990-1999 represented 629.1 million EURO. The budget for 1999 was 21 million EURO, which was used to fund the following areas:

- the strengthening of the democratic system, judicial state, the protection of human rights and rights of minorities, especially of Roma (0.5 million EURO)

- the economic and social cohesion including the support of small and middle sized companies and support of employment (5.35 million EURO)

- the strengthening of the abilities of the institutions and civil service to implement the *acquis* especially in the field of public finance, protection of health and security at the work place and the environment (5.8 million EURO)

- justice and internal affairs, including the struggle against organized crime and economic criminality, protection of frontiers and the strengthening of the judicial system (4 million EURO)

- participation in different programs of the EU (4 million EURO) and the programme TEMPUS (1 million EURO)

Other financial sources were granted for cross border cooperation and international programs such as TAIEX programmes for small and middle sized companies, and projects for the building of infrastructure.[41]

In the fall 1999 when the Report was published eight chapters of the negotiations were closed and seven were still open. The Report was very critical of the slowness of the adoption of the *acquis*, which had to overcome; complicated and bureaucratic problems in the ministries, three readings in the Parliament, problems generated by minority government, and the reluctance of the previous governments to the whole process.

The Report was also very critical when referring to the reform of the civil service. This very long and painful process started soon after 1989. Several teams were established to prepare the document. It is due for completion in 2002.[42] In the part dealing with minorities the Report stated that the status of the Roma had not improved enough. Seventy per cent of Roma children attended special schools for backward children, unemployment among the Roma population was 70-90 per cent. The governmental action plan in 1997 called for the establishment of Roma advisers and assistants in the ministries, district councils, and schools. Preparatory schools for Roma children were also founded. The Interdepartmental Commission for Roma Questions was already in place, but the health and housing situation of the Roma population still had not improved.

The micro-economic situation according to the Report remained problematic, real GDP was decreasing, unemployment had grown and real incomes had dropped. The recession was proving to be much more serious, deep and long-lasting. The outlook was not over optimistic.[43]

The Czech political elite took the 1999 Report very seriously and the government now put in a tremendous effort to regain its place as the flag ship of countries negotiating full membership in the EU. This effort was mentioned in the document of the European parliament '*The Czech Republic and the Enlargement of the European Union*', published in March 2000.[44]

The Briefing of the European Parliament mentioned that the minority government of Miloš Zeman had re-negotiated and amended the opposition agreement between the governing social democratic party and the major opposition party ODS, led by Vaclav Klaus. Part of it was a clause dealing with more collaboration on preparation for EU accession. In spite of the fact that there was an increased effort from the side of the Czech government the Briefing of the European Parliament repeated many reservations stated earlier by the Commission.

The Czech political élites and Czech media eagerly awaited the '*2000 Regular Report from the Commission on the Czech Republic's Progress towards Accession.*'

The Report studied the relations between the EU and the Czech Republic. Besides PHARE, two new programmes were introduced;[45] SAPARD provides aid for agricultural and rural development and ISPA finances infrastructures projects in the field of environment and transport.

The evaluation of criteria for membership started with political criteria. The 2000 Report accepted positively that the Parliament improved its functioning by introducing a fast track for EC related draft laws. Since 1999 a significant acceleration in the legislative process was noted. The main failure is considered to be the absence of the Act on the Civil Service. Anti-corruption measures have not yet gone far enough and with regard to judicial reform, the training of the judges has still to be completed.

The Czech government also adopted a document 'Concept of the Government Policy towards Members of the Roma Community' focusing on the key areas of education, employment, housing and the fight against discrimination of the Roma. The schools included in their syllabus multi-cultural educational programs and made information about Romany culture more widely available. More positive steps were also taken in the field of housing, with regard to Roma assistants and the creation of preparatory schools for Roma children.[46]

In the part dealing with economic criteria the Report stated that the macroeconomic situation has improved and the three years recession came to an end in the middle of 1999. The Czech Republic also accelerated structural reforms, an example can be seen in the processing of sale of the Czech Saving Bank [Česká spořitelna] and preparations for privatising the largest commercial bank in the country [Komerční banka] in 2001.

The improvement of the situation is also indicated by the increase in foreign direct investment, which in 1999 represented an inflow of 4.79 billion EUR, which made up 9.2 per cent of GDP, and was more than the double the level of 1998.[47] There could be no doubt that the overall business climate in the Czech Republic had improved.[48] However, the 2000 Report noted still not enough had been done to fight corruption and bad loans still comprise twenty six per cent of GDP.[49]

The chapter dealing with the ability to meet the obligations of EU membership is divided into twenty nine parts. These are structured in accordance with the list of twenty-nine negotiating chapters covering the following areas: sectoral policies, economic and fiscal affairs, economic and social cohesion, innovation, quality of life and the environment, justice, external policies, and financial questions.

In general the Report for the year 2000 acknowledged the progress done in many fields, but also drew attention to many problems still to be tackled, such as reform of the civil service and the judiciary, and work relating to the protection of human rights.

High expectations of Czech politicians and the professionals in the area of European integration were dealt a blow by the section entitled, 'The Strategy of the Enlargement', which accompanied the Report. The document stated that the Czech economy *could be considered* to be a market economy whilst the economy of countries such as Poland, Hungary and Estonia *'are market economies'*.[50] These disputes between representatives of the EU and the Czech government were overshadowed by the results of the Nice Summit, which have been welcomed by Czech officials.

Czechs and the EU

Regular reports and comments of the EU to the Czech government have been a positive factor in the transition process. However, to promote democracy 'as a way of life', and to make the process truly democratic, citizens have to make their decision with the full knowledge of the facts.

An important factor influencing the attitude of the Czech elite is the level of support of the population for accession.[51] The positive attitude of Czech citizens towards the EU can be encouraged by a more open approach from the government with regard to accession, something which has not always been present in the past.[52] Greater knowledge about the EU has led to greater support for it.[53] The Ministry of Foreign Affairs 'has specified the aims, principles and tools of the Communication Strategy and defined target groups . . . We carry out some projects, with for example, Czech TV, regional dailies and specialized magazines. We issue various publications . . . we plan to launch specialized Internet sites.'[54] As pointed out by the main negotiator for the accession Pavel Telička. All these activities are supposed to prepare the citizens for the referendum and to give them knowledge necessary to make their choice freely and democratically.[55]

The Czech internal debate about European integration can be divided into three periods:

1. 1989-1991 - mainly connected with a slogan 'back to Europe'

2. 1991-1997/8 - the period of formation of political attitudes about the EU

3. 1997/8 - period of forming attitudes about specific aspects of European integration[56]

The main support for joining the EU comes from young people, with higher education and a right wing political orientation. The best-informed social

groups are young people and entrepreneurs from small and bigger companies. The less informed are old people, housewives and people living in the
country.

Table 1:[57] Do you trust the European Union?

Age	18-29	30-44	45-59	60-
Yes	21%	17%	13%	8%
More yes	48%	46%	40%	38%
More no	24%	28%	33%	35%
No	7%	9%	14%	19%

Table 2:[58] Do you trust the European Union?

Education	basic	apprentice	High school	University
Yes	9%	12%	19%	27%
More yes	35%	45%	46%	50%
More no	37%	30%	29%	18%
No	18%	13%	6%	5%

The most desired expectations of Czech society are:

- the improvement of economic situation

- cooperation on European level

- the freedom of movement of persons, capital, services and goods

- the improvement of the work of the legislature

But there are also worries connected with joining the EU such as:

- the cost, higher taxes

- unequal position of the Czech Republic

- the loss of sovereignty

- economic dependence

- the influx of foreigners

- the growth of unemployment

- competition for Czech enterprises

- the decline of agriculture

- the decline of industry[59]

The analysis done by the governmental team for the Communication strategy came to the conclusion that knowledge about the EU among Czech citizens is quite vague. Only forty six per cent of population have a general idea what the EU is about. There is a crucial educational role to be played by the media, but only 26 per cent give a professional analyses.[60] There is also an important role for the government itself. According to the First Deputy Minister of Foreign Affairs and the main negotiator of the Czech Republic, Pavel Telička, the Regular Report of the Commission in the fall 1999 which heavily criticized the attitude of the Czech Republic towards the Accession had a sobering affect on the leadership. This was a 'turning point' for the Czech government and led to a new will to reach a consensus within Czech society and members of the political elite. European integration now became topic number one and began to play a unifying role in the country. Proof of this can be seen in the agreements reached between the main political parties: the ODS and social democrats, which speeded up the process.[61]

Public Debate

Till recently the main protagonists of the debate dealing with Europe were President Václav Havel and the former Prime Minister Václav Klaus. Havel presents himself as a federalist, a politically and economically integrated Europe is for him a natural framework for the vital development of the Czech nation.[62] In his speech in Strasbourg in February 2000 Havel stressed the necessity of the further democratization of Central Europe and the 'Europeanisation' of civil society. He also proposed the creation of a European Constitution, which was accepted quite warmly by EMPs. However, his proposal to create an upper House of the European Parliament fell on deaf ears.[63]

Václav Klaus, the President of the Parliament and a former Prime Minister claims to be a 'eurorealist', but many perceive him more as a 'eurosceptic'. Klaus stresses the role of the national state as a space for political sovereignty. He sees the EU as an inter-governmental organization cooperating mainly in the framework of the liberalization of the market and trade.[64] His party, The Civic Democratic Party (ODS) nonetheless has maintained a policy of seeking membership of the EU. In spite of the fact that several top politicians of ODS headed by Václav Klaus himself are quite careful and 'suspicious' vis-à-vis the EU the party as a whole is very pro-European.[65]

Social democrats (ČSSD) formerly criticised the eurosceptic approach of their conservative counterparts in the ODS. The ČSSD as the governmental party, feels responsible for the negative reports of the EU Commission and has recently moved to speed up the accession process. The approach of ČSSD is based on shared values with other socialist, social democratic and labour parties and their ideas of a Europe which pays heeds to social issues and has a social charter. The Union of Freedom (US) which was formed after the split of ODS in 1997 claims to be a euro-optimistic. They support the further deepening and widening of the EU and have tried to project their views on Europe as one of the most important differences between themselves and ODS. The Christian and Democratic Union - Czechoslovak People Party (KDU-ČSL) understand the EU as a fulfillment of their Christian democratic values. The Communist Party (KSČM) has an ambivalent approach towards the EU, the members in general (mainly representatives of older generation) are not keen on EU membership, although the leadership of the party is more open to accession.[66]

Table 3:[67] Do you trust the European Union?

Membership in Communist Party	Member before 1989	Never was a member
Yes	10%	16%
More yes	32%	47%
More no	37%	28%
No	21%	9%

From the beginning of 1999 a sort of lethargic Czech society became more aware of the necessity of an open discussion about the Czech membership in the EU. Several NGOs actively supported Czech membership of the EU (Impuls 99, Děkujeme, Odejděte). The number of discussions about the EU in the mass media is growing. This is due not only to the success of the government's Communication Strategy, but also the realisation by common citizens that membership in the EU will impact directly on their lives.[68]

What are the main resources for information about the EU?

Direct communication: political elites
                                 journalists
                                 social networks including NGOs
Indirect communication: civil servants and trainers
                                 Professionals[69]

The main topics, which are communicated, are more general dealing with the foundation, functioning and aims of the EU and more concrete referring to the changes we can expect due to our membership. Only from the fall 1999 after the highly critical Regular Report from the EU has the discussion about internal aspects of the accession become widespread throughout Czech society. Step by step European Integration has became a domestic issue and is no longer confined to foreign policy.

Conclusion

'Europe' and the EU have played a crucial part in the Czech Republic's democratic transition. Following the pre-accession strategy for full membership in the EU, the Czech Republic is now much closer to becoming a viable and stable democracy with a prosperous market economy and a modern effective state responsive to the needs of its citizens. Czech society now has a rare historical opportunity to take control of its own affairs and to steer the country 'back to Europe'. This process is not going to be easy. Czech citizens with the full knowledge of the facts have to make their own choices.

Lenka_rovna@hotmail.com

Notes

1 To name but a few; M.G. Roskin, *The Rebirth of East Europe* (London: Prentice Hall, 1991), G. Stokes, *The Wall Came Tumbling Down* (Oxford, 1993); Rothschild, *Return to Diversity* (Oxford, 1993), Jiří Vykoukal, *Bohuslav Litera, Miroslav Tejchman, Východ, Vznik vývoj a rozpad sovětského bloku, 1944-1989*, (*The East, The Creation, Development and the Fall of the Soviet Bloc*), (Praha: Libri, 2000).

2 Václav Havel, *Letní přemítání*, (*Summer meditation*) (Praha: Odeon, 1991), p. 64.

3 '. . . in five countries [Czech republic, Hungary, Poland, Estonia, Slovenia] and in most of Eastern Europe, political developments in the 1990s can be regarded as having been broadly satisfactory, especially given the economic and social difficulties which these countries underwent. . . . Support for democracy is widespread, although not overwhelming', 'Democracy in five Candidate Countries' a paper given by J. Blondel, Seminar, 'The New European Borders', (Trieste, 27-28 November 1998).

4 At least compared to the case in Hungary, see G. Ilonszki, 'Consolidation of the Hungarian Democracy', Draft paper presented at the International Conference, 'Perspectives on Democratic Consolidation in Central and Eastern Europe' (Tallin, Estonia, 19-22 November 1998).

5 D. A. Rustow 'Transitions to democracy, toward a dynamic model', *Comparative Politics*, 3 April 1970, pp. 337-364.

6 V. Dvořáková, J. Kunc, *O přechodech k demokracii* (*About transitions to democracy*), (Praha: SLON, 1994).

7 Blondel, 'Democracy in Five Candidate Countries'.

8 M. Potůček, *Nejen trh, Role trhu, státu a občanského sektoru v proměnách české společnosti*, (Not Only the Market, The Role of the Market, State and Civil Sector in the Changes of Czech Society), (Praha: SLON, 1997), p. 167.

9 M. Potůček, *Nejen trh*, p. 167.

10 Blondel, 'Democracy in Five Candidate Countries, p. 4.

11 See, Jiří Kunc, ed. *Demokracie a ústavnost* (*Democracy and Constitutionalism*), (Praha: Universita Karlova, 1996).

12 See, V. Dvořáková, A. Gerloch, *Krystalizace struktury politických stran v České republice po roce 1989, Česká společnost pro politické vědy*, (Praha, 1996).

13 'The Czech economy is already doing badly; GDP fell by 2,9 per cent in the twelve months to the third quarter of 2000. It has yet to recover from its currency crisis in 1997, when interest rates were raised sharply to defend the koruna. The Czechs are also paying the price for half-baked economic reforms. Their privatization scheme put a premium on speed rather than rational restructuring. The banks, still state-owned, have been repeatedly bailed out. Perhaps because they do not

have a large foreign debt to service, the Czechs appear complacent about the need to shake up their economy further', *The Economist*, 13 February 1999, p. 84.

[14]   *The Economist*, 5 August, 2000, p. 100.

[15]   The Interview with the Minister of Labour and Social Affairs Vladimír Špidla, *Mlada Fronta Dnes*, 13 February 1999, pp. 1, 15.

[16]   'Almost certainly, one important factor has influenced these polities in the direction of a stable democratic path, namely the fact, that they have wished to join the European Union as soon as possible: such developments occurred earlier in the case of Spain, Portugal and Greece. It is therefore critical that the Union should not delay the admission of the five countries to the point where they might show less goodwill'. Blondel, 'Democracy in Five Countries', p. 4.

[17]   *The Economist*, 13 February 1999, p. 84.

[18]   See Blondel, 'Democracy in Five Countries'.

[19]   Czech Republic can export seventy per cent of all Czech products without customs and restrictions, on the other hand sixty per cent of European export is influenced by these restrictions. Due to the fact that the rate for agricultural products is six per cent, in fact the Czech Republic has the most advantageous agreement among Central/Eastern European countries. (Gerhard Sabathil, 'Česká snaha o přijetí do západních institucí a odpověď' z Essenu', *Mezinárodní politika* 1, 1995, p. 6.

[20]   Gerhard Sabathil, 'Česká snaha o přijetí do západních institucí a odpověď' z Essenu' (Czech Effort to be Accepted to Western Institutions and an Answer from Essen), *Mezinárodní politika*, 1, 1995, p. 7.

[21]   Membership requires: that the candidate country has achieved stability of institutions guaranteeing democracy, the rule of law, human rights and respect for and protection of minorities; the existence of functioning market economy, as well as the capacity to cope with competitive pressure and market forces within the Union.

[22]   *Předvstupní strategie Evropské Unie pro přidružené země střední Evropy*, (*The Pre-Accession Strategy of EU for Associated Countries of Central Europe*), (European Commission, DG IA, 1994), p. 5.

[23]   *Předvstupní strategie Evropské Unie pro přidružené země střední Evropy*, (*The Pre-Accession Strategy of EU for Associated Countries of Central Europe*).

[24]   'particulary through; the development of a market economy; the adjustment of their administrative structures; the creation of a stable economic and monetary environment'. *Agenda 2000, Commission Opinion on the Czech Republic's Application for membership of the European Union* (Brussels, July 15, 1997), p. 2.

[25]   *Agenda 2000*.

[26]   Gerhard Sabathil, 'Příprava české republiky pro vstup do EU' ('The Preparation of the Czech Republic to the EU'), *Mezinárodní politika*, 1, 1999, p. 10.

27   Gerhard Sabathil, 'Česká snaha o přijetí', pp. 10, 11.

28   Barbara Lippertová, Strategické otázky rozšiřování Evropské unie na východ po
     lucemburském summitu, (The Strategic Questions of the Enlargement of European
     Union to East after Luxembourg Summit), *Mezinárodní vztahy*, 2, 1998, pp. 17-27.

29   Pavel Telička, Tempo jednání o přistoupení závisí na dořešení vnitřních problémů
     EU, (The Speed of Negotiations about Joining Depends on Solving Internal Problems
     of EU), *Mezinárodní politika*, 1, 1999, pp. 4, 5.

30   Petr Greger, 'K vybranným právním aspektům a souvislostem Amsterodamské
     smlouvy', ('Selected Judicial Aspects and Connections of the Amsterdam Treaty'),
     Mezinárodní vztahy, 2, 1998, pp. 5-16.

31   'EU Membership Talks Launched', An Interview with Pavel Telièka, Deputy Czech
     Minister of foreign Affairs and the chief negotiator for accession of the Czech
     Republic to the European Union, November-December 1998, pp. 1-6.

32   Petr Greger, 'Český právní stát v bruselském prizmatu'. ('Czech Rule of Law from
     the Perspective of Brussels'), *Mezinárodní politika*, 1, 1999, pp. 8, 9.

33   In accordance with the guidance provided by these Council Conclusions, the
     progress report on the Czech Republic follows the same structure as the Opinion.
     It describes the relations between the Czech Republic and the Union, particulary
     in the framework of the European Agreement; analyses the situation in respect of
     the political conditions set by the European Council (democracy, rule of law, human
     rights, protection of minorities); assesses the Czech Republic's situation and
     prospects in respect of the economic conditions mentioned by the European Council
     (a functioning market economy, capacity to cope with competitive pressure and
     market forces within the Union); addresses the question of the Czech Republic's
     capacity to meet the demands of the *acquis*, as expressed in the Treaty, the sec-
     ondary legislation and the policies of the Union. *Regular Report from the Commission
     on Czech Republic's Progress Towards Accession* (Brussels, November 1998).

34   *Regular Report.*

35   *Regular Report.*

36   *Regular Report.*

37   Petr Greger, 'Český právní stát v bruselském prizmatu', *Mezinárodní politika*, 1,
     1999, p. 9.

38   *Regular Report from the Commission on Czech Republic's Progress Towards Accession*,
     (Brussels, November 1998).

39   http://www.euroskop.cz/rc_pripravacr_zprava1999.html.

40   http://www.euroskop.cz/rc_pripravacr_zprava1999.html.

41   http://www.euroskop.cz/rc_pripravacr_zprava1999.html, p. 9.

42   In 1998-1999 I took part in the Board of Advisors for the Reform of Civil Service.
     The author took part in preparation of one of many proposals for the establish-

ment of the Institute for Public Administration, a kind of Civil Service College. The project was paid for by a grant from PHARE. At present the author is a part of another team preparing the teaching modules for the traning of civil servants.

[43] Fortunately it did not prove to be right. The slow improvement ocurred in the first half of 2000. See, *The Economist*, 4 August, 2000, p. 100.

[44] 'The Czech Republic and the Enlargement of the European Union', *Briefing No. 4, European Parliament*, (Luxemburg, 22 March 2000).

[45] Under the PHARE framework the Czech Republic will receive in 2000-2002 79 million EURO annually, *2000 Regular Report from the Commission on the Czech Republic's Progress towards Accession*, p. 9.

[46] *2000 Regular Report*, pp. 25, 26.

[47] For a more detailed economic evaluation see: *Transition Report 2000*, November 14, 2000 (European Bank for Reconstructuring and Development) http://www.ebrd.com.

[48] *Transition Report 2000*, pp. 28-38.

[49] *Transition Report 2000*, p. 90.

[50] 'Diplomaté si hodlají na EU stěžovat', ('Diplomats intend to complain about the EU'), *Mlada Fronta Dnes*, November 11, 2000, p. 6.

[51] '. . . although the level of knowledge of these issues still remains rather low among the public. This, of course, is not a fault of the public; rather it is a result of the current state of our relationship with the EU. There is a lack of information about the most important matters, about the actual impacts of such policies of the EU on individual areas of people lives.' [An Interview with Pavel Teličkа, Deputy Czech Minister of Foreign Affairs and the Chief Negotiator for accession of the Czech Republic to the European Union, *EuroInfo*, November-December 1998, pp. 4, 5.

[52] Peter Bugge, 'České vnímání perspektivy členství v EU, Havel vs. Klaus' (Czech Perceptions about the Perspectives for EU Membership), *Politologická revue*, 2, 1998, pp. 76-110.

[53] The Support for the Entry to the EU in percentage:

	V.93	III.96	XI.96	I.97	IX.97	II.98
YES	66	42	51	58	58	61
NO	12	21	26	23	22	15
DOES NOT						
KNOW	22	37	23	19	20	24

(Pramen: IVVM) 'Zpráva o vývoji české společnosti, 1989-1998', (The Report about the Development of Czech Society, 1989-1998), Editor Jiří Večerník, the research team led by Petr Matějů, p. 319. The slogan "back to Europe" is founding a real shape and structure.

54   www.euroskop.cz.

55   www.euroskop.cz, pp. 28-38.

56   Miroslav Mareš, 'České politické strany a evropská integrace', ('Czech Political Parties and European Integration'), *Integrace*, 1/2000, p. 15.

57   *STEM, Trends* 2/2000, p. 3.

58   *STEM*, p. 3.

59   *Communication Strategy of the Czech Government, Presentation of STEM and Sofres-Factum*, (Ministry of Foreign Affairs, Prague), March 3, 2000.

60   *Communication Strategy.*

61   Pavel Telička, 'The Negotiation Process and Internal Preparation of the Czech Republic for membership in the EU', *Integrace*, March, 2000, in: www.integrace.cz.

62   Bugge, 'České vnímání perspektivy členství v EU', p. 103.

63   Kateřina Šafaříková, 'Václav Havel ve Štrasburku opět navrhl některé změny Evropské Unie' ('Václav Havel again Suggested Some Changes to the EU'), *Lidové noviny*, 17 February 2000, p. 3.

64   Bugge, 'České vnímání perspektivy', p. 103.

65   Members of parties trust in the EU.

      ODS   79%
      US   81%
      KDU/ČSL   83%
      ČSSD   52%
      KSČM   24%

Source: STEM, *Trendy*, February, 2000.

66   See: Mareš, 'České politické strany', pp. 15-20.

67   *STEM, Trendy*, 2 (2000), p. 5.

68   According to an opinion poll conducted in February 2000, people in the Czech Republic trust:

      EU   58%
      NATO   53%
      Czech government   24%

Source: STEM, *Trendy*, 1994-2000.

69   *Communication Strategy, Presentation of STEM and Sofres-Factum, Ministry of Foreign Affauirs* (Prague, March 13, 2000).

Heather Field

Awkward States: EU Enlargement and Slovakia, Croatia and Serbia

ABSTRACT

Slovakia, Croatia and Slovenia constitute 'awkward states' in the
context of EU enlargement because their progress towards membership has been slower than that of some other closely-situated
countries of Central and Eastern Europe (CEE). This article considers the background and issues relating to EU enlargement, and
how the individual 'awkward states' have failed to meet criteria
for membership, or to seek it in the first place. A major finding
is that political change has been and remains the key factor in
turning 'awkward' states into suitable and enthusiastic would be
members. In this context Slovakia is already there, Croatia is on
its way, but in Serbia such change is only just now in prospect.
Economic and human rights issues are important, and the question of the future movement of the gypsy population may delay
Slovakian membership, but such factors appear to play a secondary role to that of political change towards more democratic governments and policies. Repression of the media is a common
characteristic of states which remain 'awkward' in this context.

The prospective eastwards enlargement of the European Union (EU) involves the potential membership of ten to fifteen applicant countries in Central
and Eastern Europe (CEE). The analysis undertaken
here considers the issue of 'awkward states' in terms

of prospective and potential applicant countries for membership, focusing in particular on Slovakia, Croatia and Serbia.[1] It looks at why Slovakia is now a 'rehabilitated' prospective member which might even be included in the first round of entrants, and Croatia has commenced its path towards acceptance as a prospective member, but Serbia remains a last 'domino' or 'nut to crack'. This latter situation is in the sense that Serbia's government and most of its population do not seek or desire EU membership, and its recent history and lack of adequate democratic credentials presently exclude it from acceptance as an applicant. Considerations with respect to 'awkward states' include explicit and implicit EU membership criteria and their ability to meet these. They also include the factors and rationales which lie behind eastwards enlargement of the EU in terms of the national interests and views of the EU's member states and of the applicant country. Where Serbia is concerned the manipulation of media, popular culture and identity, as well as the outcomes of the wars in which it has been involved, have been important in securing continued support for the government's positions. They have also fostered an implicit resistance to 'Europeanisation', except among opposition elites such as the Belgrade student body. A further relevant point is the disproportionately high weighting of small states in Council voting and other decision making and its prospective impact. This results in the situation that larger collective political entities are more desirable than smaller fragmented ones from the standpoint of the impact of their membership on EU decision making.

The first part of the article considers the background and progress of membership negotiations. This is followed by an analysis of membership criteria and of attitudes towards membership. The last major part focuses on each of the three countries, and on EU decision-making issues.

The progress of the CEE countries towards EU membership has been relatively slow. In 1995 German Chancellor Helmut Kohl mentioned the year 2000 as a prospective entry date into the EU for Poland to the Polish parliament or *sejm*. However, he later had to back down on this and say that he had meant only that by 2000 the Poles would have been informed of their prospective date of entry[2] French President Jacques Chirac had also mentioned 2000 as a point of reference for enlargement.[3]

Membership negotiations for a possible 'first round' enlargement entry group consisting of the Czech Republic, Estonia, Hungary, Poland and Slovenia opened with discussions on 30 March 1998, and more formal negotiations on 10 November. A reception for all applicant countries held on 12 March 1998 was also attended by Bulgaria, Cyprus, Latvia, Lithuania, Romania and Slovakia, which were considered to be prospective 'second round' applicant countries. Turkey had also been invited, but failed to attend. A change of government in Malta in 1998 resulted in the incoming Christian Democratic Party government seeking the re-activation of Malta's earlier membership application. The 1998 Slovakian elections also brought a change of government, and a stronger desire to pursue EU membership.

In 1999 Germany urged the EU to start negotiations with all applicant countries and not just the 'first wave' ones selected in late 1997, after Austria, Sweden, Finland, France and Denmark indicated support for a 'regatta option' of opening negotiations with all applicants at the same time.[4] The adoption of the commission's *Agenda 2000* plan for enlargement on a so-called 5+1 model of negotiations with the five leading applicant countries from 30 March 1998 led to complaints from Slovakia and other applicant countries designated for 'second round' membership that it could lead to a 'New Yalta' and division of Europe.[5] The institution of an individual screening process for each applicant from 31 March 1998 has allowed Slovakia to be selected from the earlier group of prospective second-round entrants, with Lithuania, to continue scheduled negotiations.

There have been moves by the EU to offer special 'association agreements' to Albania, Bosnia, Croatia, Macedonia and even possibly Yugoslavia, opening up the prospect of a wider 'second round' or additional 'third round' enlargement which could bring the total number of EU member states to thirty-two.[6] This followed a German proposal for a commitment by the EU to admit the above countries as members at some point,[7] and a 'blueprint' for such a step in a working document of the Centre for European Policy Studies (CEPS).[8] On 27 May 1999 the EU proposed a new relationship with Macedonia and FYROM. German Foreign Minister Joschka Fischer was described as having 'dangled the carrot of membership' before the countries of the region, offering a 'stability pact'. He also said that this should not be considered as a shortcut to EU membership: 'Each country would be considered on its merits and compliance with the EU conditions of respect for democracy, human rights, peaceful relations and an open economy'.[9]

The conditions for membership of CEE and other applicant countries are of both explicit and implicit in nature. The June 1992 meeting of the European Council in Lisbon set out economic and political conditions for membership, and the requirement that candidates must demonstrate adequate respect for human rights and meet conditions of European identity and democratic status.[10] Key conditions for membership were laid down for the opening of accession negotiations by the Copenhagen European Council in June 1993, as follows:[11]

• the existence of stable institutions ensuring democracy, the rule of law, human rights and the protection of minorities;
• the development of a viable market economy capable of withstanding the pressure of competition and the forces of the EU's Single Market; and
• the ability to assume the obligations arising out of accession, and to subscribe to the objectives of political, economic and monetary union.

Following the setting of these the European Commission adopted an 'objectivity frame' to the selection of candidates, appraising the performance of each relative to the criteria.[12]

The first of the above conditions has been problematic for all of the 'awkward states' considered here, and only Slovakia meets the second and third conditions. Government pressures and controls on the media have been a source of criticism for all three countries, and remain a crucial problem in Serbia. Key issues with respect to applicants overall include: free movement of labour, which relates to the movement of both workers in general and of Roma minorities, the freeing up of sales of land, the level of support to be provided to agriculture, and closure or upgrading of inadequately safe nuclear power facilities.

The major debates or discourses relevant to enlargement and 'awkward states' reflect different theoretical perspectives, and the differing positions of participants in the debate. There are different constructions of the EU, and of its eastwards enlargement.[13] One of the discourses in favour of enlargement is that it is an historic opportunity,[14] which if lost may not return.[15] Coffey[16] speaks of a moral obligation on the part of the west to help the former communist countries of central and eastern Europe, on the basis that it earlier encouraged them to overthrow communism. The EU's progress towards enlargement has been seen by Holman and Van der Pijl as being driven by the interests of the European bourgeoisie or capitalist class,[17] and by Preston as reflecting the concern of the EU to maximise the benefits to current members.[18] The increased degree of security afforded to Foreign Direct Investment (FDI) in the CEE applicant countries has been described as the most important source of gains from their prospective membership.[19] It can also be seen as a factor behind support for enlargement from industry or capitalist interests. Enlargement is also encouraged by factors such as the prospective economic gains from resource complementarity, and from economies of scale.[20] However, the latter are increasingly less evident in the present 'information age' and trend towards greater importance of smaller and medium sized enterprises.[21] EU business will benefit from access to a relatively poorly paid additional workforce, albeit one which is not as highly skilled as that in the present EU.[22]

Enlargement moves have been criticised for not focusing on a wider Europe, but instead encouraging Russia, Ukraine and Turkey to feel excluded due to the construction of a 'hub and spoke' pattern of bilateral relations with neighbouring countries.[23] The nature of relations between the EU and the applicant countries has been criticised as 'an exercise in subtle racism using colonialist control mechanisms',[24] which tends to have a gendered characterisation in which the West European 'hero' saves the more passive and feminine East.[25]

Slovakia can be seen as an obvious possible candidate for EU membership, partly due to its location in Central Europe. Also, prior to 1993, the present Slovakian territory and the territory which was to become the present Czech Republic, now one of the leading entrants for membership, constituted Czechoslovakia. Surveys have indicated a high level of support for EU membership there, falling from eighty six per cent in 1994 to fifty seven per cent in 1996, recovering slightly to sixty two per cent in 1997.

The rationale for Croatian and especially Serbian membership differs from that for applicant countries in general, although it is similar to that for other states in South East Europe. The desire to include Croatia and Serbia in the

eventual EU could be considered to be implicitly exemplified by German
Foreign Minister Joschka Fischer's description of the full accomplishment of
European unification as not just a historical duty, but even more so one which
is in Germany's future interests.[26] Friis has argued that policy problems with
respect to enlargement are socially constructed,[27] while Davis has stressed
the importance of ideas and communicative action.[28] Both take the view that
governments do not necessarily know what their preferences and national
interests are, but search for these and define them over time. However, the
EU itself has a clear preference for continued enlargement so long as there
are prospective European candidates, and this reflects political and economic
self-interest and is hence consistent with rational choice theory and the view
that institutions know and look after their own interests and preferences.
There has nevertheless been controversy over policy choices. The initial EU
perspective on Yugoslavia was that the federation should be maintained, that
'ideas of self-determination were against the grain of European development',
and events in Yugoslavia (were) spoiling the European idea.[29] The perspective changed over time, and Fotopoulos argues that EU elites supported war
in Yugoslavia in terms of Nato's defence of Kosovo because it would 'indirectly bring the full integration of the Balkans into the EU'.[30]

The 'awkwardness' of Slovakia arose largely due to the policies of former
prime minister Vladimir Meciar when leader of the largest party in the government, the Movement for a Democratic Slovakia (HZDS), 1994-98. Slovakia
applied for EU membership on 27 June 1995. It was the only candidate country which the EU considered to fail to meet the democratic criteria for membership at that time.[31]

In the June 1990 elections Public Against Violence (PAV) had come first in
Slovakia with twenty nine per cent of the national assembly vote. In March
1991 it split into a federalist faction led by Fedor Gal and a more nationalist
faction led by Meciar called Public Against Violence - For a Democratic
Slovakia (VPN-ZDS).[32] Meciar won the first three elections he contested as
prime minister after 1989. Although the second Meciar government was
brought down in March 1994 and replaced by a broad left-right coalition, following the September/October 1994 elections his HZDS was able to form a
majority government with the aid of the extreme left Workers' Association
of Slovakia and the extreme right Slovak National Party.[33]

Problems between the government and the presidency of Slovakia were a concern for the EU. President Michael Kovac could himself have been considered a defector from Meciar's HZDS party, having given up his affiliation with it on taking up presidential office. The no confidence vote which removed the Meciar government temporarily from office in March 1994 followed a critical speech by the president on the state of the nation. In 1995 President Kovac's son was kidnapped and transported to Austria; he was wanted for questioning at that time by German police in relation to a fraud case. A number of questionable actions were undertaken towards former supporters who had left the party, including an attempt to remove the mandate of Frantisek Gaulieder when he left the HZDS parliamentary faction to sit as an independent.[34] The head of the Slovak Information Service (SIS), Vladimir Mitro, confirmed in 1999 that there had been 'enormous abuses of power' by the Service. According to him, under Meciar it had sought to slander Hungary's name in the region and to foster suspicion between Germany and Austria. It had put under covert surveillance members of Meciar's coalition partners and opposition parties, as well as a former defence minister, the head of the army, church officials and President Michael Kovac, and had also undertaken the kidnapping of Michal Kovac's son in 1995. He claimed that it had devised a campaign to try to convince Slovakians that the nation should fall back under the Russian sphere of influence, and that through 'Operation Dezo' it had fostered racial hated against the Czech Republic's gypsy minority 'in order to prevent' that country's 'accession into euroatlantic integration structures'. Meciar denied this and asserted that the accusations were 'all lies' in a letter to Czech Prime Minister Milos Zeman. In response to the allegations police had requested that parliament remove the immunity from prosecution of Ivan Lexa, the former head of the SIS and an HDZS MP.[35]

There were strong EU concerns when Meciar avoided allowing the position of president to be filled when it became vacant on 2 March 1998, allowing the President's powers to be exercised by the government. In February 1997 the EU urged the Slovak government to press ahead with economic reforms and bringing its laws into line with EU requirements. Enlargement Commissioner Hans Van den Broek said, pointing to Slovakia's shaky democratic record, that it would be regrettable if doubts over Slovakia's ability to satisfy the political criteria for EU membership jeopardised its accession to the Community.[36] In spite of this a new Slovakian election law was introduced in May 1998 four months before a general election. It skewed election coverage in favour of the ruling three-party coalition dominated by the HZDS and restricted all election broadcasting to the state-owned Slovak television and radio, which tended to be strongly in favour of the government. Fines were to be levied on any private TV and radio stations, these being generally hostile to the government, covering the election.[37]

Prior to the 1998 election Meciar had also considered making a number of changes to the political system to improve his own and his party's political chances. These included re-writing the election laws to allow only party leaders' names to go on the ballot paper, which would have assisted his HZDS party as he was much more popular than the party itself. He also considered abolishing the existing seven per cent coalition threshold with respect to taking up seats in parliament with a five per cent party one, and replacing the existing cross-party election supervisory committee with an 'electoral court' appointed by the government.[38]

These actions resulted in criticisms and opposition from domestic elites. The chancellors of six universities and colleges joined Catholic bishops in a call for political reforms and for a defence of civil liberties. They asked for standards of 'objective journalism' rather than the manipulation of news by the state-run media.[39] Meciar had already put the universities offside by getting a law passed in 1996 which allowed the government to intervene in matters under the jurisdiction of universities and faculties, deans and academic senates, also museum directors and the director of the National Theatre.[40]

The government continued to play down the importance of EU membership for Slovakia, and to take actions calculated to fail to meet EU-required standards. When Polish President Aleksander Kwasniewski commented that Slovakia's domestic political situation had made it a lesser candidate for EU membership than its neighbours, it responded that 'Slovakia does not consider the process of integration into European Union structures as a race.'[41] Meciar himself said that the EU needed Slovakia as 'geopolitically an exceptionally well-situated country', implicitly a bridge between east and west.[42] A history book for Slovakian schools, Milan S. Durica's *Dejiny Slovenska a Slovakov*, the production of which the EU had provided financial assistance for, turned out to attempt to play down Slovak involvement in the World

War II Holocaust, causing embarrassment to the EU which found itself helping to prevent distribution of the book to Slovak high schools.[43]

Under Meciar Slovakia had also shown reluctance to comply with EU wishes
in terms of both economic policy and that on minority and human rights. Its
economic achievements had nevertheless been significant, and better than
those of some of the more favoured applicant countries. In 1997 it had achieved
a growth rate of over four per cent and a GDP per head level equivalent to
that of fourteen per cent of the EU average; in 1998 growth was running at
around six per cent. Continued support for Meciar had arisen partly because
of these achievements. In the earlier post-communist years Slovakia had found
itself burdened by having a substantial but uncompetitive arms industry, and
an unemployment rate nearly twice that of the Czech Republic. In 1996 the
rate was still 11.6 per cent in Slovakia compared to six per cent in the Czech
Republic, but Slovakia had the lowest inflation rate in Central Europe. However,
it had been relatively unsuccessful in attracting Foreign Direct Investment
(FDI), receiving only US$1.4 billion in 1989-97 compared with US$7.8 billion
in the Czech Republic, US$18.0 billion in Hungary and US$25.6 billion in
Poland. Prospective foreign investors were frightened by the huge current
account deficit in Slovakia.[44] However, the situation that a sustained growth
rate of around four per cent of GDP was achieved in Slovakia with only relatively small inflows of FDI suggests that the government's general economic
policy was relatively successful. Nevertheless, in 1996 many banks were close
to insolvency. The government had gone into reverse on privatisation, halt-
ing the use of vouchers and selling off state companies mostly to those who
ran them. The latter tended to be former communist officials friendly with
Meciar. As a result of this *nomenklatura* privatisation over half of the country's private companies had been sold to friends of Meciar's party, mostly at
knockdown prices, and with finance from state banks. A reported example
of this was the take-over of control of the country's largest insurance company, Slovenska Pojistovna, by the steel company VSZ. The former head of
VSZ and its largest shareholder happened to be Meciar's election campaign
manager.[45]

The population of Slovakia was optimistic and approving of small-scale privatisation, but only in Bratislava was there a relatively high level of support
for more general privatisation, with twenty four per cent of those surveyed

being in favour. In the major regions of Slovakia the levels were eighteen, fourteen and seventeen per cent, compared with forty per cent in the Czech Republic.[46] The lack of progress towards privatisation on the part of the Meciar government was hence not inconsistent with popular views. This lack of progress, and an initial refusal to phase out a ten per cent import surcharge imposed during a period of economic difficulty, led to the EU threatening in 1995 to cancel anticipated further macro-financial assistance.[47] Nevertheless, Slovakia was a relatively industrialised economy where only 9.7 per cent of the labour force was employed in agriculture. Its exclusion in 1997 from the list of countries expected to be included in the initial enlargement was based on its failure to meet required democratic standards. Commissioner Van den Broek had issued a warning that only democratic countries with independent judiciaries would be acceptable for membership.[48] The European Commission also told Slovakia to hold free and fair presidential, national and local elections in 1998 to expedite membership.[49]

Minority rights issues have also been an impediment to membership for Slovakia, as with a number of CEE applicant countries. The Commission's 1997 Opinion on the membership of Slovakia was submitted to the Council and the European Parliament on 15 July[50] as part of the Agenda 2000 assessment arrangements. It commented relatively favourably on the extent to which economic criteria had been met, but negatively on political achievements. It also referred to the treatment of the Hungarian minority, which still lacked the benefit of a law on use of minority languages, although the government had undertaken to adopt one, and it said that the situation of the Roma needed attention. The Meciar government's response was to downplay these criticisms. It argued that a language law for the Hungarian minority was not necessary, and none was forthcoming.[51]

The problem with the Hungarian minority in Slovakia is seen by Auer[52] as reflecting the situation that a culturally defined nationalism can be as damaging and divisive as arrangements under the communist system. Slovak nationalists including Meciar have accused their political opponents of not being Slovak enough. Citizenship in Slovakia cannot be based solely on a culturally or ethnically defined nation, as this would exclude the large Hungarian minority and others. Extreme Slovak nationalists attempt to invalidate Hungarian minority claims for more cultural autonomy and rights by referring to the thousand years of Slavic settlement of Slovakia, and consider themselves to be more 'indigenous' than the Hungarian tribes.[53]

The lack of a general language law resulted in concerns for example over parents no longer being permitted to use Hungarian Christian names when registering babies.[54] The government argued that there had been no ban on particular names, and that 'only allowing the choice of first names from an officially approved list was a legacy of the former communist regime'.[55]

The 1998 general election resulted in the replacement of the Meciar government by the centrist government of Mikulas Dzurinda. The incoming Slovak Democratic Coalition (SDK) was composed of five parties. As well as the new Party of Civic Understanding (SOP), it included the Hungarian Coalition and the reformed communist Party of the Democratic Left. The inclusion of the Hungarian minority's party in the governing coalition signified a movement towards greater minority rights. The election of Rudolf Schuster as president of Slovakia in 1999, beating Vladimir Meciar's candidacy and obtaining a fifty seven per cent share of the vote, removed any remaining potential objections to Slovakian membership of the EU on the basis of democratic status. Schuster has since adopted a stance relatively independent of party politics, and been praised for this even by Meciar's party. Meciar himself had bowed out as head of the government on 30 September 1998 in a televised tearful farewell to the Slovak nation during which he sang 'Disappointed I am leaving you . . . I haven't hurt any of you'.

The new Slovak government was given a 'warm welcome' by EU governments, and an assurance that with respect to enlargement it could expect to 'board the train soon'. In practice this has not been so easily achieved, but it is still possible that Slovakia will be included in the first group of CEE entrants to the EU. Slovakia and Lithuania are the only two members of the second group of applicants with which the European Commission will continue scheduled association negotiations.[56]

Certain problems do remain. With respect to audio-visual policy the *Television Without Frontiers* directive[57] is required to be applied on a mandatory basis by the applicant countries even though this is not the case for the existing member states. A November 1998 Commission report (COM(98)703 final) on the situation in Slovakia stated that the directive had not yet been fully complied with.[58] The situation with regard to the Roma minority remains a possible barrier to entry. The persecution of Roma has been regarded as being most severe in Slovakia and Romania, although also meriting criticism in the Czech Republic.[59] Meciar earlier referred to the Roma as a 'problem group that is growing in size' and with respect to which there was 'extended reproduction of socially inadaptable populations'.[60] He later dropped this attitude in return for their political support. An exodus of Roma from Slovakia resulted in the UK reintroducing visa requirements in October 1998,[61] as did Iceland that year and Finland, Norway and Denmark in 1999. Given the extent of the discrimination and disadvantage to the Roma in Slovakia (and some other CEE countries), their lack of integration into society, and the greater safety and better welfare state arrangements in western Europe, it is unrealistic to assume that free movement provisions could be adopted without a major flow of Roma westwards. Kolankiewicz[62] says that that it is above all the position of the gypsies that poses a problem for the new Europe. What is required is EU funding of pan-European Roma arrangements, run by Roma themselves and not the host countries, to improve education and training and raise living standards.

Moreover, the new democratic government has not yet been able to bring about improvements in economic terms or with respect to the level of political stability. Unemployment rose to 17.7 per cent in 1999 and the standard of living of the average citizen declined. Dzurinda's own party, the Christian Democrats, will not be joining the SDK in the next elections. However, the SDK's affiliated parties continue to cooperate for fear of a political return by Meciar. Corruption scandals have led to the resignation of several cabinet members, include two heads of the National Property fund which oversees the privatisation of state assets. There have been revelations of financial assistance being given to the ruling party by companies which later received contracts ahead of others offering lower quotations.[63] Nevertheless there is much to encourage optimism with regard to Slovakia. A 1998 survey indicated that office space there cost only US$30 000 for a five year lease of 186 square metres, whereas in Ukraine the same leased space cost around $450 000, reflecting red tape, legal difficulties, and corruption.[64] Two instances relating to the behaviour of 'ordinary Slovakians' also suggest relative honesty. The driver of an Opel Astra from Germany to Bulgaria in 1999, according to the editor of a Slovak daily who accompanied him the whole way, was required to hand over bribes at all border crossings except the one from the Czech Republic into Slovakia.[65] With regard to the Sydney Olympic bid, whereas delegates were in many cases seeking personal benefits or benefits for their countries in return for their support, the Slovakian delegate and his wife were described as 'very honest' and surprised their hosts with their humble tastes and honesty.[66]

Croatia has only recently begun to be considered acceptable as a prospective EU member. In this it follows Slovenia which is well on the way to membership in the first group of applicant countries, and Macedonia which has only since the Kosovo crisis begun to be considered an acceptable potential applicant. On 19 July 2000 the European Commission proposed the opening of negotiations for a Stabilisation and Association Agreement with the Republic of Croatia. The decision was described as 'a major step forward in EU/Croatia bilateral relations' and one which followed the election of a new Croatian political leadership advocating radical political and economic reform. The new agreement will be the second one to be reached under the EU Stabilisation and Association Process launched in May 1999 to try and bring political and economic stability to the region. It will include provisions for political dialogue, incentives for greater regional cooperation, the creation of a free trade area with the EU after a transitional period, provisions on the movement of workers, freedom of establishment and so on, and cooperation in all fields of Community interest, including justice and home affairs. The first such agreement is presently being negotiated with Macedonia.[67] The agreement with Croatia could be in place by the end of the year 2000.[68] Croatia is the 'jewel in the crown' of the EU's strategy for South-East Europe[69] in view of the swift changes achieved there. It has been meeting EU policy aims for the region with respect to the return of refugees and to the handing over of war crimes suspects to the International Criminal Tribunal for former Yugoslavia. The latter policy has not been popular with the electorate, with 4000 demonstrating at the US Embassy after Croat General Tihomir Blaskic was sentenced to forty-five years in prison for 'appalling war crime'. Croatia criticised his sentence as too harsh and wishes for it to be served on Croatian soil. Croatia has also won EU approval for democratisation of the media, and for taking the first steps towards structural economic reform.[70] It can be contrasted with Serbia, which has not undertaken any similar steps.

Croatia was not earlier acceptable as a candidate for EU membership due to the relatively undemocratic nature of the Croatian Democratic Union (HDZ), the party of President Franjo Tudjman, and various other grounds. Tudjman was a former wartime partisan and Yugoslav National Army (JNA) general who became the first president of independent Croatia. The HDZ came to power in 1990, and on 23 December 1991 Germany indicated it would recognise the independence of Croatia with effect from 15 January 1992. Britain and France did not readily agree to do the same,[71] but nevertheless in the event the EC recognised the independence of Slovenia and Macedonia and on a conditional basis with respect to minority rights that of Croatia.

Tudjman sought to allay the fears of the Serb minority in Croatia by giving a formal official apology for the wartime Ustasha regime, which was estimated to have killed around a sixth of the Serbian population of Croatia.[72] However, remarks by him such as 'Thank God my wife is not a Jew or a Serb'[73] were not calculated to allay these fears. He chose the traditional red and white chequered Croat flag as the flag of the new Croatia, a decision much resented by the Serb population in the Krajina and elsewhere in Croatia. Milan Babic, Mayor of the Krajina capital of Knin, had asked on 12 August 1990 for guarantees on behalf of the Krajina Serbs that the chequered flag would never fly over Knin as under it 'their fathers and grandfathers had been murdered', also that Croat police would not be allowed into the area, nor Serb police required to wear black uniforms.[74] August 1995 was to see the chequered Croat flag indeed flying over Knin, and President Tudjman kissing the flag, raising a clenched fist and shedding tears of triumph at the Croatian victory of Operation Storm which had overrun the Krajina in three days starting from August 4, destroying the myth of Serb invincibility.[75] Some 150 000 Serb inhabitants of the Krajina were put to flight, crossing into Serbia at the rate of 1000 an hour. Thus was the earlier expulsion of some 200 000 Croat inhabitants of the Krajina by the Serbs there in 1991 reversed.[76]

The clearing of Serbs from the Krajina in August 1995 followed the mass slaughter of up to 8000 Muslim men and youths in the UN's supposed 'safe haven' of Srebenica in July when the enclave was overrun by Bosnian Serb forces. In the United States Newt Gingrich, speaker of the House of Representatives called it the 'worst humiliation for the western democracies since the 1930s'.[77] US Secretary of State Madeleine Albright, visiting one of the

mass graves being uncovered there the following year, described it as
'the most disgusting sight for a human being to see'.[78] Nearly 4000 bags of
human remains from Srebenica's mass graves now await DNA testing in stor-
age in nearby Tuzla. The town's Muslim defenders had themselves undertaken massacres in Serb villages around the town, for example at Kravica on
7 January 1993,[79] and Vlasenica.[80] According to Colonel Thomas Karremans,
the commander of the Dutch UN battalion responsible for the defence of
Srebenica when it fell, some two hundred of the surrounding Serb villages
had been burned by its Muslim defenders and even after the fall and
massacre of Srebenica it was 'still hard to tell the good guys from the bad
ones over there'.[81] However, the greatest number of murders, injuries and
rapes were inflicted by Serb forces, mostly of an irregular or paramilitary
nature.

President Tudjman used the state-owned media to support his political interests, hence failing to meet western democratic standards. In 1996 some 100,000
people protested against his shutting down of 'Radio 101', the only independent station in Zagreb, and the government was forced to back down.[82]
There were problems with corruption in his party, with some members having enriched themselves through the process of privatisation of state assets,
though Tudjman himself was regarded as relatively untainted by corruption.
Elections held on 15 June 1997 were described as 'free but not fair' by international observers and he obtained sixty one per cent of the vote, compared
with the twenty two per cent and eighteen per cent obtained by the other
two challengers respectively.[83]

Croatia under Tudjman was criticised by US Secretary of State Madeleine
Albright for failing to guarantee the security of refugee Serbs returning home
to Croatia. The situation of returnees and would-be returnees was to remain
difficult until the election of Stipe Mesic as president of Croatia in February
2000, a few weeks after a reforming government had taken office there. He
issued an immediate invitation to 300,000 ethnic-Serb refugees to return to
Croatia. Mesic had been a high ranking figure in Tudjman's Croatian Democratic
Union until he broke with Tudjman to establish the Croatian Independent
Democratic Party.[84] Tudjman died in 1999, having failed to make a full accom-
modation with the western powers and having for example in 1996 argued
that Bosnia had no future as an independent state.[85]

Croatia was badly affected by the break-up of Yusolavia and war during the early 1990s, when national income per head fell from US $3865 in 1990 to US $2693 in 1994, but by 1998 this had recovered to US $4544, a figure comparable to that of other applicant countries for EU membership.

With regard to Serbia, the European Commission says that 'Europe stands ready to welcome Serbia as soon as the present Serbian regime is replaced by leaders committed, like Croatia's, to democracy, the rule of law and economic and political reform'.[86] At the European Council Feira summit on 19-20 June 2000 the EU's leaders spoke for the first time of the states of former Yugoslavia as potential EU members, rather than on an individual case-by-case basis.[87] They encouraged the opposition in Serbia to continue its activities, and warned ethnic Albanian leaders in Kosovo to ensure the safety of the Serbian minority there and facilitate the return of refugees.[88] The EU's foreign ministers had earlier discussed issues which included supporting Yugoslavia's 300 independent media outlets and linking Serbian towns with towns in the fifteen member states. Foreign policy representative Javier Solana has stressed the need for the EU to bond with the people of Serbia and ensure the region does not become 'even more shut off'.[89] Commission President Romano Prodi told Zoran Djindjic, the leader of Serbia's Democratic Party, that:[90]

> It is the regime in Belgrade and its policies which are continuing to deny
> the Federal Republic of Yugoslavia its place in Europe, a place to which it
> will be wholeheartedly welcomed once a democratic government is in place.

Commissioner for External Relations Chris Patten added his voice to Prodi's and Solana's, speaking of the support the EU is giving to the area in terms of financial assistance to refugee aid, institutional reform, and infrastructure, and over 28,000 troops serving in Kosovo, and that the 'road to Europe' is open to Serbia.[91]

However, as Shelley comments, hopes that such 'mighty weapons' as town-twinning are going to oust the Milosevic government are far-fetched.[92] In spite of the EU's support for the Serbian opposition, Otpor student opposition activists are at the time of writing being arrested,[93] and the movement's active members consist increasingly of high school students, whose relative youth does not make them immune from arrest.[94]

The problem for prospects of EU membership for Serbia, or for that matter the Federal Republic of Yugoslavia which includes at least notionally Monte-negro and Kosovo, is that it has not undergone acceptable political change. This is because the regime is headed by President Slobodan Milosevic, the governing coalition being comprised of Milosevic's Socialist Party of Serbia (SPS), the Serbian Radical Party (SRS) of Vojislav Seselj, the Socialist People's Party (SPP), and the Serbian People's Party (XND). The government of Serbia proper consists of a not dissimilar coalition of the SPS, SRS, and the Yugoslav Left (JUL) party headed by Slobodan (Sloba) Milosevic's wife Mirjana (Mira).

The Milosevic government has been responsible for the waging of war against breakaway Slovenia and then Croatia, for supporting independent Serb forces waging war and carrying out atrocities in Bosnia-Herzegovina, and for 'eth-nic cleansing' exercises in Kosovo in 1999 which led to the occupation of the region by a KFOR force. It prepared the ground for action by the Bosnian Serbs by transferring Yugoslav People's Army (JNA) officers who were from Bosnia back there, contrary to earlier arrangements whereby the majority of JNA officers and conscripts would serve in regions or republics other than their home ones.[95]

One of the problems facing the achievement of political change in a more democratic direction and one more respectful of human rights has been that the closest contender to Milosevic has earlier been the extreme right-wing leader of the paramilitary 'White Eagles', Vojislav Seselj of the Radical Party. In the 1997 general election his party won eighty seats in the 250 seat assem-bly, only eighteen behind Milosevic's Socialists, with the pro-Monarchist Serbian Renewal Movement getting forty-five seats and seven smaller par-ties obtaining a total of fifteen seats.[96] Seselj's party's aims included a redraw-ing of Serbia's boundaries and the annexation of most of Croatia.[97] In the early 1990s his 'White Eagle' paramilitaries were associated with some of the worst atrocities of the wars in Croatia and Bosnia, including mass murder and rape, and he was described as 'one of the cruellest commanders of this war' during the Bosnian war.[98] In the topsy-turvy world that is present day Serbia, it is Seselj who has been giving lectures in, and sitting on the Board of, the Faculty of Law of Belgrade University.[99]

Student protests in Belgrade against the wars have been put down with police batons, water cannon and the bringing of tanks into the city. In 1993 protest leader and opposition figure Vuk Draskovic was arrested and badly beaten and tortured after leading protests against the Bosnian war, and has since had apparent attempts made against his life. In 1998 the government ended the autonomy of the universities. The repression of the media and closure of opposition radio and television stations has continued and been stepped up. Public support for Milosevic had been largely retained in spite of the war and the damage inflicted by the NATO bombardment over the attempted ethnic cleansing of Kosovo. This is because of the misrepresentations of the state-controlled media, and the continued tendency of a majority of rural Serbs to support his government and policies.

However, at the time of writing Vojislav Kostunica, the leading Serb presidential candidate of the Democratic Opposition of Serbia (DOS), appears set to gain a majority of votes over Milosevic in the presidential election on 24 September. One of the difficulties facing Serbian membership of the EU, and that of Bosnia or of Kosovo as a separate entity, will be the application of provisions on the movement of workers and freedom of establishment. This is because the wars of the past decade in former Yugoslavia have been mostly over the issue of who is allowed to live, work, run a business and so on, where. However, Serbia has by far the largest population of expellee refugees, hence would benefit most from this part of the *acquis* and from EU pressures on ex-Yugoslavia for the return of refugees and the restitution of their property. Such pressures are already leading to a permitted return of Serb refugees from the Krajina and Slavonia into Croatia, albeit on a small scale so far. Hence having lost the wars Serbia can still win the peace, in terms of a better deal for Serbs in Croatia and possibly Kosovo, with EU membership.

The smallness of the political entities involved in EU enlargement to take in former Yugoslavia is likely to create problems for the EU's decision making system in a way that the original Federal Republic of Yugoslavia would not have done. This is because of the extent to which the present system enhances the proportion of votes going to small countries in the Council, and the representation in the EP of the very smallest political entities, and the continued availability of a veto by individual member states. The present EU Intergovernmental Conference is seeking to achieve changes in some of these to facilitate eastwards enlargement. There is likely to be some pressure to prevent further splintering into newer and smaller states, for example on the part of Kosovo, and even to attempt to 're-federalise', although this presently seems unattainable.

In conclusion, Slovakia has ceased to be an 'awkward state' and such barrers as remain are likely to be due to economic factors and the risk of movement of the Roma population. Croatia is on its way to ceasing to be an 'awkward state', though while the government is committed to the changes necessary to achieve membership there is still some resistance on the part of the electorate to such matters as the delivery of alleged war criminals and the return of refugees. Serbia under the Milosevic government remains obstinately 'awkward', but there is likely to be swift and far-ranging political change there in the near future. In all three countries the failure of government to accept and pursue democratic norms has been the main cause of 'awkwardness', and once political change is achieved movement towards meeting other conditions can be swift.

Griffith University
h.field@mailbox.gu.edu.au

Notes

[1] The name 'Serbia' is used here and not that of Yugoslavia to reflect the current reality that Kosovo is under the control of the KFOR UN force and administration, and Montenegro has been taking an increasingly independent and separatist line. Also, the EU has been differentiating between the three entities in a manner indicating that they are *de facto* seen presently as separate states at least for the purposes of trade concessions.

[2] 'Germany and Eastern Europe: Just Do It', *The Economist*, 15 July 1995, pp. 39-40.

[3] Graham Avery and Fraser Cameron, *The Enlargement of the European Union* (Sheffield: Sheffield Academic Press, 1998), p. 41.

[4] Lykke Friis, 'The End of the Beginning of Eastern Enlargement - Luxembourg Summit and Agenda-setting', *European Integration Online Papers (EioP)* 2(7) 1981 p. 15, http://eiop.or.at/eiop.or.at/eiop/texte/1998-007.htm.

[5] Friis, 'End of the Beginning', p. 6.

[6] *European Voice*, 3 June 1999.

[7] *New Europe*, 31 May, 1998.

[8] Centre for European Policy Studies (CEPS) (1999), *A System for Post-War South-East Europe*, Brussels, 3 May.

[9] *New Europe*, 7 June 1999.

10 Helene Sjursen, 'Enlarging the Union', in *New Challenges to the European Union* (Aldershot: Dartmouth, 1997).

11 'EU Enlargement - Greater Coordination Essential', *European Union News* 16(7) 1998, 2, October/November.

12 Friis, *End of the Beginning*, p. 8.

13 Thomas Diez, 'Governance - a Matter of Discourse: Discursive Nodal Points in the British Debate Over Europe', paper presented to the Biennial Convention of the European Community Studies Association (ECSA), Seattle, 28 May - 1 June 1997.

14 Commission of the European Communities, 'Europe and the challenge of enlargement', *Bulletin of the European Communities 1992*, Supplement 3/92, 9.

15 The Federal Trust, Security of the Union: the intergovernmental conference of the European Union (Federal Trust: London, 1995).

16 Peter Coffey, *The Future of Europe* (London: Edward Elgar, 1995), pp. 96-7.

17 Otto Holman and Kees van der Pijl, 'The Capitalist Class in the Union', in *The Impact of European Integration* (Westport, Conn.: Praeger, 1996), pp. 55-74.

18 Christopher Preston, *Enlargement and Integration in the European Union* (London: Routledge, 1997), p. 9.

19 Alan Mayhew, *Recreating Europe: The European Union's Policy Towards Central and Eastern Europe* (Cambridge: Cambridge University Press, 1998), p. 198.

20 Heather Field, 'Enlargement of the European Union', *Contemporary European Studies Association of Australia (CESAA) Review* 25 1999, pp. 19-30.

21 Walter Mattli, *The Logic of Regional Integration* (Cambridge: Cambridge University Press, 1999).

22 Heather Field and James Goodman, 'Transforming Europe: New Zones of Dependency', *Democracy and Nature*, 5(2) 1999, pp. 217-38.

23 *Financial Times*, 16 September 1998.

24 Idas Daskalovski, 'Go East! Racism and the EU', *Central Europe Review*, 2(24) 2000, pp. 1-13, http://www.ce-review.org/00/24/daskalovski24.html.

25 Anne Gatensby and Nora Jung, 'The Political Economy of the Gendered Language of Technology Transfer to Eastern Europe', in *Desperately Seeking Sisterhood* (London: Taylor and Francis, 1997, pp. 169-177, 174-5.

26 Joschka Fischer, '*Bundesminister Joschka Fischer am 03.12.1999 vor dem Deutschen Bundestag (Auszuege)*' (Federal Minister Joschka Fischer on 3 December 1999 Addressing the German Parliament (Extract)', Auswärtiges Amt (Foreign Ministry), http://www.auswaertiges-amt.de/6_archiv/99/r/r991203a.htm, '*Die Vollendung der Europäischen Einheit is nicht nur eine historische Verpflichtung; sie liegt vielmehr auch im Interesse der Zukunft unseres Landes*'.

27 Friis, *End of the Beginning*, p. 1.

28 Michael Davis, 'European Union Relations with the Baltic States', paper presented at the fourth UACES research conference (University of Sheffield: 8-10 September 1999).

29 James Gow, 'Security and Democarcy: the EU and Central and Eastern Europe', in *Back to Europe: Central and Eastern Europe and the European Union* (London: UCL Press, 1999), pp. 23-36, 25.

30 Takis Fotopoulos, 'The First War of the Internationalised Market Economy', *Democracy and Nature*, 5(2) 1999, pp. 357-81, 364.

31 Karen Henderson, 'The Slovak Case of EU Enlargement: Foreign Policy and Domestic Political Conflict', paper presented to the ECPR standing group on international relations/international studies association joint conference in Vienna, 16-19 September 1998.

32 F. Stephen Larrabee, 'Democratisation and Change in Eastern Europe', in *The Shape of the New Europe* (New York: Council on Foreign Relations, 1992), pp. 130-71, 138.

33 Karen Henderson, 'Slovakia and the Democratic Criteria for EU Accession', in *Back to Europe: Central and Eastern Europe and the European Union* (London: UCL Press, 1999), pp. 221-40.

34 Henderson, 'Slovakia', p. 229.

35 *New Europe*, 1 March 1999.

36 *The European*, 20 February 1997.

37 *The European*, 7 September 1998.

38 'Slovakia: A Meciar Coup?', *The Economist*, 7 February 1998, p. 57.

39 *The Times Higher*, 15 May 1998.

40 'A Slovak Premier Cum Theatre Critic', *The Economist*, 9 November 1996, p. 70.

41 *The European*, 22 February 1996.

42 Henderson, 'Slovakia', p. 18.

43 Stefan Auer, 'Reflections on Nationalism and Minority Rights in Central Europe', unpublished paper, University of Melbourne, 1998.

44 *New Europe*, 30 August 1998.

45 The Economist, 'Central Europe Survey: Slowcoach Slovakia', *The Economist*, 18 November 1995, p. 19.

46 Iveta Radicova, 'Ethics in Business in Slovakia: A Sociological Survey', in *Business Ethics in East Central Europe* (Heidelberg: Springer Verlag, 1997), pp. 110-30, 111.

47 'Accession to the European Union of the Countries of Central and Eastern Europe: Situation, Costs, Prospects', *Eur-op News*, 5(1) 1996, 4, (Spring).

48 *The European*, 26 June 1997.

49 *New Europe*, 8 February 1998.

50 Commission of the European Communities, 'Commission Opinion on Slovakia's

Application for Membership of the European Union', (*Bulletin of the European Union 1997*), supplement 9/97.

51 Avery and Cameron, *Enlargement*, pp. 124-5.

52 Stefan Auer, 'Two Types of Nationalism in Europe?' *Russian and Euro-Asian Bulletin* 6(12) 1997, pp. 1-10.

53 Auer, *Reflections*, p. 23.

54 Burton Bollag, 'Blaming It All On Everyone But Himself', *The European 1994*, 15 April.

55 Milos Ruppeldt, Embassy of the Slovak Republic, 'Choosing Names from an Official List', letter to the editor, *The European 1994*, 22 April, p. 8.

56 *New Europe*, 2 July 2000.

57 Commission of the European Communities, 'Audio-Visual: Applicant Countries and the Community Acquis', (*SCADplus: AUDIO-VISUAL 2000*), 26 May, p. 1, http://europa.eu.int/scadplus/leg/en/lvb/e20109.htm.

58 Council of the European Communities, 'Directive on the Coordination of Certain Provisions Laid Down by Law, Regulation or Administrative Action in Member States Concerning the Pursuit of Television Broadcasting Activities' (89/552/EEC) *Official Journal* L298, 1989, 17 October, pp. 23-30.

59 Milada Vachudova and Tim Snyder, 'Are Transitions Transitory? Two Types of Political Change in Eastern Europe Since 1989', *East European Politics and Societies*, 11(1) 1997, pp. 1-35.

60 'His Struggle', *The Economist*, 18 November 1993, p. 52.

61 *The Times Higher*, 16 October 1998, p. 11.

62 George Kolankiewicz, 'The Other Europe: Different Roads to Modernity in Eastern and Central Europe', in *Europe's Fragmented Identities and the Frontiers of Citizenship* (London: Pinter, 1993), pp. 106-30, 118.

63 Michael J. Kopanic, 'Slovakia: Success Abroad, Questions at Home', *Central Europe Review*, 1(25) 1999, pp. 1-4, 13 December, http//www.ce-review.org/99/25/kopanic25. html.

64 Rupert Wright, 'Office in Slovakia, Phone in Baku', *The European 1997*, 16 March, p. 62.

65 Daniel Butora, 'Only Halfway to Freedom', *Transitions* 6(2) 1999, pp. 39-40.

66 *The Australian*, 5 May 1999.

67 Commission of the European Communities, *Major Step in EU Balkan Stabilisation Efforts: Commission Proposes Croatian Association with the EU*, Brussels 19 July 2000, http://europa.eu.int/rapid/startc . . . txt=gt&doc=IP/00/806/0/RAPID&lg=EN.

68 'Association Deal for Croatia?' *European Union News* 18(5) 2000, p. 3.

69 *European Voice*, 6 July 2000.

70 'Croatia: Edgy Start', The *Economist*, 8 April, 2000, pp. 60-61.

71   *New Europe*, 18 June 2000.

72   *The European*, 26 October 1995.

73   Laura Silber and Allan Little, *The Death of Yugoslavia* (London: Penguin, 1995).

74   Stjepan G. Mestrovic, 'Introduction', in *Genocide After Emotion: The Postemotional Balkan War* (London: Routledge, 1996), p. 19.

75   Silber and Little, *Death of Yugoslavia*, p. 92.

76   'Croatia's Blitzkrieg', *The Economist*, 12 August 1995, p. 47.

77   'The Flight of the Krajina Serbs', *The Economist*, 12 August 1995, p. 48.

78   Greg Campbell, *The Road to Kosovo* (Boulder, Col.: Westview, 1999), p. 58.

79   *The European*, 16 May 1996.

80   Tim Judah, 'The Family Angle', *Transitions*, 5(11) 1998, pp. 65-7.

81   *The European*, 16 May 1996.

82   'Black and Grey', *The Economist*, 5 August 1995, p. 46.

83   'Croatia and Serbia: End of Era?' *The Economist*, 30 November 1996, pp. 54-55.

84   *The European*, 19 June 1997.

85   Sabrina Ramet, *Balkan Babel: The Disintegration of Yugoslavia from the Death of Tito to Ethnic War* (Boulder, Colorado: Westview, 1996), p. 209.

86   'Europe's Last Strongmen', *The Economist*, 7 December 1996, pp. 17-18.

87   *The Economist*, 7 December, 1996, pp. 17-18.

88   Commission of the European Communities, *Major Step*.

89   'EU to Hold a Summit with Former Yugoslav Republics', *EurActiv 2000*, 21 June, http://www.euractiv.com/egi-bin/eu . . . t.exe/9430?1100=1&204&0IDN=1500473.

90   *New Europe*, 16 April 2000.

91   *New Europe*, 2 July 2000.

92   Chris Patten, 'South East Europe - Joining the European Mainstream', London, 2000, http://europa.eu.int/comm/comm/external . . . ions/news/patten/speech_00_259.htm, 7 July 2000.

93   John Shelley, 'Union Steps Up Efforts to Topple Milosevic Regime', *European Voice*, 6 July 200, p. 13.

94   Slobodan Jaksic (former Belgrade Law Faculty student), personal communication.

95   'Five Otpor Members Detained, Three Spend Night In Police', and 'Arrested for Otpor Posters', *FreeB92 News* 20 August 2000, also 'Otpor Arrests' and 'Otpor Arrests Continue in Vojvodina', 14 August, http://news.freeb92.net /index.phtml.2.

96   Silber and Little, *Death of Yugoslavia*, p. 240.

97   *The European*, 25 September 1997.

98   For example, in the ethnic cleansing of the village of Brezovo Polje near Brcko in northern Bosnia in 1992 even the local Serb troops who claimed to be under orders to rape the girls from the village during their deportation tried to protect the women from Seselj's subordinates, assuring the latter that they did not need to

worry, as the girls had already been raped (Stiglmayer, *Rapes in Bosnia-Herzegovina*, 160). The White Eagles have been associated with some of the most vile atrocities of the Bosnian war.

[99] Alexandra Stiglmayer, 'The Rapes in Bosnia-Herzegovina', in *Mass Rape: The War Against Women in Bosnia-Herzegovina* (Lincoln: University of Nebraska Press, 1994), pp. 82-169, 160.

David Brown

The New Hurdle: The Prospects for Polish And Estonian Accession To 'Pillar III' in the Post-Tampere European Union

ABSTRACT

During the current enlargement process, the issues surrounding the Third Pillar of the European Union, with the exception of elements of the asylum and immigration *acquis* (which were subsequently transferred to the European Community pillar at Amsterdam), have been relatively marginalised. At one stage, it was even suggested that a partial accession could take place, with entrance to Pillars Two and Three considered of little difficulty to the applicant states from central and eastern Europe, while the more complex elements of the Community *acquis* would be postponed to a later date. This paper, by critically examining the likely solutions offered by two of the original 'first wave' candidates, Poland and Estonia, will suggest that accession to the internal security agenda of the European Union will be a far greater obstacle than originally imagined. Through a detailed empirical assessment of the administrative and logistic capacities required for full implementation of the 'Tampere agenda' - the latest development to the internal security *acquis*, agreed at the Tampere European Council of October 1999 - it will be demonstrated that neither of them is within reach of successfully completing the Justice and Home Affairs *acquis* within the timetable currently being suggested.

In December 1999, two European Council meetings were held in Helsinki and Tampere. In different ways, the agreements made at both meetings would significantly affect the prospects for enlargement of the European Union to the applicant states of central and eastern Europe. At Helsinki, which was the last European Council meeting under the Finnish Presidency, the member states endorsed the 'regatta' model of enlargement negotiation,[1] opening the accession process to all those excluded from the initial 'first wave' decision.[2] The Estonian Foreign Minister, Toomas Ilves, commented that 'the situation has ... changed ... all of the twelve applicants are now in the same boat', adding that it was no longer guaranteed that the initial front-runners would complete accession procedures first.[3] Rather than demonstrate preferential treatment to the original 'first wave' states, the position of the European Union, post-Helsinki, is 'that each candidate country will be able to join when it is ready, and, if Poland is not ready, it will have to wait'.[4] In contrast, while the agenda of the special European Council meeting at Tampere did not dwell on the question of enlargement, the first ever European Council meeting dedicated solely to Pillar Three matters will also have important consequences for the applicant states. In agreeing the priorities for the European Union in the field of internal security - a matter rarely discussed in conjunction with the current enlargement process[5] - the member states have established the markers by which all applicants will be judged.

At Tampere, the European Commission also agreed to operate a 'scoreboard', which 'would show year by year and publicly how matters are progressing and where blockages lie'.[6] This was a device used very effectively in the drive towards implementing the Single Internal Market, and would be a first step towards tackling the 'implementation gap' that clearly exists between the rhetoric and reality of 'an area of freedom, security and justice'. The purpose of this article is to offer a similar assessment for two of the most prominent candidates for accession, Poland and Estonia, who were both within the initial 'first wave' of accession candidates. In order to make the assessment as current as possible, the agreements reached at Tampere will be utilised as the best available guide to the future intentions of the European Union in the field of internal security. The focus of the paper will not be on the potentially deleterious consequences of the proposed enlargement to central and eastern Europe, such as the penetration from Russian organised crime and the over-dramatised surge in illegal immigration. Instead, the article will examine the likely solutions offered by Poland and Estonia, through a detailed empirical assessment of the administrative and logistic capacities required for full implementation of the 'Tampere agenda'. It will be suggsted that, while neither of them is within reach of successfully completing the Justice and Home Affairs *acquis* within the timetable currently being suggested, on most of the Tampere agenda, Poland is in a slightly more advantageous position.[7] This is contrary to the current speculation concerning the state of negotiations between Poland and the European Union, which has led some commentators to conclude that 'Poland could be left out of the first wave of entrants'.[8]

Before examining the specific progress made in both states, a brief summary of the 'Tampere agenda' is necessary. Paavo Lipponen, the Finnish Prime Minister, hailed the 'ten milestones of Tampere',[9] which are listed within the Presidency Conclusions. While the scope of this paper is too small to fully explore all ten elements of the Tampere programme, key decisions can be identified in three main areas: immigration and asylum matters, judicial co-operation and increased police co-operation between the member states of the European Union. For immigration and asylum, where there is the greatest degree of consensus amongst the fifteen member states, moves were made towards a common asylum system, which would, in part, establish a common asylum determination procedure for the whole European Union.[10] More importantly for the states of central and eastern Europe, continued emphasis was placed on the concept of immigration control, with plans for more severe sentencing for traffickers, strengthened external border controls and a greater role for Europol (the European Police Office). It had its powers augmented by "authorising it to ask Member States to initiate, conduct or co-ordinate investigations or to create joint investigative teams in certain areas of crime".[11] Europol also received a further boost with the planned establishment of a new forum for European police chiefs to support its work.[12] However, the 'milestones' that received the most publicity concern the third main area, that of judicial co-operation. While it has been felt, in the past, that judicial co-operation has been the poor relation of the Third Pillar, failing to keep pace with the developments in the policing field, the plans agreed at Tampere, if fully completed, would see the creation of a 'European area of justice'.[13] For example, a new organisation, Eurojust, has been suggested, in order to 'ensure that criminal investigations launched by Europol will result in the bringing of charges and the securing of convictions'.[14] While it must be noted that certain states, such as the United Kingdom, remain opposed to the creation of a single, harmonised judicial area,[15] this paper is more concerned with the position of Poland and Estonia on these issues. It would seem clear that, while Helsinki took the enlargement process one step further forward, the Tampere agenda, ironically, focused on those areas wherein lies the biggest difficulties for the applicant states.

The first problem to be considered when assessing the likelihood of Poland and Estonia being able to meet the requirements of the 'Tampere agenda' for immigration and asylum matters concerns the external border regime, consistently the key compensatory measure since its proposition in the 1989 Palma Document. While it is clear that both states have serious problems in attempting to achieve the agreed minimum standards required to operate a European Union external border regime, the problems differ significantly in nature. In the case of Estonia, for example, it is the final demarcation of the border itself that remains uncertain. As O'Dowd has pointed out, 'if there is to be a 'fortress Europe', its eastern line has yet to be settled'.[16] While the detailed negotiations with the Russian government on demarcation of their joint border were concluded in March 1999, seven years after the initial process began, the full ratification process has yet to be completed.[17] The actual process of negotiations that took place is also worth further consideration, as it demonstrates the necessity of making concessions to the Russian negotiating position in order to reach agreement. While the Estonian Government would have liked the border between the states to return to the position outlined in the Treaty of Tartu (1920), which would involve part of the Pechory region becoming Estonian territory,[18] this proved to be a significant stumbling block. Eventually, it was agreed to remove all reference to previous treaties, and attempt to concentrate on a technical agreement between the two states, a substantive concession to the Russian negotiating position.[19] Even following this diplomatic manoeuvre, announced by the then Estonian Prime Minister, Andres Tarand, in November 1996, it took another two years to reach the stage of initialling the document.[20] While the Estonian Foreign Minister is correct in his assessment that 'a signed agreement has more worth than any political speech or statement',[21] the final implementation of the agreement is not a foregone conclusion.

The issue seems to be loaded with such historical and political significance for the Russian government that even the celebration of the eightieth anniversary of the Treaty of Tartu in Estonia evinced a stern rebuke from the Russian ambassador. Alexei Glukhov stated that 'the Tartu peace agreement . . . is an event belonging to the days gone by',[22] and implied that such celebrations would not assist the good neighbourly relations required for stability in the region. The reaction of newly elected Russian President, Vladimir Putin, is also not known, and, realistically, he could yet demand even further concessions from the Estonian government in return for the final demarcation of their mutual border. It is also worth putting such matters into context. It should, therefore, be noted that, in the first six months of 1998, the last published statistics available from the Estonian Statistical Office; there was an 8.2 per cent decline in the number of crossings of the mutual Estonian-Russian border.[23] This would seem to suggest that there need not be as great a sense of urgency about finalising an agreement as is currently displayed by the Estonian government (under pressure from the existing member states of the European Union), as the border is not as porous as in previous years. It should also be remembered that there has been no such agreement between Latvia and Russia, with the Russian government continuing to stall over the necessity of guarantees for the Russian diaspora within Latvia.[24] Significantly, the position of the European Union in both of these disputes has been to argue that the differences in opinion over the exact positioning of the inter-state border will not prevent either Estonia or Latvia from becoming members of the European Union.

This would be in line with the conclusions of a group of Estonian academics and experts in international law, established in 1996, to examine whether Russia's refusal to recognise the Treaty of Tartu as a legal basis for negotiation affected the legal continuity of the Estonian State. The group argued that there was no impact on the legal continuity of the Estonian state,[25] although, as the commission was established by an Estonian government in the midst of negotiations with the Russians, such a conclusion cannot have been unexpected. Significantly, such a conclusion would be in stark contrast to the current rhetoric of certain member states, notably Austria and the United Kingdom. It would also be out of synch with the conclusions of the Tampere Council, which placed considerable emphasis upon achieving agreed standards of immigration and border control across all of the territory of the European Union. Tony Blair, for example, commented that 'it is important for countries to protect their own boundaries, and to protect them . . . against illegal immigration'.[26] While Estonia cannot agree, once and for all, a demarcated border with Russia, it would seem unlikely that any agreed standards could even be judged, let alone met. If Estonia was still permitted to accede without final agreement on the mutual border with Russia, this would send out a dangerous signal to the other applicant states, concerning the flexibility of the *acquis communautaire*.

While there is no ambiguity over the legal status of Poland's shared borders, its geographical position does place it next to three non-European Union states, namely Belarus, the Ukraine and the Russian enclave of Kaliningrad. Grabbe has pointed out that 'much of this long border is "green", running through open country and mountains', which would make the level of control necessary 'difficult and costly to patrol'.[27] Poland also has a specific problem relating to the timetable for eventually meeting the standards laid down as part of the Schengen Convention, which has now replaced the defunct External Frontiers Convention as the basis for the so-called 'ring of steel'. In the last Commission Report on Poland, the assessment was made that 'the requirements of an external European Union border are seemingly proceeding in an ad hoc manner'.[28] The Commission could find 'no overall plan . . . which can quantify either the budget required . . . [nor] the number of years needed for achieving even the minimum standards currently expected'.[29] Significantly, while there were still substantial shortages of manpower and equipment highlighted in the Estonian assessment, the Commission was able to estimate a completion date for the Estonian Border Guard reform programme. Although the nine year estimate for Estonia[30] contrasts sharply with the Estonian government's somewhat optimistic declaration that 'January 2003 denotes . . . the moment when we can assure ourselves and the whole world that Estonia is no longer a country in transition',[31] there is a definite plan and timetable to work towards. While the source of the problem is different to that of Estonia, the end result - an inability to even begin to assess whether Poland is capable of meeting the Schengen standards - is the same.

There are other general areas of concern that deserve to be highlighted when discussing the issues of immigration and asylum. The question of resources, indicated earlier in the paper, is a source of concern for all applicant states, although both Poland and Estonia have had a longer period of time to redress any resource imbalance. In Poland's case, the problem seems to be less to do with the level of resources than the actual prioritisation and division of the finances available. For example, despite an overall increase in the budget for border matters, from EURO 107 to 132 million in 1999, the Commission still concluded that the Polish Border Guard was 'under-performing owing to a lack of adequate equipment, infrastructure and operational budget'.[32] The devil, as always, is in the detail, and, behind the headline increase, only seven million is reserved for investment in equipment and a mere EURO 400,000 for staffing.[33] This does not seem adequate to alleviate the current problems in recruitment and staffing, especially given that the same report also estimates that there was a thirty two per cent vacancy rate in the Polish Border Guard, within the context of an overall increase in staffing levels. The situation is made even more complicated for Poland, ironically, due to the differing priorities of the most vehement supporter of their candidacy, Germany.

While continued transfer of staff from mutual borders with European Union member states would alleviate reported manpower shortages at the eastern border, the timing of this switch will be crucial. At present in Poland, only 8300 guards have been assigned to the eastern border, out of a total of over 18,000 in 1998.[34] Rather than simply begin the process of redistributing the bulk of the Polish Border Guard to the more crucial eastern border, which would allow them to more speedily meet the requirements of the *acquis communautaire*, the Polish government have continued, as noted earlier, to employ more staff. This has knock-on consequences for training and experience levels, increasing 'the difficulties of dealing with sophisticated . . . crime . . . and the development of adequate criminal intelligence structures'.[35] Perhaps more importantly, the failure simply to work within the current staffing levels highlights a central dilemma of the current enlargement process. A substantial re-weighting of the relative strengths of the eastern and western borders of Poland, in favour of the eastern border, may, currently, be in the interest of Poland (and will certainly be in the long-term interests of the other member states). The complicating factor is that it remains more advantageous for Germany and other front-line member states to maintain a strong western border for as long as possible. As an illustration, in 1998, there was a recorded 'reduction of forty per cent on illegal crossings . . . on the Western border',[36] yet the overall number of illegal crossings of Polish borders increased. This may be good news for Germany, which is able to utilise Poland as a convenient buffer zone, but does not aid Poland's chances of meeting the necessary border control standards required as part of accession. Poland will only be judged on the capability of its eastern border guard to meet the Schengen criteria (as the mutual border with Germany would become an internal border of the European Union when Poland accedes). Therefore, it is of greater concern for Poland to see extra resources and manpower targeted there, a fact recognised in the Polish Strategy on Integrated Border Management, which states that the eastern borders of Poland should have priority in all EU-related funding.[37] However, the priorities dictated by the re-admission agreement with the Schengen states and the need for Germany, in particular, to protect its own borders in the meantime have led to a continued distortion in the balance between the eastern and western Polish borders.

While Poland, reluctantly, seems prepared to act as a buffer zone for its western neighbours, there is no question of Estonia playing the same role. In fact, the insistence of the Estonian government on an immigration quota - based on a 0.05 per cent share of the total Estonian resident population[38] - seems to suggest an unwillingness to ever act in the way that Poland has done. While, as a result of its geographical position, Estonia does not face the same dilemma as its Polish counterpart, such a policy will only complicate another area where progress is required if the European Union is to agree a common European immigration and asylum policy. Given that the current state of negotiations within the European Union on the issue of burden-sharing has been described by one Commission official as having reached a 'total political impasse',[39] the more compliant Polish attitude will only benefit any future attempts to reach agreement on the subject.

In fact, in the general area of asylum matters, Poland seems to be better prepared than Estonia to meet the challenges of membership. The overall asylum numbers, while substantially higher than those of Estonia, do indicate a more optimistic downward trend. In 1998, 3100 immigrants applied for asylum, compared to the previous year's total of 3531,[40] figures that, admittedly, dwarf the twenty five outstanding Estonian cases awaiting processing in July 1998.[41] Yet, once again, a more detailed examination makes less comfortable reading for Estonia, especially when the prevailing trends for both states are contrasted. As noted above, Poland has, since 1998, begun to register a decrease in the overall number of asylum cases to be processed, helped by the introduction of 'a special office to deal with all asylum-related issues'.[42] Unlike

Estonia, Poland has begun to establish the necessary infrastructure required to 'fast-track' and remove 'manifestly unfounded' asylum seekers and economic migrants. This suggests that Poland, in relative terms, is closer to the European Union's agreed position, and therefore better placed to participate in the common asylum system suggested at Tampere.

Estonia, by way of a contrast, has failed to even establish the necessary administrative structures required for full participation in any agreed 'common asylum system'. This has led to Estonia's poor record in asylum processing. While only fifteen cases were registered in the Commission report in 1998, none of them had been processed over fifteen months later. The Commission was unable, in its report, to even indicate at what stage within the process each case was at, or even suggest whether the processing had even begun. To make matters worse, another thirteen cases have entered the asylum process according to the 1999 report.[43] The Commission has suggested that such delays have developed, in part, due to the lack of experience demonstrated by the elements of the Estonian administrative structure that are in place. The official explanation offered for the delay that developed in 1998-1999 centred on the fact that the regulations necessary to implement the Refugees Act (9 July 1998) were not actually in place. However, as well as offering a timely warning to the European Union that it must concentrate on full implementation, rather than simple ratification of legislation, this excuse is no longer valid. The regulations are now in place, yet the backlog has actually worsened.[44] This suggests that the problem is more deep-rooted than the Estonian administration was originally suggesting, and will take a substantial reform programme to resolve.

The second area where both states face significant problems in creating the administrative apparatus, let alone meet the standards of the current member states, is the area of judicial co-operation in criminal matters. This was the area that garnered the most attention at the Tampere summit, with agreements made on Eurojust and the mutual recognition of judgements in criminal matters. Even the possibility of eventually moving towards a European *corpus juris* was raised in discussion. The Finnish Presidency recognised the agreements at Tampere as laying the foundations for a common 'European judicial area, by making the methods and practices of justice systems more commensurate'.[45] In fact, the shift of emphasis to questions of European judicial co-operation has been explained as providing the 'second major engine, alongside the launch of the Euro, to drive a new wave of integration'.[46] While not all of the current member states consider this to be the way forward for the European Union, the focus on judicial co-operation in criminal matters creates an even more substantive obstacle for the applicant states, which demonstrate severe shortcomings in this particular field. The gap between the applicant states and even the current level of co-operation in this area belies the argument that the deepening and widening of integration can happen simultaneously. The applicant states will always, by definition, be playing 'catch up' with the current member states, as the *acquis communautaire* will not remain static during the accession process. If, as is suggested, progress is made in this specific area, however necessary to operationalise 'the area of freedom, security and justice', the likelihood of the applicant states being able to meet the demands of membership will diminish substantially.

The record of Estonia in this area is hardly edifying, with the European Commission recognising a failure on the part of the Estonian government to put in place the necessary foundations for any future system of judicial co-operation. One of the main problems in this area is the continued reliance on judges trained and employed within the preceding Communist era. This problem was highlighted in the 1998 report, which noted that 192 of the 221 existing judges had been trained under the previous Communist regime, where priorities were somewhat different to that which is required to be a member of the European Union.[47] As a result, the Commission has called for a programme of retraining for existing judges in European Community law, and suggested that this 'training should be accompanied by an increase in the number of judges'.[48] However, despite the importance placed on this issue by the Commission, the 1999 report actually registers a decrease in the overall number of the Estonian judiciary. While the decline has only been slight, from 221 to 219, the Estonian government has found itself more, rather than less reliant on the judges trained under the old system. In contrast, the police forces immediately attempted some form of ideological purge of those trained in the Communist era.

It is difficult to imagine the other member states being content with a perceived Communist inspired judiciary of the Estonian administration participating fully within the envisaged European judicial system, especially as such a system will depend greatly on mutual trust and informal contacts. Plans for mutual recognition of judgements, where each state would accept court rulings from other states, are already under attack. For example, Ann Widdecombe, the Shadow Home Secretary, insisted that 'Britain must retain control over its own system of prosecution . . . we must not yield these rights to any other power'.[49] If the plans are eliciting such vehement opposition while the only proposed participants in such a system would be the 'safe' countries of the European Union, it is not difficult to imagine the reluctance likely to be expressed at Estonia's future participation, should the current situation continue.

While the Commission was unable to make any clear cut judgement on Poland's chances of effectively operating a system of mutual recognition - commenting in October of last year that 'comprehensive information is lacking on the state of co-operation and the application of mutual legal assistance' - there are some indications that progress is actually being made. While there still remains, as with Estonia, a 'large backlog of pending cases and a poor allocation of human resources',[50] Poland at least strikes a positive note where recruitment is concerned. There was an increase registered in 1999, although (perhaps significantly) the 1998 figure, by which any detailed comparison could be made, is not included in any Commission report. Initially, Poland had also faced considerable problems with a perception of overt Communist influence within the judiciary. In an attempt to rectify this situation, Poland created the Vetting Court, an idea suggested by the Commission in its 1998 Report. The Court will be able to examine any government officer or member of the judicial system regarding their involvement in the Communist regime, and, while it has no power to force resignations, critical opinions have, in the past, resulted in just that outcome.[51] This stands in sharp contrast to Estonia, which, as noted above, remains overtly reliant on those trained and employed during the preceding Communist regime. The Vetting Court will have an important role to play in reassuring potential partners within any future European judicial system.

Such reassurance will become even more difficult to achieve in the light of the first ever report by the Ministry of Internal Affairs into corruption in the field of public administration. This report highlighted the judiciary as one of 'the public services most vulnerable to corrupt practices',[52] although Poland has attempted to address this through measures such as the establishment of a hotline to anonymously report cases of bribery. These are aimed at restoring, not only public confidence, but also international confidence in the judicial and police structures of the state. However, there is a considerable mountain still to be climbed, more so in the field of police co-operation. The Commission indicates that 'regrettably, there is a general lack of a long-term and integrated anti-corruption strategy in the public administration',[53] and notes, with particular concern, that 'the Polish authorities . . . have not responded adequately in relation to the importance of the issue'.[54] The report also accepts that corruption amongst the various Polish police forces is 'widespread', although it seems to dismiss this with the unfortunate assessment that the problem is 'essentially . . . confined to the lower ranks'.[55] As it will be the lower ranks that will have to implement any measures agreed by the proposed forum of European police chiefs, or operate alongside Europol (as suggested at Tampere), then this is not a problem that can be dismissed lightly.

It is also not a new problem. In 1997, the International Crime Victim Survey indicated that, along with the Czech Republic, Poland had the dubious distinction of having the highest level of corruption of any state recorded in the survey.[56] Even after a decade of reform in the sphere of policing, with the Police Act of 1990 creating a completely new police force to replace its discredited predecessor, the public tends to remain highly suspicious of their local police force. The fact that the survey recognised an 'almost triple increase in the number of responses indicating policemen as officials that demanded a bribe' (from just over eleven per cent to almost a third of those interviewed)[57] is clear evidence of this trend. Given that the main thrust of European police co-operation, such as the role primarily envisaged for Europol, is targeted on information exchange, which is, in itself, predicated on the existence of mutual confidence and trust in the 'competent authorities' of the other member states, surveys such as this cannot be ignored. The Pre-Accession Pact, for example, attaches 'great importance to the mutual exchange of law enforcement intelligence, while safeguarding the protection of data'.[58] While Poland's Accession Partnership stated that 'corruption has to be addressed and accountability enhanced',[59] the European Commission's findings seem to suggest that this pledge will require greater effort than has been put in up to now.

The situation for Poland is further complicated when an issue that rarely gets taken into consideration within the academic sphere is highlighted. The prominent role taken by the secret services within the Polish internal security field will make an already difficult background for transfer of information between states even more complex. The European Commission agreed, stating that 'the role of the Secret Services could hamper co-operation with the European Union, since information often cannot be easily released by the Polish authorities without violating official secret constraints'.[60] Damage has already been done by the culture of continued secrecy that depicts the Polish internal security field. While certain matters that fall within the remit of the Secret Services are, understandably, sensitive, such reliance on 'official secret' status is adversely affecting Poland's participation in mutual criminal assistance with its potential European Union partners. Their different interpretation of the level of transparency required in such matters 'inhibits much of the international dialogue',[61] and leads to 'a great majority of requests for mutual assistance simply [being] denied, because they are held to be secret by the Polish authorities'.[62] This could have a reciprocal impact on Polish requests for information, with states unsure of whether they should share information freely with a state that would not respond the same way for them.

Estonia would also, it is assumed, be likely to give the secret service within their state the same title, given the reaction of Prime Minister Laar to Russian claims that the Estonian government has allowed NATO to establish spy centres on Estonian territory.[63] Rather than attempt to ameliorate Russian concerns, especially when the Estonians still require final Russian agreement on the demarcated mutual border, Laar simply pointed out that he 'would be much more concerned if the development of such Estonian structures did not cause headaches to anyone'.[64] The reference to 'development' of such structures, and the prominent defence issued by the Prime Minister would seem to suggest that the Estonian secret service is valued in the same way as their Polish counterparts, regardless of the consequences. However, it would be interesting to speculate whether Laar's reaction would be as defensive if this issue causes 'headaches' for its potential European Union partners.

There is also a question mark over whether the security services of any state should be considered a 'competent authority', and therefore have access to any information passed within the European policing sphere. Willy

Bruggemann, the Deputy Director of Europol, the agency that would be working closely with both post-accession states, seemed to suggest that secret service organisations would be considered as 'competent', as long as the signatory
state indicated that that was the case.[65] According to a Commission official,
the Convention text refers solely to 'any other public-law agencies',[66] without making any specific mention of the secret or intelligence services. In both
cases, given the prominent role that they have played thus far, it is difficult
to imagine them not being given that label, although, incidentally, Poland
has not placed the same emphasis on co-operation with Europol as existing
member states have.

However, according to Article 15 (paragraph 2) of the Convention, 'member
states may use the data for other, in particular also intelligence and secret
service, purposes with the prior consent of the unit which communicated the
data'.[67] The separation of the intelligence and secret services from other 'competent authorities', which are referred to in the following paragraph, seems,
however, to contradict the Bruggemann position. There would seem, according to Article 15, to be different rules regarding the use and access to data,
depending on whether the request was made by the security service or another
'competent authority'. In the latter case, 'personal data retrieved . . . shall be
used in accordance with the laws . . . of the authority which uses the data',[68]
removing the need to obtain prior permission from the national unit which
placed the data within the system in the first place. This ensures that the
secret services, which are unlikely to have many operating rules and regulation (at least not published), do not have the right to unconstrained access.
It also suggests that there is a difference between the intelligence services, on
one hand, and the 'competent authorities' that will be involved in the day-
to-day information transfer that will constitute much of the European police
co-operation agenda. Therefore, the continued prominence of the secret services, while possibly legally permitted to be involved within the wider European
policing sphere, will place yet another political obstacle in the way of both
states' desire to be fully involved in the on-going development of police cooperation.

In conclusion, with even the briefest survey of some of the key issues that
are likely to dominate the internal security agenda over the next decade, it
is clear that neither Poland nor Estonia are overtly well prepared to incor-

porate the Tampere agenda within their administrative structures. On asylum matters, while the scale of the problem is far greater in Poland, the infrastructure seems to be in place and the trend of speedily reducing the number of asylum requests is in line with the prevailing viewpoint of the current European Union membership. Estonia must also resolve the outstanding issue of its border with Russia, and should not rely too heavily on the assurances of the European Union that it will not allow Russia to exercise a veto over the process of enlargement. It would be politically difficult to justify such a precedent, of allowing a state into the European Union without full and legitimate recognition of all of its borders, and would only give encouragement to Latvia that there was no need to finalise an agreement with Russia in order to ensure membership. While both have problems in the judicial field, again, it seems that only Poland, which is rumoured to be falling behind in the accession 'race', has any potential solutions in place. Yet, in the crucial field of police co-operation and the increased mandate of Europol, Estonia seems to have the advantage. While the self-imposed deadline of 2003 seems particularly optimistic given the need to embed the new administrative infrastructure, if Estonia does finish the accession process ahead of Poland, the European Union will have given its clearest indication yet of where its priorities lie within the remit of Pillar Three.

University of Aberdeen
pol108@abdn.ac.uk

Notes

[1]   See the first section of the 'Helsinki Presidency Conclusions', 10-11 December 1999, entitled 'Preparing for Enlargement', (Luxembourg: Office for the Official Publications of the European Union, 1999).

[2]   For details of the enlargement process, see G. Avery and F. Cameron, *The Enlargement of the European Union*, (Sheffield: Sheffield Academic Press, 1998).

[3]   'Foreign Minister Ilves sees 2000 as Decisive for Estonia's Bid for European Union', *Estonian Review*, 16-22 January 2000, p. 2; http://www.vm.ee/eng/review/2000, 23 March 2000.

[4]   *European Voice*, 2 March 2000, http://www.european-voice.com/thisweek/index.html, 30 March 2000.

[5]   For detailed texts dealing solely with the impact of enlargement on *Third Pillar* matters, see for example M. Popowski, 'Co-operation between Poland and the

European Union within the Framework of the *Third Pillar* of the Treaty on European Union' in R. Bieber and J. Monar, (eds), *Justice and Home Affairs in the European Union*, (Brussels: European Inter-University Press, 1995); H. Grabbe, *The Sharp Edges of Europe: Security Implications of Extending European Union Border Policies Eastwards*, (Paris: Institute for Security Studies of the Western European Union, 2000).

6   Dr. Romano Prodi, President of the European Commission, Speech at the Special Meeting of the European Council at Tampere, 15 October 1999, http://presidency.finland.fi, 16 January 2000.

7   Helmut Kohl, the former Chancellor of Germany, argued that it would be 'unacceptable to Germans if, in the long term, the Western frontier of Poland or of the Czech Republic were to become the eastern frontier of the European Union'.

8   *European Voice*, 2 March 2000.

9   Paavo Lipponen, Prime Minister of Finland, 'Speech to the Plenary Session of the European Parliament', 27 October 1999, http://www.presidency.finland.fi, 16 December 1999.

10 See the Tampere Presidency Conclusions for further details of the agreements reached by the member states, European Council Presidency Conclusions, 'Tampere European Council on 15-16th October 1999', (Luxembourg: Office for the Official Publications of the European Union, 1999).

11 See *Tampere Presidency Conclusions*.

12 See *Tampere Persidency Conclusions*.

13 Paavo Lipponen, 'Speech to Plenary Session'.

14 See the *Tampere Presidency Conclusions* for further details.

15 For example, in responding to a question in the House of Commons on 19 October 1999, the Prime Minister stated that 'There are people who are talking about a European Public Prosecutor . . . but we have not agreed to that and there is no active proposal on it', *Hansard*, 19 October 1999, Column 264, http://www.publications.parliament.uk/pa/cm199899/cmhansrd/vo991019/.

16 Liam O'Dowd and Thomas M. Wilson, 'Frontiers of sovereignty in the new Europe' in Liam O'Dowd (ed), *Borders, Nations and States*, (Aldershot: Avebury Press, 1996), p. 13.

17 See, *Estonia Today*, March 1999, http://www.vm.ee/eng/estoday/1999/o3border.html, 28 November, 1999.

18 As reported by Dr Graeme Herd, lecturer in the Department of Politics and International Relations, University of Aberdeen.

19 *Estonia Today*, March, 1999.

20 *Estonia Today*, March, 1999.

21 *Estonian Review*, January 2000, p.?, http://www.vm.ee/eng/review/2000, 23 March, 2000.

[22]   'Estonia Celebrated the Eightieth Anniversary of the Tartu Peace Treaty', *Estonian Review*, 23 March, 2000, http://www.vm.ee/eng/review/2000.

[23]   *Estonia Today*, 28 November, 1999, http://www.vm.ee/eng/estoday/1998/border.html.

[24]   Margita Markevica, 'The Impact of Identity on the Latvian policy of dual-containment', presentation on behalf of the Defence and Internal Affairs Commission of Latvia, 11 March 2000.

[25]   *Estonia Today*, March 1999.

[26]   *Hansard*, 19 October 1999, Column 264.

[27]   Grabbe, *The Sharp Edges*, p. 14.

[28]   Commission of the European Communities, 'Regular Report from the Commission on Progress towards Accession by Poland', (Luxembourg: Office for Official Publications of the European Communities, 1999).

[29]   'Regular Report . . . Poland'.

[30]   Commision of the European Communities, 'Regular Report from the Commission on Progress towards Accession by Estonia', (Luxembourg: Office for Official Publications of the European Communities, 1999).

[31]   Estonian Prime Minister Mart Laar, cited in, 'Estonia will complete reforms in 2003', *Estonian Review*, 23 March, 2000, http://www.vm.ee/eng/review/1999.

[32]   'Regular Report . : . Poland', p. 73.

[33]   'Regular Report . . . Poland', p. 72.

[34]   'Regular Report . . . Poland', p. 72

[35]   'Regular Report . . . Poland, p. 52.

[36]   'Regular Report . . . Poland', p. 73.

[37]   Jan Truszcynski, *Problems Concerning the Implementation of the Justice and Home Affairs Acquis by the Candidate Countries: a Polish View*, (Paris: Cicero Foundation, 2000), p. 10.

[38]   'European Union citizens can apply for residence permits in Estonia', *Estonian Review*, 5 January 2000, http://www.vm.ee/eng/review/2000, 23 March 2000, p. 4.

[39]   Interview with the author, 14 July 1999.

[40]   'Regular Report . . . Poland', p. 52.

[41]   'Regular Report . . . Estonia', p. 49.

[42]   See 'Regular Report . . . Poland'.

[43]   See 'Regular Report . . . Estonia', p. 48.

[44]   'Regular Report . . . Estonia', p. 48.

[45]   'Presidency Week 11-17 October 1999', Press Release of the Finnish Presidency on the Tampere Summit, http://www.presidency.finland.fi, 16 January 2000.

[46]   For details see, http://www.presidency.finland.fi.

[47] See 'Regular Report . . . Estonia'.

[48] See 'Regular Report . . . Estonia'.

[49] *The Times*, 16 October 1999.

[50] See 'Regular Report . . . Estonia'.

[51] 'Regular Report . . . Poland', p. 53.

[52] 'Regular Report . . . Poland', p. 16.

[53] 'Regular Report . . . Poland', p. 53.

[54] 'Regular Report . . . Poland', p. 53.

[55] 'Regular Report . . . Poland', p. 74.

[56] Andrzej Siemaszko, *The International Crime Victim Survey in Poland - 1996*, (Warsaw: Institute of Justice, 1997), p. 10.

[57] Siemaszko, The *International*, p. 6.

[58] Justice and Home Affairs Council, 'The Pre-Accession Pact on Organised Crime Between the Member States of the European Union and the Applicant Countries of Central and Eastern Europe and Cyprus', (OJ C220, May, 1998).

[59] Details can be found in the European Commission's 'Poland - Accession Partnership', 18 February 1999.

[60] 'Regular Report . . . Poland', p. 53.

[61] 'Regular Report . . . Poland', p. 72.

[62] 'Regular Report . . . Poland', p. 72.

[63] 'Russian unease over Estonian Secret Services', *Estonian Review*, 3 February, 2000, http://www.vm.ee/eng/review/2000, 23, March 2000, p. 3.

[64] Estonian Prime Minister Mart Laar cited in 'Russian unease', p. 3.

[65] As cited by Dr. Willy Bruggemann in an interview conducted at the Stakis Treetops Hotel, Aberdeen, 12 May 1998.

[66] Interview with the author, 17 June 1999.

[67] Justice and Home Affairs Council, 'Council Act of 26th July, Drawing up the Convention, based on Article K: 3 of the Treaty on European Union, on the establishment of a European Police Office', (Luxembourg: Office for Official Publications of the European Communities, 1995).

[68] 'Council Act of 26th July', Article 15 (1).